# LIFE IN THE FORESTS

OF

# THE FAR EAST.

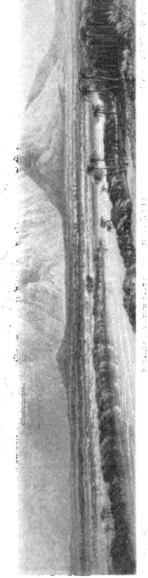

# LIFE IN THE FORESTS

OF

# THE FAR EAST.

BY

## SPENSER ST. JOHN, F.R.G.S., F.E.S.,

FORMERLY H.M.'S CONSUL-GENERAL IN THE GREAT ISLAND OF BORNEO,
AND NOW
H.M.'S CHARGÉ D'AFFAIRES TO THE REPUBLIC OF HAYTI.

*WITH NUMEROUS ILLUSTRATIONS.*

IN TWO VOLUMES.

## VOL. I.

## LONDON:
SMITH, ELDER AND CO., 65, CORNHILL.

M.DCCC.LXII.

# PREFACE.

—◦◦—

I have explained in a short introduction the object and plan of the present volumes, and have little more to say, beyond a reference to the assistance I have received, and the plates and maps which accompany and illustrate them. In order to prevent mistakes, and correct my own impressions, I submitted a series of questions to four gentlemen who were intimately acquainted with the Dayak tribes, and they gave me most useful information in reply. To Mr. Charles Johnson and the Rev. William Chalmers I am indebted for very copious and valuable notes on the Sea and Land Dayaks; and to the Rev. Walter Chambers and the Rev. William Gomez for more concise, yet still interesting accounts of the tribes with whom they live.

To Mr. Hugh Low, the Colonial Treasurer of Labuan, I am under special obligations, as he freely placed at my disposal the journals he had kept during our joint expeditions, as well as those relating to some

districts which I have not visited. It is to be regretted that he has not himself prepared a work on
the North-West Coast, as no man possesses more
varied experience or a more intimate knowledge of
the people.

With regard to the plates contained in this work,
I am indebted to the courtesy of George Bentham,
Esq., the President of the Linnean Society, for permission to engrave the figures of the Nepenthes from
the admirable ones published in Vol. XXII. of that
Society's Transactions, and which being of the size
of life are the more valuable.

I have inserted, with Dr. Hooker's permission, his
description of the Bornean Nepenthes; and it will
always be a subject of regret that the British Government did not carry out their original intention of
sending this able botanist to investigate the Flora of
Borneo, which is perhaps as extraordinary as any in
the world.

I have also to thank the Rev. Charles Johnson, of
White Lackington, and Charles Benyon, Esq., for
the photographs which they placed at my disposal,
and which have enabled me to insert, among other
plates, the most life-like pictures of the Land and
Sea Dayaks I have ever seen. To the Society for the
Propagation of the Gospel I am also indebted for
their generous offer to place all their drawings at my
disposal.

I must likewise draw attention to the exquisite manner in which the plates of the Nepenthes are coloured, and to the beauty of the engravings in general. They are admirably illustrative of the country, and·do very great credit to the lithographers, Messrs. Day and Son, and to their excellent draughts-men. I ought also to mention that the Nepenthes are drawn less than half the natural size, as it was found impracticable to introduce the full size without many folds, which would have speedily destroyed the beauty of the plates.

I will add a few words respecting the maps. The one of the districts around Kina Balu was constructed from the observations made during our two expedi-tions to that mountain. The map of the Limbang and Baram rivers is the result of many observations, and with regard to the position of the main moun-tains, I think substantially correct, as they were fixed with the aid of the best instruments. The third map is inserted in order to give a general idea of the North-West Coast, though the run of the rivers is often laid down by conjecture.

# CONTENTS.

## CHAPTER I.

### THE SEA DAYAKS.

## CHAPTER II.

### SOCIAL LIFE OF THE SEA DAYAKS.

## CHAPTER III.

### THE KAYANS OF BARAM.

## Chapter IV.

### THE LAND DAYAKS.

# CHAPTER V.

## LAND DAYAKS OF SIRAMBAU.—THEIR SOCIAL LIFE.

# CHAPTER VI.

## SOCIAL LIFE OF THE LAND DAYAKS—*Continued.*

## Chapter VII.

### THE SAMARAHAN RIVER AND THE CAVES OF SIRIH.

## Chapter VIII.

### THE MOUNTAIN OF KINA BALU.

#### FIRST EXPEDITION.

## Chapter IX.

### SECOND ASCENT OF KINA BALU.

PAGE

## CHAPTER X.

### SECOND ASCENT OF KINA BALU—*Continued.*

## CHAPTER XI.

THE PHYSICAL AND POLITICAL GEOGRAPHY OF THE
DISTRICTS LYING BETWEEN GAYA BAY AND THE
TAMPASUK RIVER; WITH A GEOGRAPHICAL
SKETCH OF MALUDU BAY AND THE NORTH-EAST
COAST OF BORNEO.

# LIST OF ILLUSTRATIONS.

## MAPS.

# ERRATA.

———•◦•———

Page 317, line 9, *for* "four," *read* "fourteen."
   ,,    ,, 17, *for* "was," *read* "that of the others is."

*c*

LIFE IN THE

# ·FORESTS OF THE FAR EAST.

## INTRODUCTION.

THE wild tribes of BORNEO, and the not less wild interior of the country, are scarcely known to European readers, as no one who has travelled in the Island during the last fourteen years has given his impressions to the public.

My official position afforded me many facilities for gratifying my fondness for exploring new countries, and traversing more of the north of Borneo than any previous traveller, besides enabling me to gain more intimate and varied experience of the inhabitants.

In the following pages I have treated of the tribes in groups, and have endeavoured to give an individual interest to each; while, to preserve the freshness of my first impressions, I have copied my journal written at the time, only correcting such errors as are inseparable from first observations, and comparing them with the result of subsequent experience.

Preserving the natural order of travel, I commence with an account of my expeditions among the tribes living in the neighbourhood of Sarawak; then follow narratives of two ascents of the great mountain of Kina Balu, the loftiest mountain of insular Asia, of which I have given a full account, as it is a part of Borneo but little known, and rendered still more curious by the traces we find of former Chinese intercourse with this part of the island; my personal narrative being concluded by the journal of a distant expedition I made to explore the interior of the country lying to the south and south-east of Brunei, the capital of Borneo Proper.

The starting-point of the first journeys was Kuching, the capital of Sarawak, where I was stationed in the acting appointment of H. M.'s Commissioner in Borneo. I lived so many years among the Dayaks, that the information I give of their mode of life may be relied on; and I have received so much assistance from others better acquainted with individual tribes, that I can place before the public, with great confidence in the correctness of detail, the chapters on the Manners and Customs of these people. I persuade myself that the more the natives of Borneo are studied, the more lively will be the interest felt in them. The energy displayed by the Sea Dayaks, gives much hope of their advancement in civilization at a future time; and a few years of quiet and steady government would produce a great change in their condition. The Land Dayaks scarcely display the same aptitude for improvement, but patience may do much with them also; their modes of thought, their customs, and the traces of Hinduism in their religion, render them a very singular and interesting people.

Of the Kayans we know less; and I have only been able to give an account of one journey I made among them, very slightly corrected by subsequent experience. They are a strange, warlike race, who are destined greatly to influence the surrounding tribes. They have already penetrated to within thirty miles of Brunei, the capital, spreading desolation in their path.

For ten years, every time I had entered the bay near the Brunei river, I had speculated on what kind of country and people lay beyond the distant ranges of mountains that, on a clear day, appeared to extend, one behind the other, as far as the eye could reach. I constantly made inquiries, but never could find even a Malay who had gone more than a few days' journey up the Limbang, the largest river which falls into the bay. In 1856, I took up my permanent residence in Brunei as Consul-General, and, after many minor attempts, I was at last enabled to organize an expedition to penetrate into the interior, and, hoping it might prove interesting, every evening, with but two exceptions, I wrote in my journal an account of the day's proceedings. I have printed it, as far as possible, in the same words in which it was originally composed. As this country was never before visited by Malay or European, I hope there will be found in my narrative some fresh and interesting matter.

The Malays being a people about whom much has been written, I have refrained from dwelling on their characteristics.

1—2

I conclude with a sketch of the present condition of Brunei and Sarawak, of the Chinese settlers, and of the two missions which have been sent to Borneo, one Roman Catholic, the other Protestant.

It was with much regret that I gave up the idea of penetrating to the opposite side of Borneo, starting from the capital, and crossing the island to Kotei or Baluñg-an, on the eastern coast; but the expense would have been too great: otherwise, with my previous experience of Borneo travelling, I should have had no hesitation in attempting the expedition.

Having thus briefly indicated the plan of the work, I will commence with an account of my journeys among the Sea Dayaks.

# CHAPTER I.

## THE SEA DAYAKS.

THE Sea Dayaks are so called from their familiarity
with the sea, though many live as far inland as any
of the other aborigines. They inhabit the districts
lying to the eastward of Sadong, and extend along

the coast to the great river of Rejang. They are the most numerous and warlike of the Dayaks; and the most powerful of their sections formerly indulged in the exciting pastime of piracy and head-hunting. The next river to the east of Sadong is the Sibuyau, whose inhabitants were scattered and had fled to the districts around Sarawak.

The first village of these Sibuyaus, to whom we paid a long visit, was situated on the Lundu, the most westerly river in the Sarawak territories.

We started in March; and the north-east monsoon still blowing occasionally, made it necessary to watch our time for venturing to sea, as the waves would soon have swamped our long native prahu.

From the Santubong entrance of the Sarawak River to the Lundu, there are passages which run behind the jungle that skirts the sea-shore, enabling canoes to hold communication between those places thirty miles apart without venturing to sea; but our boat being fifty feet long was unable to pass at one place, so during a lull in the weather we pushed out, calling at the little island of Sampadien, where Mr. Crookshank was preparing the ground for a cocoanut plantation. He brought us down a fine haunch of venison, covered with a layer of fat, a very rare thing in Borneo, where the deer generally are destitute of that sign of good condition. He had employed himself the first few days in clearing the island of game, and his dogs had on the previous evening been fortunate enough to bring this fine animal to bay, when he speared it with his own hands.

Pushing off quickly, as the sea breeze was blowing

in strongly, we sailed and pulled away for the river
of Sampadien, and after a narrow escape from not
hitting the right channel, found ourselves clear of
the breakers and safe in still water. An inland
passage then took us to the Lundu.

The banks of this river are very flat and the plains
extend for a considerable distance, but the scene is
redeemed from tameness by the mountains of Gading
and Poè. There is a flourishing appearance about
the place; all were engaged in some occupation. We
were received by Kalong, the Orang Kaya's eldest
son, the chief himself being absent collecting the
fruit of the mangkawan, from which a good vegetable
oil is extracted: the natives use it for candles and
for cookery, but it is also exported in quantities to
Europe.

The landing-place is very picturesque, being overshadowed by a grove of magnificent palms, under
which were drawn up the war-boats of the tribe.
A passage raised on posts three feet above the ground,
led to the great village-house, which extended far on
either side, and was then hidden among the fruit-
trees. It was the longest I had seen, measuring
534 feet, and contained nearly five hundred people.
There are various lesser houses about of Malays and
Dayaks, forming a population of about a thousand.
The Orang Kaya lived in the largest house, which
was certainly a remarkably fine one: the broad
verandah, or common room, stretched uninterruptedly
the whole length, and afforded ample space for the
occupations of the tribe. The divisions appropriated
to each family were comparatively large, and all had
an air of comfort; while in front of the house were

bamboo platforms, on which the rice is dried and beaten out.

No village in Sarawak is blessed with greater prosperity than this. The old Orang Kaya, being of a most determined character, has reversed the usual order of things; and the Malays, instead of being the governors, are the governed. Having for years been little exposed to exactions, they are flourishing and exhibit an air of great contentment.

They made us comfortable in the long public room, and placed benches around a table for our accommodation. I confess to prefer the clean matted floor. After the first burst of curiosity was over, the people went on with their usual avocations, and did not make themselves uncomfortable about us.

We walked in the evening among the Chinese gardens extending over about a hundred acres of ground, and neatly planted with various kinds of vegetables, among which beans and sweet potatoes appeared most numerous. There were here about two hundred Chinese, most of them but lately arrived, so that the cultivated ground was continually increasing. A large market was found for their sweet potatoes among the sago growers and workers of the rivers to the north.

Next day we started for a waterfall, which we were told was to be found on the sides of the Gading mountain, a few miles below the village. After leaving our boat, the path lay through a jungle of fruit-trees; but as we ascended the spur of the mountain these ceased. In about an hour we came to a very deep ravine, where the thundering noise of falling water gave notice of the presence of a cataract. This is by far the finest I have yet seen: the stream, tumbling down the sides of the mountain, forms a succession of noble falls: the first we saw dashed in broken masses over the rocks above, and then descended like a huge pillar of foam into a deep, gloomy basin, while on either side of it rose smooth rocks, crowned with lofty trees, and dense underwood, that threw their dark shadows into the pool.

A slight detour brought us to a spot above the cascade, and then we could perceive that it was but the first of a succession. One view, where six hundred feet of fall was at once visible, is extremely fine : the water now gliding over the smoothest granite rock, then broken into foam by numerous obstructions, then tumbling in masses into deep basins,—the deafening roar, the noble trees rising amid the surrounding crags, the deep verdure, the brightness of the tropical sun, reflected from burning polished surfaces, then deep shade and cooling air. This varied scene was indeed worth a visit. We ascended to the top of the mountain, though warned of the danger we incurred from a ferocious dragon which guarded the summit.

The Sibuyaus are only interlopers in the Lundu, as there is a tribe, the original inhabitants of the country, who still live here. One day we visited them.

After pulling a few miles up the river we reached a landing place, where the chief of the true Lundus was waiting to guide us to his village. For six or seven miles our path lay through the jungle over undulating ground, and we found the houses situated at the commencement of a great valley lying between the moun-

tains of Poè and Gading. The soil is here excellent,
but now little of it is tilled, though there are
thousands of acres around that might support an
immense population. Most of it, however, had, in
former times, been cleared, as we saw but very little
old forest.

The Lundu houses, on the top of a low hill, are
but few in number, neat and new. The tribe, however, has fallen; they fear there is a curse on them. A
thousand families, they say, once cultivated this
valley, but now they are reduced to ten, not by the
ravages of war, but by diseases sent by the spirits.
They complain bitterly that they have no families, that
their women are not fertile; indeed, there were but
three or four children in the whole place. The men
were fine-looking, and the women well favoured and
healthy—remarkably clean and free from disease.
We could only account for their decreasing numbers
by their constant intermarriages: we advised them to
seek husbands and wives among the neighbouring
tribes, but this is difficult. Their village is a well-
drained, airy spot.

On our return, one of those sudden squalls came on
that are so frequent in Borneo: we were among the
decayed trees that still stood on the site of an old
farm. As a heavier gust swept from the hills, the
half-rotten timber tottered and fell with a crash
around us, rendering our walk extremely dangerous.
I was not sorry, therefore, to find myself in the boat
on the broad river. The banks are tolerably well
cleared by Chinese, Malays, Millanaus, and Dayaks.
A few months after this, a sudden squall struck the
British brig "Amelia," and capsized her: ninety-three

went down with her, but twenty escaped in the jolly-boat.

In the evening Kalong's wife was taken in the pains of child-birth. The Rev. F. Dougall, now Bishop of Labuan, offered his medical assistance, as it was evident the case was a serious one, but they preferred following their own customs. The child died, and we left the mother very ill.

A young girl, bitten by a snake, was brought in; the wound was rubbed with a piece of deer's horn, she became drowsy and slept for several hours, but in the morning she was about her usual occupations.

A year after this visit, the Rev. W. Gomez was established there, to endeavour to convert the Sibuyau Dayaks. At first, he did not press religious instruction upon them, but opened a school. I mention this circumstance on account of the very remarkable tact he must have exercised to induce the children to attend as they did. His system of punishment was admirable, but difficult to be followed with English boys. He merely refused to hear the offending child's lesson, and told him to go home. A friend, who often watched the progress of the school, has told me that instead of going home the little fellows would sob and cry and remain in a quiet part of the school till they thought Mr. Gomez had relented. They would rarely return to their parents, if it could be avoided, before their lessons were said.

On our journey along the coast, while walking at the edge of the jungle, a favourite dog of mine was seized by a boa-constrictor, perhaps twelve feet in length. Fortunately, Captain Brooke was near, and sent a charge of shot into the reptile, which then let go its hold and made off.  The dog had a wound on the side of his neck.

The natives tell many stories of these monstrous snakes; but rejecting the testimony of those who say they have seen them so large as to mistake them for trees, I will mention three cases where the animals were measured.  A boa one night got into a closely-latticed place under a Dayak house, and finding it could not drag away a pig which it had killed there, on account of the wooden bars, swallowed the beast on the spot.  In the morning the owner was astonished to find the new occupant of the sty; but as the reptile was gorged, he had no difficulty in destroying it. Its body was brought to Sarawak and measured by Mr. Ruppell, when it was found to be nineteen feet in length.

The next was killed in Labuan, and without head and a large portion of its neck, it measured above twenty feet.  I heard the story told how the reptile was secured.  One day, a dog belonging to Mr. Coulson disappeared, and a servant averred that it was taken by an enormous snake.  The following week, as the same servant was laying the cloth for dinner, he saw, to his horror, a huge snake dart at a dog, that was quietly dozing in the verandah, and carry it off.  The master, alarmed at the cries of his follower, rushed out, and, on hearing the cause, gave chase, spear in hand, followed by all his household. They tracked the reptile to his lair, and found the dead dog opposite a hole in a hollow tree; placing a man with a drawn sword to watch there, Mr. Coulson thrust a spear into an upper hole, and struck the boa, which, feeling the wound, put its head out of the entrance, and instantly lost it by a blow from the Malay. I believe that when it was drawn from its hiding-place it measured about twenty-four feet; the before-mentioned length was taken by me from the mutilated skin.

Mr. Coulson was also fortunate enough to secure the largest boa that has ever been obtained by a European in the north-west part of Borneo.

In March, 1859, a Malay, his wife, and child, accompanied by a little dog, were walking from the Eastern Archipelago Company's house, at the entrance of the Brunei towards the sea-beach. The path was narrow; the little dog trotted on first, followed by the others in Indian file. Just as they reached the shore, a boa darted on the dog and dragged him into the bushes. The Malays fled back to the house, where they found Mr. Coulson, who, on hearing of the great size of the serpent, determined to attempt the capture of its skin. He loaded a Minié rifle, and requested three English companions who happened to be there to accompany him with drawn swords. He made them promise to follow his directions. His intention was to walk up to within a fathom of the boa, and then shoot him through the head; if he were seized, then his companions were to rush in with their swords, but not before, as he wished to preserve the skin uninjured. They found the reptile on the same spot where it had killed the dog, that still lay partly encoiled: on the approach of the party, it raised its head, and made slight angry darts towards them, but still keeping hold of its prey. Mr. Coulson coolly approached to within five feet of the animal, which kept raising and depressing its head, and, seizing a favourable opportunity, fired; the ball passed through its brain and it lay dead at his feet—a prize worthily gained. They raised the boa up while still making strong muscular movements, and carried it back to the house; there they measured it—it was twenty-six feet two inches. Mr. Coulson immediately skinned it, and, shortly after, brought it up to the consulate. When I measured it, it had lost two inches, and was exactly twenty-six feet in length.

These boas must have occasionally desperate struggles with the wild pigs. I one day came upon a spot where the ground was torn up for a circle of eight or nine feet, and the branches around were broken. The boar, however, had evidently succumbed, as we could trace with ease the course it had been dragged through the jungle. We followed a little distance, but evidently no one was very anxious in pursuit. I knew the animal killed on this occasion to be a boar, from finding his broken tusk half-buried in the ground.

I may mention one or two incidents which I heard from very trustworthy Malays. Abang Hassan was working in the woods at the Santubong entrance of the Sarawak river, when he came upon a huge boa, completely torpid; it had swallowed one of the large deer, whose horns, he said, could be distinctly traced under the reptile's skin. He cut it open and found that the deer was still perfectly fresh. The boa measured about nineteen feet.

Abang Buyong, a man whose word is trusted by all the Europeans who know him, told us that one

day he was walking through the jungle with a drawn
sword, looking for rattans, when he was suddenly
seized by the leg; he instinctively cut at the animal,
and fortunate for him that he was so quick, as he had
struck off the head of a huge boa before it had time
to wind its coils around him. He said he carefully
measured him, and it was seven Malay fathoms long—
that is, from thirty-five to thirty-seven feet. Dozens of
other stories rise to my memory, but they were told
me by men in whom I have not equal confidence.
The largest I have myself killed was fourteen feet.

I will mention an incident that took place in July,
1861, during the Sarawak expedition to the Muka
river. A Malay, subject to fits of delirium, sprang
up suddenly one day in a boat, drew a sword, killed
two and wounded several men; he then dashed overboard, and fled into the jungle. Ten days after, he
was found wandering starving on the beach. He
appeared quite in his senses, and perfectly unaware
of the act he had committed. He said, one night
that threatened heavy rain, he crawled into a hollow
tree to sleep. He was suddenly awakened by a choking
sensation in his throat. He instinctively put up both
his hands, and tore away what had seized him; it
was a huge boa, which in the confined space could
not coil around him. The Malay quickly got out of
the serpent's lair and fled, leaving his sword behind
him. When found, there were the marks of the fangs
on the sides of the torn wound, which was festering.
The last news I heard of the man was that he was
expected to die.

Many persons are very partial to small boas, as
wherever they take up their abode all rats disappear;

therefore they are seldom disturbed when found in granaries or the roofs of houses, though the reptile has as great a partiality for eggs as for vermin. Our servants killed one, and found fourteen eggs in its stomach.

Passing, on our way to the great tribes of Sea Dayaks, through Sarawak, we picked up our home letters and newspapers, and transferred our baggage to a larger prahu, very comfortably fitted up, with a spacious cabin in the centre.

At Muaratabas we joined the *Jolly Bachelor* pinnace, sending our boat on in shore. Setting sail with a fair breeze, we soon reached the entrance of the Batang Lupar, which is marked by two conical hills, —one the island of Trisauh, in the centre of the river, the other on the right bank. During our passage we observed some of those floating islands which wander over the face of the sea, at the mercy of wind and wave. I remember once that the signal-man gave notice that a three-masted vessel was ahead. We all fixed our telescopes on her, as at sea the slightest incident awakens interest: her masts appeared to rake in an extraordinary manner. As we steamed towards her our mistake was soon discovered; it was a floating island, with unusually tall nipa palms upon it, that were bending gracefully before the breeze.

On one occasion a man was found at sea making one of these his resting-place. Doubtless he abandoned his island home cheerfully, though he fell into the hands of enemies. He told us that his pirate companions, in hurried flight, had left him on the bank of a hostile river, and so seeing a diminutive island floating to the sea, he swam off and got upon it, and he had been there many days, living upon the fruit he had found on the palm stems.

The origin of the islands is this: The stream occasionally wears away the steep bank under the closely united roots of the nipa, and some sudden flood, pressing with unusual force on the loosened earth, tears away a large portion of the shore, which floats to the mouth of the river to be carried by the tides and currents far out to sea. Some fifteen miles off Baram Point, mariners tell of a great collection of floating trees and sea-weed, that forms an almost impassable barrier to ships in a light breeze. Some action of the currents appears to cause this assemblage of floating timber always to keep near one spot, and to move with a gyrating motion.

The Batang Lupar is in breadth from two to three miles, and occasionally more: we never had a cast of less than three fathoms on the bar, and inside it deepens to six. The banks are low, composed entirely of alluvial soil. Wind and tide soon carried us to our first night's resting-place at the mouth of the Lingga river, some twenty miles from the *embouchure* of the Batang Lupar. It is small, and its banks have the usual flat appearance, relieved, however, by some distant hills and the mountain of Lesong (a mortar), from a fancied resemblance to that article to be seen in every Malay house.

We found our boat here, together with a large force from Sarawak. I had taken advantage of the chance to accompany Captain Brooke on one of his tours through the Sarawak territories. This was to induce all the branches of the Sea Dayaks to make

peace with each other, and with the towns of the
coast, some of which they had so long harried.

While business detains the force at the mouth of the
Lingga, I will describe Banting, the chief town of the
Balau Dayaks, about ten miles up that stream.   There
are here about thirty long village houses, half at the
foot of a low hill, the others scattered on its face, completely embowered in fruit-trees.  From the spot where
Mr. Chambers, the missionary, has built his house,
there is a lovely view,—more lovely to those who have
long been accustomed to jungle than to any others.
For here we have the Lingga river meandering among
what appear to be extensive green fields, reminding
me of our lovely meadows at home.   We must not,
however, examine them too closely, or I fear they
will be found swamps of rushes and gigantic grass.
Still the land is not the less valuable, being admirably adapted in its present state for the best rice
cultivation.

The Lingga river is famous for its alligators, which
are both large and fierce; but, from superstitions
to which I shall afterwards refer, the natives seldom
destroy them.  In Sarawak there is no such prejudice.
It is a well-known fact, that no alligator will take a
bait that is in any way fixed to the shore.  The usual
mode of catching them is to fasten a dog, a cat, or a
monkey to a four or five fathom rattan, with an iron
hook or a short stick lightly fastened up the side of
the bait.  The rattan is then beaten out into fibre
for a fathom, to prevent its being bitten through by
the animal when it has swallowed the tempting
morsel.  Near a spot known to be frequented by
alligators, the bait, with this long appendage, is

placed on a branch about six feet above high-water mark. The cries of the bound animal soon attract the reptile; he springs out of the water and seizes it in his ponderous jaws. The natives say he is cunning enough to try if it be fastened to the bank; but the real fact appears to be that the alligator never eats its food until it is rather high. So that when fastened, finding he cannot take away his prize to the place where he usually conceals his food, he naturally lets it go. Gasing, a Dayak chief, saved his life when seized by an alligator, by laying hold of a post in the water: the animal gave two or three tugs, but finding its prey immovable, let go.

Two or three days after the bait has been taken, the Malays seek for the end of the long rattan fastened to it. When found, they give it a slight pull, which breaks the threads that fasten the stick up the side of the bait, and it spreads across the alligator's stomach. They then haul it towards them. It never appears to struggle, but permits its captors to bind its legs over its back. Till this is done they speak to it with the utmost respect, and address it in a soothing voice; but as soon as it is secured they raise a yell of triumph, and take it in procession down the river to the landing-place. It is then dragged ashore amid many expressions of condolence at the pain it must be suffering from the rough stones; but being safely ashore, their tone is jeering, as they address it as Rajah, Datu, and grandfather. It then receives its death at the hands of the public executioner. Its stomach is afterwards ripped open, to see if it be a man-eater. I have often seen the buttons of a woman's jacket, or the tail of a Chinese, taken out.

The alligator always appears to swallow its food whole. Some men are very expert in catching these reptiles; I remember one Malay, who came over from the Dutch possessions, capturing thirteen during a few months, and as the Sarawak Government pay three shillings and sixpence for every foot the beast measures, the man made a large sum.

Alligators sometimes attain to a very large size. I have never measured one above seventeen feet six inches, but I saw a well-known animal, the terror of the Siol branch of the Sarawak, that must have been at least twenty-four or twenty-five feet long. The natives say the alligator dies if wounded about the body, as the river-worms get into the injured part, and prevent its healing; many have been found dying on the banks from gunshot wounds. In the rivers are occasionally found curious balls of hair, five or six inches in diameter, that are ejected from these reptiles' stomachs,—the indigestible remains of animals captured.

I once lost an acquaintance in Sarawak who was killed by an alligator. He was seized round the chest by the jaws of an enormous beast that swam with his prey along the surface of the water. His children, who had accompanied him to bathe, ran along the banks of the river shouting to him to push out the animal's eyes; they say he looked at them, but that he neither moved nor spoke, paralyzed, as it were, by the grip.

I am very partial to this tribe of Lingga Dayaks; they have always shown so unmistakable a preference for the English—faithful under every temptation, and ready at a moment's warning to back them up with a force of a thousand men.

The lads, too, have a spirit more akin to English youths than I have yet seen among the other tribes. I well remember the delight with which they learnt the games we taught them—joining in prisoner's base with readiness, hauling at the rope, and shouting with laughter at French and English, represented by the names of two Dayak tribes.   There is good material to work on here, and it could not be in better hands than those of their present missionary, Mr. Chambers.   That his teaching has made any marked difference in their conduct I do not suppose, but he has influenced them, and his influence is yearly increasing.

It is pleasing to record a little success here, at the Quop, and at Lundu, or we should have to pronounce the Borneo mission a complete failure.

The largest orang-utans I have ever heard of are in the Batang Lupar districts.   Mr. Crymble, of Sarawak, saw a very fine one on shore, and landing, fired and struck him, but the beast dashed away among the lofty trees; seven times he was shot at, but only the eighth ball took fatal effect, and he came crashing down, and fell under a heap of twigs that he had torn in vain endeavours to arrest his descent. The natives refused to approach him, saying it was a trick—he was hiding to spring upon them as they approached.   Mr. Crymble, however, soon uncovered him, and measured his length as he lay : it was five feet two inches, measuring fairly from the head to the heel.   The head and arms were brought in, and we measured them: the face was fifteen inches broad, including the enormous callosities that stick out on either side ; its length was fourteen inches ; round the wrist was twelve inches, and the upper arm seventeen. I mention this size particularly, as my friend, Mr. Wallace, who had more opportunities than any one else to study these animals, never shot one much over four feet, and perhaps may doubt the existence of larger animals; but he unfortunately sought them in the Sadong river, where only the smaller species exists.

The Dayaks tell many stories of the male orang-utans in old times carrying off their young girls, and of the latter becoming pregnant by them; but they are, perhaps, merely traditions. I have read somewhere of a huge male carrying off a Dutch girl, who was, however, immediately rescued by her father and a party of Javanese soldiers, before any injury beyond fright had occurred to her.

During the time I lived at Sarawak, we had many tame orang-utans; among others, a half-grown female called Betsy. She was an affectionate, gentle creature that might have been allowed perfect liberty, had she not taken too great a liking for the cabbage of the cultivated palms. When she climbed up one of these, she would commence tearing away the leaves to get at the coveted morsel, but shaking or striking the tree with a stick, would induce her to come down. Her cage was large, but she had a great dislike to being alone, and would follow the men about whenever she had an opportunity. At night, or when the wind was cold, she would carefully wrap herself in a blanket or rug, and of course choose the warmest corner of her cage.

After some months, we procured a very young male, and her delight was extreme. She seemed to take the greatest care of it; but like most of the small ones brought in, it soon died.

When I lived in Brunei, a very young male was given me. Not knowing what to do with it, I handed it over to a family where there were many children. They were delighted with it, and made it a suit of clothes. To the trousers it never took kindly; but I have often seen him put on his own jacket in damp weather, though he was not particular about having it upside down or not. It was quite gentle and used to be fondled by the very smallest children.

I never saw but one full-grown orang-utan in the jungle, and he kept himself well sheltered by a large branch as he peered at us. He might have shown himself with perfect safety, as I never could bring myself to shoot at a monkey; but a friend who was collecting specimens saw an enormous one in a very high tree: he fired ten shots at him with a revolver, one of which hit him on the leg. As in the case when I saw the orang-utan, he kept himself well sheltered, but whenever a bullet glanced on a tree or branch near him, he put out his hand to feel what had struck the bark. When he found himself wounded, he removed to the topmost branches, and was quite exposed, but my friend's guns were left behind him, and he failed to obtain this specimen.

It is singular that most of the orang-utans die in captivity, from eating too much raw fruit. Betsy, that was fed principally on cooked rice, must have lived a twelvemonth with us. I was not in Sarawak when she died, and do not remember the cause.

On my return, finding that the arrangements were made, we started for a fort built at the entrance of

the Sakarang, which was under the command of Mr.
Brereton, accompanied by the Sarawak forces and the
Balau Dayaks.   The real value of the Batang Lupar
as a river adapted for ships ceases shortly after leaving
the junction, as sands begin, and a bore renders the
navigation dangerous to the inexperienced; but it presents a noble expanse of water.   As we started after
the flood tide had commenced, the bore had passed
on, and only gave notice of its late presence by a
little bubbling in the shallower places.

The banks of the river continue low, with only
an occasional rising of the land; nothing but alluvial
plains, formerly the favourite farming grounds of the
Dayaks, then completely deserted, or tenanted only
by pigs and deer; but it was expected that as soon as
the peace ceremonies were over, the natives would not
allow this rich soil to remain uncultivated, and the
expectation has been fulfilled, as this abandoned
country was, on my last visit, covered with rice farms,
while villages occupied the banks.

After we had passed Pamutus, the site of the
piratical town destroyed by Sir Henry Keppel, the
river narrows, and is not above a hundred yards
broad at the town of Sakarang, built at the con-
fluence of a river of the same name.   The fort was
rather an imposing-looking structure, though built
entirely of wood.   It was square, with flanking towers,
and its heavy armament completely commanded the
river, and rendered it secure against any Dayak force.

This country was at the time influenced, rather
than ruled, by the late Mr. Brereton, as his real
power did not extend beyond the range of his guns.
I never met a man who threw himself more enthu-

siastically into a most difficult position, or who, by his imaginative mind and yet determined will, exercised a greater power over Dayaks by the superiority of his intellect. A stranger can scarcely realize a more difficult task than that of endeavouring to rule many thousands of wild warriors without being backed by physical force ; but he did a great deal, though his exertions were too much for his strength, and he died a few years after, while engaged in his arduous task. In him the Sarawak service lost an admirable officer, and we an affectionate friend.

When we landed at the fort, we found a great crowd assembled to meet us, among whom were the principal Sakarang chiefs, as Gasing and Gila. Many were fine-looking men of independent bearing and intelligent features. There were a few women about, but until the preliminaries of peace had been settled, they were not encouraged to come into the town.

It was found impossible to inquire into the origin of many of the quarrels, so Captain Brooke settled the matter by agreeing to give each party a sacred jar (valued at 8*l.*), a spear, and a flag. This was considered by them as satisfactory, and it was immediately determined that the next day the formal ceremonies should take place to ratify the engagement.

There is comparatively little difficulty in putting a stop to the piratical acts of the Sakarangs, as the fort commands the river ; but it is almost impossible to prevent them head-hunting in the interior, there being so many unguarded outlets by which the hostile tribes can assail each other. The Bugau Dayaks— a numerous and powerful tribe, living on the Kapuas,

and tributary to the Dutch—were principally exposed
to their expeditions, and their justifiable retaliations
kept up the hostile feeling.

Whenever a head-hunting party was expected to
be on its return, a strict watch was kept to prevent
it passing the fort. One day, at sunset, a couple of
light canoes were seen stealing along the river bank,
but a shot across their bows made them pull back:
they dared not come up to the fort, having three
human heads with them. The sentries were doubled,
and Mr. Brereton kept watch himself. About two
hours before dawn, something was seen moving under
the opposite bank. A musket was fired; but as the
object continued floating by, it was thought to be a
trunk of a tree; but no sooner had it neared the
point than a yell of derision arose, as the swimming
Dayaks sprang into the boat, and pulled off in high
glee up the Sakarang.

To prevent all chance of the hostile tribes of Sakarangs and Balaus quarrelling before the treaty was
concluded, it was arranged that the latter tribe should
remain at the entrance of the Undup, a stream about
two miles below the town, and that we should drop
down to that spot next day.

We found a covered stage erected, and a crowd of
nearly a thousand Balau men around it, and in their
long war boats: the Sakarangs came also in large
force, and our mediating party of about five hundred
armed men was there likewise.

Captain Brooke clearly explained the object of the
meeting, when the topic was taken up by the Datu
Patinggi of Sarawak, who, with easy eloquence,
briefly touched on the various points in question.

The Dayak chiefs followed; each protested that it was their desire to live in peace and friendship; they promised to be as brothers and warn each other of impending dangers. They all appear to have a natural gift of uttering their sentiments freely without the slightest hesitation.

The ceremony of killing a pig for each tribe followed; it is thought more fortunate if the animal be severed in two by one stroke of the parang, half sword, half chopper. Unluckily, the Balau champion struck inartistically, and but reached half through the animal. The Sakarangs carefully selected a parang of approved sharpness, a superior one belonging to Mr. Crookshank, and choosing a Malay skilled in the use of weapons placed the half-grown pig before him. The whole assembly watched him with the greatest interest, and when he not only cut the pig through, but buried the weapon to the hilt in the mud, a slight shout of derision arose among the Sakarangs at the superior prowess of their champion. The Balaus, however, took it in good part and joined in the noise, till about two thousand men were yelling together with all the power of their lungs.

The sacred jar, the spear, and flag, were now presented to each tribe, and the assembly, no longer divided, mixed freely together. The Balaus were invited to come up to the town, and thus was commenced a good understanding which has continued without interruption to the present time—about eleven years.

There are many kinds of sacred jars. The best known are the Gusi, the Rusa, and the Naga, all most probably of Chinese origin. The Gusi, the most valu-

able of the three, is of a green colour, about eighteen
inches high, and is, from its medicinal properties,
exceedingly sought after. One fetched at Tawaran
the price of four hundred pounds sterling to be
paid in produce ; the vendor has for the last ten
years been receiving the price, which, according
to his own account, has not yet been paid, though
probably he has received fifty per cent. over the
amount agreed on from his ignorant customer. They
are most numerous in the south of Borneo. The
Naga is a jar two feet in height, and ornamented
with Chinese figures of dragons; they are not worth
above seven or eight pounds. While the Rusa is
covered with what the native artist considers a representation of some kind of deer, it is worth from fifteen
to sixteen pounds. An attempt was made to manufacture an imitation in China, but the Dayaks immediately discovered the counterfeit.

We pulled up the Sakarang river to visit Gasing
in his farmhouse, which was large, neat, and comfortable ; in form and general appearance like their usual
village houses. These Sea Dayaks are a very im-
provable people. I have mentioned the tender point
of their character as displayed in Mr. Gomez's
school at Lundu, and another is their love of imitation. A Sakarang chief noticed a path that was cut
and properly ditched near the fort, and found that in
all weathers it was dry, so he instantly made a similar
path from the landing place on the river to his house,
and I was surprised on entering it to see coloured representations of horses, knights in full armour, and ships
drawn vigorously, but very inartistically, on the plank
walls. I found, on inquiry, he had been given some

copies of the *Illustrated London News*, and had endeavoured to imitate the engravings. He used charcoal, lime, red ochre, and yellow earth as his materials.

The Sakarang women are, I think, the handsomest among the Dayaks of Borneo; they have good figures, light and elastic; with well-formed busts and very interesting, even pretty faces; with skin of so light a brown as almost to be yellow, yet a very healthy-looking yellow, with bright dark eyes, and long glistening black hair. The girls are very fond of using an oil made from the Katioh fruit, which has the scent of almonds. Their dress is not unbecoming, petticoats reaching from below the waist to the knees, and jackets ornamented with fringe. All their clothes are made from native cloth of native yarn, spun from cotton grown in the country. These girls are generally thought to be lively in conversation and quick in repartee.

The Sakarang men are clean built, upright in their gait, and of a very independent bearing. They are well behaved and gentle in their manners: and, on their own ground, superior to all others in activity. Their national dress is a chawat or waistcloth, and in warlike expeditions they are partial to bright red cloth jackets, so that when assembled at a distance, they look like a party of English soldiers. The Sakarang and Seribas men have the peculiar practice of wearing rings all along the edge of their ears, sometimes as many as a dozen. I thought this custom confined to them, but I find the Muruts of Padas, opposite Labuan, also practise it.

Their strength and activity are remarkable. I have

seen a Dayak carry a heavy Englishman down the
steepest hills; and when one of their companions is
severely wounded they bear him home, whatever may
be the distance.   They exercise a great deal from
boyhood in wrestling, swimming, running, and sham-
fighting, and are excellent jumpers.   When a little
more civilized they would make good soldiers, being
brave by nature.   They are, however, short—a man
five feet five inches high would be considered tall,
the average is perhaps five feet three inches.

We did not visit the interior of the Batang Lupar,
but it is reported to be very populous, and the Chinese
are now working gold there.   I have penetrated to
the very sources of the Sakarang, and found it, after
a couple of days' pull, much encumbered by drift-wood
and rocks, with shallow rapids over pebbly beds.
This interior is very populous, and from a view we
had on a hill over the upper part of the Seribas
River, as far as the hills in which the Kanowit rises,
we could perceive but little old forest.

I may mention that the crime of poisoning is
almost unknown on the north-west coast, but it is very
generally believed the people of the interior of the
Kapuas, a few days' walk from the Batang Lupar, are
much given to the practice.   Sherif Sahib, and many
others who visited that country, died suddenly, and
the Malays assert it was from poison; but of this
I have no proof.

Near the very sources of the Kapuas live the
Malau Dayaks, who are workers in gold and brass, and
it is very singular that members of this tribe can
wander safely through the villages of the head-hunting Seribas and Sakarang, and are never molested,—

on the contrary, they are eagerly welcomed by the female portion of the population, and the young men are not indifferent to their arrival; but the specimens of their work that I have seen do not show much advance in civilization. The Malau districts produce gold, and it is said very fine diamonds.

I will insert here an anecdote of the public executioner of Sakarang. Last year, a native was tried and condemned to death for a barbarous murder, and according to the custom in Malay countries, the next day was fixed for carrying out the sentence. A Chinese Christian lad, who was standing near the executioner, said to him earnestly, " What! no time given him for repentance?" " Repentance!" cried the executioner, contemptuously. " Repentance! he is not a British subject." A curious confusion of ideas. Both were speaking in English, and very good English.

I tasted here, for the first time, the rambi fruit, that looks something like a large grape, growing in bunches, pleasantly sweet, yet with a slight acidity, yellow skin, with the interior divided into two fleshy pulps.

At the broadest part of the Batang Lupar, nearly four miles across, I saw a herd of pigs swimming from one shore to the other. If pigs do this with ease, we need not be surprised that the tigers get over the old Singapore Strait to devour, on a low average, a man a day.

On our return, while anchored at Pamutus, we saw the bore coming up, and it was a pretty sight from our safe position. A crested wave spread from shore to shore, and rushed along with inconceivable speed, . to subside as it approached deep water, to commence

again at the sands with as great violence when it had
passed us.    At full and change, few native boats
escape which are caught on the shallows, but are
rolled over and over, and the men are dashed breathless on the bank, few escaping with life.

Some of our Malays went ashore last night to snare
deer, while the Balaus tried for pigs.   It used to be a
very favourite hunting ground of the Dayaks, who are
expert in everything appertaining to the jungle ; they
nearly always employ dogs, which are very small, not
larger than a spaniel, sagacious' and clever in the
jungle, but stupid, sleepy-looking creatures out of it,
having all the attributes of bad-looking, mongrel
curs as they lurk about the houses ; but when some
four or five are led into the jungle, dense and pathless
as it is in most places, then they are ready to attack
a wild boar ten times their size.    And the wild boar
of the East is a very formidable animal.   I have seen
one that measured forty inches high at the shoulder,
with a head nearly two feet in length.   Sir Henry
Keppel also was present when this was shot, and he
thought a small child could have sat within its jaws.
Captain Hamilton of the 21st M. N. I., a very
successful sportsman, killed one forty-two inches
high.   Native hunting with good dogs is easy work ;
the master loiters about gathering rattans, fruit, or
other things of various uses to his limited wants,
and the dogs beat the jungle for themselves, and
when they have found a scent, give tongue, and soon
run the animal to bay : the master knowing this
by the peculiar bark, follows quickly and spears the
game.

I have known as many as six or seven pigs killed

before midday by Dayaks while walking along a
beach: their dogs searching on the borders of the
forest, bring the pigs to bay, but never really attack
till the master comes with his spear to help them.
The boars are very dangerous when wounded, as they
turn furiously on the hunter, and unless he has the
means of escape by climbing a tree, he would fare
ill in spite of his sword and spear, if it were not for
the assistance of his dogs. These creatures, though
small, never give in unless severely wounded, and by
attacking the hind legs, keep the pig continually
turning round.

The Dayaks are very fond of pork, and fortunately it is so, or they would be much more easily
persuaded to become Mahomedans. They have a
sort of respect for the domestic pig, and an English
gentleman was in disgrace at Lingga on account of
allowing his dogs to hunt one that they met in the
fruit-groves, which in any civilized country would
have been considered wild. The European sportsman
said in his defence, that he could not help clapping
his hands when he heard his dogs give tongue in
chase. Upon a hot day a deer is soon run down by
them; in fact, hunters declare that they could easily
catch them themselves in very dry weather, when the
heat is extremely oppressive. The deer have regular
bathing-places to which they resort, sometimes
during the day, and at others by night.

There are, I believe, only two kinds of deer in
Borneo, one Rusa Balum, and the other Rusa Lalang.
The former frequents low swampy ground, and has
double branched horns, averaging about eighteen
inches in length. The Rusa Lalang is a small,

plump, hill deer, with short horns, and having ono fork branch near the roots.

The Dayaks say there is another kind; but after making many inquiries, it appears to be the same as Rusa Balum. Occasionally you meet with deer whose horns are completely encased in skin.

The natives snare them with rattan loops and nooses, fastened on a long rope. They are of different lengths, varying from twenty to fifty feet. A number of these attached to each other, and resting on the tops of forked sticks, they stretch across a point of land where they have previously ascertained that deer are lying. After they have arranged the snares, the party is divided, one division watching them, and the other landing on the point; barking dogs and yelling men rush up towards the snare, driving the game before them; the deer, though they sometimes lie very close, generally spring up immediately and dart off bewildered, rushing into the nooses, catching their necks or their fore legs in them; the men on the watch dash up and cut them down, or spear them before they can break through. They sometimes catch as many as twenty in one night, but generally only one or two; snaring may be carried on either in the light or dark.

The evening we set sail from the Batang Lupar, we had a discussion on Marsden's theory of the land and sea breezes; one of our party denied the correctness of the authority whom we looked upon as not to be challenged in all that relates to the Eastern Archipelago. At midnight the land breeze commenced blowing, as the ocean does retain the heat longer than the land, and at midday the sea breeze set in, which

carried us pleasantly onward, passing the mouths of
the Seribas and Kalaka, to our anchorage in the
noble river of Rejang. We did not triumph over our
adversary, but recommended him to study Marsden
more carefully. On the bar at the entrance of this
river at dead low water, we had one cast which did
not exceed three fathoms, but I do not think we were
in the centre of the channel.

At the entrance of the Rejang is a small town
of Millanaus, a people differing greatly from the
Malays in manners and customs; some converted to
Islamism are clothed like other Mahomedans, while
those who still delight in pork dress like Dayaks, to
which race they undoubtedly belong. Their houses
are built on lofty posts, or rather whole trunks of
trees are used for the purpose, to defend themselves
against the Seribas.

It is stated that at the erection of the largest house,
a deep hole was dug to receive the first post, which
was then suspended over it; a slave girl was placed in
the excavation, and at a signal the lashings were cut,
and the enormous timber descended, crushing the girl
to death. It was a sacrifice to the spirits. I once
saw a more quiet imitation of the same ceremony.
The chief of the Quop Dayaks was about to erect a
flag-staff near his house: the excavation was made,
and the timber secured, but a chicken only was thrown
in and crushed by the descending flag-staff.

I made particular inquiries of Haji Abdulraman, and
his followers, of Muka, whilst I was in Brunei last
year. They said that the Milanaus of their town who
remained unconverted to Islamism have within the last
few years sacrificed slaves at the death of a respect-

3—2

able man, and buried them with the corpse, in order that they might be ready to attend their master in the other world. This conversation took place in the presence of the Sultan, who said he had often heard the report of such acts having been committed. One of the nobles present observed that such things were rare, but that he had known of a similar sacrifice taking place among the Bisayas of the River Kalias, opposite our colony of Labuan. He said a large hole was dug in the ground, in which was placed four slaves and the body of the dead chief. A small supply of provisions was added, when beams and boughs were thrown upon the grave, and earth heaped to a great height over the whole. A prepared bamboo was allowed to convey air to those confined, who were thus left to starve. These sacrifices can seldom occur, or we should have heard more of them. There were rumours, however, that at the death of the Kayan chief Tamawan, whom I met during my expedition to the Baram, slaves were devoted to destruction, that they might follow him in the future world.

In front of the houses were erected swings for the amusement of the young lads and the little children. One about forty feet in height was fastened to strong poles arranged as a triangle, and kept firm in their position by ropes like the shrouds of a ship. From the top hung a strong cane rope, with a large ring or hoop at the end. About thirty feet on one side was erected a sloping stage as a starting-point. Mounting on this, one of the boys with a string drew the hoop towards him, and making a spring into it, away he went. Other lads were ready, who successively sprung upon the ring or seized the rope, until there were

five or six in a cluster, shouting, laughing, yelling
and swinging. For the younger children smaller ones
were erected, as it required courage and skill to play
on the larger.

The Rejang is one of the finest rivers in Borneo,
and extends far into the interior. We ascended it upwards of one hundred miles, and never had less than
four fathoms. Mr. Steel, who lived many years at
the Kanowit fort, told me that it continued navigable
for about forty miles farther, then there were dangerous rapids, but above them the water again deepened.
The Rejang has many mouths, but the principal are
the one we entered, and another to the eastward of
Cape Sirik, called Egan. Its tributaries below the
rapids are the Sirikei, the Kanowit, and the Katibas,
the last two very populous.

Above the junction, the Rejang is about a mile and
a half broad, with islets scattered over it, but afterwards it contracts to about a thousand yards, and has
a fine appearance. The scenery here is not varied by
hill or dale; the land is low, but the banks were rendered interesting by the varied tints of the jungle;
blossoms and young leaves were bursting out in every
variety of colour, from the faintest green to the
darkest brown.

The air was filled with a kind of may-fly in astonishing numbers; I have never seen anything like
it before or since: they fell by myriads into the water,
and afforded a feast to thousands of fish that rose
with a dash to the surface, covering the river with
tiny widening circles.

During our passage up we had an instance of the
insecurity to which the head-hunters formerly reduced

this country.   We landed at a place called Munggu
Ayer (water hill) to bathe; a party of our men insisted on keeping watch over us, as many people had
lost their lives here.   Being a good spot to procure
water, boats are accustomed to take in their supplies
at this well, and the Dayaks lurked in the neighbouring jungle to rush out on the unwary.

Anchored opposite the entrance of the Kanowit,
where it was intended to build a fort to stop the
exit of the fleets of Dayak boats that used to
descend this river to attack the people of the Sago
countries.   Leaving the force thus engaged, I went
and took up my residence in the village of the
Kanowit Dayaks, built opposite the entrance of that
stream.   The Rejang is here about 600 or 700 yards
broad. .

The village consisted of two long houses, one
measuring 200 feet, the other 475.   They were built
on posts about forty feet in height and some eighteen
inches in diameter.   The reason they give for making
their posts so thick is this: that when the Kayans
attack a village they drag one of their long tamuis or
war boats ashore, and, turning it over, use it as a
monstrous shield.   About fifty bear it on their heads
till they arrive at the ill-made palisades that surround
the hamlets, which they have little difficulty in demo-
lishing; they then get under the house, and endeavour to cut away the posts, being well protected from
the villagers above by their extemporized shield.   If
the posts are thin, the assailants quickly gain the
victory; if very thick, it gives the garrison time to
defeat them by allowing heavy beams and stones to
fall upon the boat, and even to bring their little brass

wall pieces to bear upon it; the Kayans will fly if
they suffer a slight loss.

The Kanowit Dayaks are a very different people
from those who live on the river of the same name;
the latter are all immigrants from the Seribas and
Sakarang. The appearance of these people is very
inferior; few of them have the fine healthy look of
those I saw about Mr. Brereton's fort.; the women are
remarkably plain, and scarcely possess what is so
common in Borneo, a bright pair of eyes; ophthalmia
is very prevalent among them, partly caused by their
extracting their eyelashes. They have another custom
which is equally inelegant; they draw down the lobes
of their ears to their shoulders, by means of heavy
lead earings.

Some of the men are curiously tatooed; a kind of
pattern covers their breast and shoulders, and sometimes extends to their knees, having much the
appearance of scale-armour. Others have their chins
ornamented to resemble beards, an appendage denied
them by nature.

I have never before entered a village without
noticing some interesting children, but I observed
none here; though active enough, they looked unhealthy and dirty.

Belabun, the chief of this tribe, has had, from his
position, a very extensive intercourse with men, particularly with the Kayans, who inhabit the upper
portion of the river. One of our objects in visiting
the country was to proceed to the interior to make
friends with the numerous Kayan chiefs who live
there; but the small-pox had, unfortunately, broken
out among them, and the ascent of the river was for-

bidden, and all had fled into the forest. I much regretted this, as I never had another opportunity of ascending the Rejang. I will not introduce here the information we collected concerning the Kayans, as I intend giving an account of the visit I made shortly after to a branch of those people who lived on the Baram.

It is singular how the story of the men with tails has spread. I have heard of it in every part I have visited, but their country is always a few days' journey farther off. The most circumstantial account I ever had was from a man who had traded much on the north-east coast of Borneo. He said he had seen and felt the tails, they were four inches long, and were very stiff, so that all the people sat on seats in which there was a hole made for this remarkable appendage to fit in.

Sherif Musahor, a chief of Arab descent, and one of the most violent men that ever tormented these countries, arriving from Siriki, came in to see us; he is a very heavy-looking fellow; at one time we were great friends, as we were equally fond of chess. It is not my object to enter into political affairs, but I may mention that having instigated the murder of two Englishmen he fled north, and after a variety of adventures found himself in 1861 at the head of a band of desperadoes at a place called Muka. Sir James Brooke had often been reported dead, and on his arrival at Sarawak the news spread like wildfire along the coast. Sherif Musahor, greatly disturbed, called before him a Madras trader and asked him, "Did you see the Rajah?"

"Yes."

"Had he all his teeth perfect?"

"Yes."

"Ah, you lie! when I saw him last he had a front tooth knocked out."

The Madras man saw the fiery look of this desperate chief, but without losing his presence of mind for a moment, answered, "What, have you not heard that the Rajah bathed in the waters of the Nile, and that it has restored his youth again?"

His reply was satisfactory to all the Mahomedans present, who believe implicitly in every wonder told in the Arabian Nights.

One afternoon, it being a very warm day, we were reclining on our mats, when a burst of wailing and howling around us told that bad news had been received. One of the chief's brothers had returned from the interior and brought the following intelligence: It appeared that about two years and a half ago, a younger brother longing to see the world, had started off to the sources of the Kapuas river, which ultimately falls into the sea at Pontianah, a Dutch settlement, taking with him thirteen young men; he travelled on till he reached a Kayan tribe with whom his people were friends, and stayed with them for a few months. One day their hosts started on a headhunting expedition, and invited seven of their guests to accompany them: the latter never returned, having all been killed by the Kayans themselves. Why or wherefore it is impossible to tell, but it is supposed that having failed in their head-hunt, and being ashamed to return to their women without these trophies, they had fallen upon their guests. Their remaining companions being in a neighbouring vil-

lage escaped. Belabun, anxious to have news of his
brother, had sent the one who had just returned to
look for him. He patiently tracked him, but meeting
with the seven survivors, he learnt the fate of his
brother; they returned overland, but the young chief,
impatient to reach home, made a bark canoe, in which
he reached the village.

Belabun and his people were greatly excited, and
moved about the house in a restless and anxious
manner, while the wailing of the female relatives was
very distressing, particularly of the young girl whom
the wanderer left as a bride.

It may appear incredible that even the wildest
people should commit so treacherous a deed, but
before the Kanowit was well guarded, a Sakarang
chief from the interior, named Buah Raya, passed with
fifty war boats and pulled up the Rejang. Arriving
at a village of Pakatan Dayaks, his allies, he took
the men as his guides to attack some Punans, who,
however, escaped; mortified at this result he killed
the guides, and on his return carried off all the
women and children as captives. This was the chief
who refused to enter an English church, saying "an
old man might die through entering the white men's
tabernacle." He would or could give no explanation
of this observation.

These Kanowits follow the Millanau custom of
sending much of a dead man's property adrift in a
frail canoe on the river: they talk of all his property, but this is confined to talk.

We heard so much of the deceased chief's goods,
which were to be thrown away, as it is considered
they belong to the departed and not to those who

remain, that we went to the place where they lay.
We found a sort of four-sided bier erected, covered
with various coloured cloths, and within it his bride
widow lay moaning and wailing, surrounded by his
favourite arms, his gongs, his ornaments, and all that
he considered valuable.    Among his treasures was
the handle of a kris, representing the figure of Budha
in the usual sitting posture, which they said had
descended to them from their ancestors.

As I expected, these valuables were not sent adrift,
but merely a few old things, that even sacrilegious
strangers would scarcely think worth plundering.

A short time before the Rejang came under Sir
James Brooke's sway, a relation of Belabun died.
Having no enemy near, he looked about for a victim.
Seeing a Dayak of the Katibas passing down the
river, he and a small party followed and overtook him
just as he reached the junction; they persuaded him
to come ashore, and then seized and killed him,
taking his head home in triumph.    As this murder
took place before Sir James Brooke's jurisdiction
extended over the country, it was difficult to bring
him to account, but on the relations coming to
demand satisfaction, Captain Brooke insisted upon
his paying the customary fine, which satisfied the
Katibas.

The second chief of this village is Sikalei, who,
when one of his children died, sallied out and killed
the first man he met—they say it was one of his own
tribe, but it was the custom to kill the first person,
even if it were a brother: fortunately they now are
brought under a Government which is strong enough
to prevent such practices.

They are a very curious people; the men dress as Dayaks, the women as Malays; and the latter part their hair in the middle, while all the other races draw it back from the forehead. They appear to be much influenced in their customs by the surrounding people; the men tatoo like Kayans, the women not.

We saw a very curious war-dance; two men, one of a Rejang tribe, the other from a distant river, commenced a sham fight, with sword and shield; one of them was dressed as a Malay, the other as a Dayak. With slow side movements of their arms and legs, advancing and retreating, cutting and guarding to a measured step, and in regular time; then they changed to quick movements, stooping low till the shield completely covered them: with a hopping, dancing motion they kept giving and receiving blows till one of them fled; the other immediately followed, but cautiously, as the fugitive was supposed to plant spikes in the path. At last they again met, and after a fierce combat one was slain, and the victor with a slow dancing step approached the body and was supposed to cut off the head of his enemy; but, on looking at it attentively, he found he had killed a friend, and showed signs of much grief. With a measured tread, he again drew near the body and pretended to restore the head; he retired and advanced several times, shaking the various limbs of the friend's body, when the slain sprang up as lively as ever, and the two wound up by a frantic dance.

I have mentioned the ceremonies that took place at the solemnization of peace between the Sakarangs and Balaus; here they were slightly different. A pig

was placed between the representatives of two tribes,
who, after calling down the vengeance of the spirits
on those who broke the treaty, plunged their spears
into the animal, and then exchanged weapons. Drawing their krises, they each bit the blade of the other's,
and so completed the affair. The sturdy chief of
Kajulo declared he considered his word as more
binding than any such ceremony.

In the neighbourhood of the Kanowit, and scattered
about these countries, are the wandering tribes of
Pakatan and Punan, which seldom build regular
houses, but prefer running up temporary huts, and
when they have exhausted the jungle around of wild
beasts and other food, they move to a new spot.
They are the great collectors of wax, edible birds'
nests, camphor and rattans. They are popularly said
to be fairer than the other inhabitants of Borneo, as
they are never exposed to the sun, living in the
thickest part of the old forest. Those we have seen
were certainly darker, but they themselves assert that
their women are fairer. It is probable that exposure to
the air has as much effect upon them as exposure to
the sun. I have often met with their little huts in
the forest and used them as night lodgings, but I
have never come across these wild tribes. I have
seen individual men, but never communities.

The Pakatans and Punans are the true manufac-
turers of the Sumpitan, or blow-pipe; and in their
hands it is a formidable weapon. It is curious to
examine this product of their skill; and we cannot
but admire the accuracy with which the hole is
drilled through a hard wood shaft some seven or
eight feet long.

I had often heard of the deadly effect of the poison into which the arrow was dipped, but always disbelieved the bulk of the native stories, though I must believe in the evidence we have lately had. In 1859, the Kanowit tribe, instigated by Sherif Musahor, murdered two English gentlemen, and then fled into the interior. Mr. Johnson, who led the attack on them, tells me he lost thirty men by wounds from the poisoned arrows. He found the bodies of Dayaks who had gone out as skirmishers without a mark, beyond the simple puncture where a drop of blood rested on the wound. One man was struck near him ; he instantly had the arrow extracted, the wound sucked, a glass of brandy administered, and the patient sent off to the boats about four miles distant. Two companions supported him, and they had strict orders not to allow him to sleep till he reached the landing-place : they made him keep awake, and he recovered. As it is common to destroy deer, wild boars and other creatures with these arrows, no doubt man also can be killed.

I will now give an account of the manners and customs of the Sea Dayaks.

# CHAPTER II.

## SOCIAL LIFE OF THE SEA DAYAKS.

*At the Birth of Children.*—The Sea Dayaks naturally
look upon this as a very ordinary event; occasionally
guns are fired to celebrate it, but even that practice has
almost fallen into disuse. However, a few months
after the birth of the infant, the Sakarang Dayaks
give a feast in its honour, which generally takes place
before they commence preparing their land for the
rice crop, and another after the harvest to " launch
the child" on the world. During these feasts the
manang, or priest, waves the odoriferous areca-blossom

over the babe, and moves about the house chanting
monotonous tunes. The festival lasts a day and a
night. The Dayak women suffer very little at their
confinements, and seldom remain quiet beyond a few
days. They are very anxious to have children, but if
they have a preference, it is for boys; and when the
only child is a daughter, they often make a vow to
fire guns and give a feast, should the next prove a
son.

It is very singular, that though these Dayaks are
exceedingly fond of their offspring, yet infanticide
sometimes occurs among the Batang Lupars; arising,
it is said, from a selfish feeling of affection. One
man confessed to Mr. Johnson that he had put an
infant to death, because all the children born to him
previously had died just as they arrived at an age when
he could fondly love them. He said he could not endure
to think that it should occur to him again. But this
must have been a rare instance, since they feel acutely
the loss of their children, and wander about incon-
solable, and mope, and often refuse to work for
months. They do not bear misfortunes well; even the
loss of houses by fire, or their crops from bad seasons,
disheartens them to an extent that is surprising to
those who have watched the conduct of the Scribas
Dayaks. The piratical pursuits in which these latter
delighted have certainly given great energy to their
character; and they recover immediately from the
effects of the destruction of their villages and of their
property, and set to work to create more wealth.

The Sea Dayaks, as I have observed, generally prefer male children; and the more mischievous and
boisterous they are when young the greater the

delight they afford their parents. The observation,
" He is very wicked," is the greatest praise. They
indulge them in everything, and at home give way to
their caprices· in an extraordinary manner. If the
parents are affectionate to their children, the latter
warmly return it. Instances have even occurred
when, oppressed by sorrow at the reproaches of a
father, a child has privately taken poison and destroyed himself.

Like other tribes in the same state of civilization,
the Dayaks are fond of oratory; and while the elders
are discoursing· or delivering long speeches, the young
lads look gravely on, never indulging in a laugh,
which would be regarded as a serious offence.

The Dayaks are a very sociable people, and love to
have their families around them; grandfathers spoil
their grandchildren; and during the heavy work of the
harvest, the very old ones stay at home surrounded
by merry groups of young ones.

Strangers are generally very welcome; and it would
be an annoying idea to enter into their heads that
they were considered either mean or inhospitable. So
the wayfarer is presented on his arrival with the best
food in the house. Occasionally it is not very welcome to a European, as it too often consists of fish
that emits a very high scent, or eggs of a very ancient
date; but there is generally some fruit, or a little
clean boiled rice. I was once presented with some
preserved durian fruit, which stank so fearfully as to
drive my friends completely out of the house. But
the greatest luxury that can be presented to a native
is always forthcoming, and that is the box of areca
nuts, and the other chewing condiments.

Parents and children, brothers and sisters, very
seldom quarrel; when they do so, it is from having
married into a family with whom afterwards they may
have disputes about land.   One would imagine that
was a subject not likely to create dissensions in a
country like Borneo; but there are favourite farming
grounds and boundaries are not very settled. . It
used to be the practice not to have recourse to
arms on those occasions, but the two parties collecting
their relatives and friends would fight with sticks for
the coveted spot.   Now, however, their disputes are
brought to their chiefs, or the nearest English officer.

*Marriage.*—Among the Sibuyau Dayaks of Lundu,
no ceremony attends a betrothement, but when
the consent of the parents of the bride has been
obtained, an early day is appointed for the marriage.
As a general rule, the husband follows the wife, that
is, lives with and works for the parents of the latter.
On the wedding day, the bride and bridegroom are
brought from opposite ends of the village to the spot
where the ceremony is to be performed.   They are
made to sit on two bars of iron, that blessings as
lasting, and health as vigorous, as the metal may
attend the pair.   A cigar and betel leaf prepared with
the areca nut are next put into the hands of the bride
and bridegroom.   One of the priests then waves two
fowls over the heads of the couple, and in a long address to the Supreme Being, calls down blessings upon
the pair, and implores that peace and happiness may
attend the union. After the heads of the affianced have
been knocked against each other three or four times,
the bridegroom puts the prepared siri leaf and the cigar
into the mouth of the bride, while she does the same

to him, whom she thus acknowledges as her husband. The fowls are then killed, and the blood caught in two cups, and from its colour the priest foretels the future happiness or misery of the newly married. The ceremony is closed by a feast, with dancing and noisy music.

It is worthy of remark that the respect paid by a son-in-law to the father of his wife is greater than that paid to his own father. He treats him with much ceremony, must never pronounce his name, nor must he take the liberty of eating off the same plate, or drinking out of the same cup, or even of lying down on the same mat.

Among the Balaus, or Sea Dayaks of Lingga, there is also no ceremony at a betrothement; in fact, Mr. Chambers informs me that the word is not known in their language. Indeed their manners preclude the necessity of any such formal arrangement.

Marriage itself is a very simple affair, and is not accompanied by any long rite. However, as it is different from that practised in Lundu, I will enter into particulars.

Two or three days previous to the ceremony, the mother of the bridegroom usually gives the bride's relations a plate or a basin. The wedding takes place at the house of the girl, and the rite is called blah pinang, or the splitting of the prepared areca nut. It is divided into three portions, and the mother, after placing them in a little basket, and covering them over with a red cloth, sets them on a raised altar in front of the bride's house. The respective friends of the families then meet in conclave and enjoy the native luxury of prepared areca nut;

and it is now determined what shall be the fine paid
in case the husband should separate from his wife
after she shall be declared pregnant, or after she has
borne a child. This is a very necessary precaution,
as I shall have presently to show.

I may notice that among these Dayaks there is great
pride of birth, and that parents will seldom consent
to their daughter's marrying a man of very inferior
condition. Many lamentable occurrences have arisen
from this, among other causes, which I will mention
when treating of love. As a general rule, if the
bride be an only daughter, or of higher rank, the
husband joins her family—if he be of higher rank, or
an only son, she follows him, and then she is conducted
under a canopy of red cloth to the house of his
parents. If they should be of equal condition and
similarly circumstanced, they divide their time among
their respective families, until they set up housekeeping on their own account.

There are three subjects of which I must now
treat,—and they are the chastity of the women, love,
and divorce. I find it difficult to reconcile the statements that I have to make; they are modest, and yet
unchaste, love warmly and yet divorce easily, but are
generally faithful to their husbands when married.

In looking over the notes I have collected, both of
my own and those that I have received from my
friends, I find them apparently irreconcilable; but I
will endeavour to make them intelligible.

The Sibuyaus, though they do not consider the
sexual intercourse of their young people as a positive
crime, yet are careful of the honour of their daughters, as they attach an idea of great indecency to pro-

miscuous connection. They are far advanced beyond
their brethren in this respect, and are of opinion that
an unmarried girl proving with child must be offensive
to the superior powers, who, instead of always chas-
tising the individual, punish the tribe by misfortunes
happening to its members. They, therefore, on the
discovery of the pregnancy fine the lovers, and
sacrifice a pig to propitiate offended Heaven, and
to avert that sickness or those misfortunes that
might otherwise follow ; and they inflict heavy mulcts
for every one who may have suffered from any
severe accident, or who may have been drowned
within a month before the religious atonement was
made ; lighter fines are levied if a person be simply
wounded.

As these pecuniary demands fall upon the families
of both parties, great care is taken of the young girls,
and seldom is it found necessary to sacrifice the pig.
After marriage the women also are generally chaste,
though cases of adultery are occasionally brought
before the Orang Kayas.

Among the Dayaks on the Batang Lupar, however,
unchastity is more common ; but the favours of the
women are generally confined to their own countrymen, and usually to one lover. Should the girl prove
with child, it is an understanding between them that
they marry, and men seldom, by denying, refuse to
fulfil their engagements. Should, however, the girl
be unable to name the father, she is exposed to the
reproaches of her relatives, and many to escape them
have taken poison. In respectable families they sacrifice a pig, and sprinkle the doors with its blood, to
wash away the sin ; and the erring maiden's position

is rendered so uncomfortable that she generally tries
to get away from home.

In the account of the Land Dayaks, I will mention
the manner in which the young lover approaches the
curtains of his mistress.  As this seldom ends in immorality, it may be likened to the Welch and Af-
ghan bundling.  The Sea Dayaks have the same
practice of seeking the girls at night; and as the
favoured lover is seldom refused entrance to the
curtains, it may be compared to the system of com-
pany-keeping which obtains in many of our agricultural counties, where the brides have children a
couple of months after marriage.  The morality of
the Sea Dayaks is, perhaps, superior to the Malays,
but inferior to that of the Land Dayaks.

During one of my visits to the Sakarang I heard
a story which is rather French in its termination.  A
young man proposed to a girl and was accepted by
her, but her parents refused to give their consent, as
he was of very inferior birth.  Every means was tried
to soften their hearts, but they were obstinate, and
endeavoured to induce her to give up her lover and
marry another.  In their despair the lovers retired to
the jungle, and swallowed the poisonous juice of the
tuba plant: next morning they were found dead, with
their cold and stiff arms entwined round each other.
Cases are not of very rare occurrence among the
Sakarang Dayaks, where disappointed love has sought
solace in the grave.

Of the warmth of married affection, I have never
heard a more striking instance than the following :—
the story has been told before, but it is worth repeating.  Ijau, a Balau chief, was bathing with his wife

in the Lingga river, a place notorious for man-eating alligators, when Indra Lela, a Malay, passing in a boat remarked,—"I have just seen a very large animal swimming up the stream." Upon hearing this, Ijau told his wife to go up the steps and he would follow; she got safely up, but he, stopping to wash his feet, was seized by the alligator, dragged into the middle of the stream, and disappeared from view. His wife hearing a cry turned round, and seeing her husband's fate sprang into the river, shrieking,—"Take me also," and dived down at the spot where she had seen the alligator sink with his prey. No persuasion could induce her to come out of the water: she swam about, diving in all the places most dreaded from being a resort of ferocious reptiles, seeking to die with her husband; at last her friends came down and forcibly removed her to their house.

About two miles below the town of Kuching, is a place called Tanah Putih. Here a man and his wife were working in a small canoe, when an alligator seized the latter by the thigh and bore her along the surface of the water, calling for that help, which her husband swimming after, in vain endeavoured to afford. The bold fellow with a kris in his mouth neared the reptile, but as soon as he was heard, the beast sank with his shrieking prey and ended a scene almost too painful for description. Two days after-wards the body, unmangled, was found hidden in some bushes, which partly confirms my previous remark, that alligators do not immediately swallow their prey.

Husbands and wives appear to pass their lives very

agreeably together, which may partly be caused by
the facility of divorce. Many men and women have
been married seven or eight times before they find the
partner with whom they desire to spend the rest of
their lives. I saw a young girl of seventeen who had
already had three husbands. These divorces take
place at varied times, from a few days after marriage,
to one or two years. However, after the birth of a
child, they seldom seek to separate, and if they do
the husband is fined, but not the wife. The work of
the family is divided, though perhaps the female has
most continued labour. The man builds and repairs
the houses and boats, fells all the heavy timber at the
farm, brings home the firewood, and very often nurses
the baby. The wives are very domestic, and in their
way carefully attend to household duties ; they cook,
clean the rice, feed the pigs and poultry, spin the
yarn, weave the cloth, and make the clothes. A wife
is also expected to be polite to visitors, to bring out
her finest mats, and offer the interminable areca nut
to her guests.

As the wife works hard, she is generally very
strong and capable of taking her own part. She is
very jealous of her husband, much more so than he is
of her. If he be found flirting with another woman,
the wife may inflict a severe thrashing on her, but
only with sticks, while if the offending woman have a
husband, he may do the same to the man. To
escape these domestic broils, he generally starts off
into the jungle, and pretends to or really does go
head-hunting.

The causes of divorce are innumerable, but incom-
patibility of temper is perhaps the most common ;

when they are tired of each other they do not say so,
but put the fault upon an unfavourable omen or a bad
dream, either of which is allowed to be a legitimate
cause of divorce. Should they, however, be still fond
of each other, the sacrifice of a pig will effectually
prevent any misfortune happening to them from
neglecting to separate. Partners often divorce from
pique, or from a petty quarrel, and are then allowed
to come together again without any fresh marriage
ceremony. Among the Balau Dayaks, it is necessary
for the offended husband to send a ring to his wife,
before the marriage can be considered as finally dissolved, without which, should they marry again,
they would be liable to be punished for infidelity.

I may add, that as the wife does an equal share of
work with her husband, at a divorce she is entitled to
half the wealth created by their mutual labours.

*Burials.*—Among the Sea Dayaks, corpses are
usually buried; although, should a man express a wish
to share the privilege of the priests and be, like them,
exposed on a raised platform, the relations are bound
to comply with this request.

Immediately the breath has left the body, the
female relations commence loud and melancholy
laments; they wash the corpse, and dress it in its
finest garments, and often, if a man, fully armed, and
bear it forth to the great common hall, where it is
surrounded by its friends to be mourned over. In
some villages a hireling leads the lament, which is
continued till the corpse leaves the house. Before
this takes place, however, the body is rolled up in
cloths and fine mats, kept together by pieces of
bamboo tied on with rattans, and taken to the burial-

ground. A fowl is then killed as a sacrifice to the spirit who guards the earth, and they commence digging the grave from two and a half to four and a half feet deep, according to the person's rank ; deeper than five feet would be unlawful. Whilst this operation is going on, others fell a large tree, and cutting off about six feet, split it in two, and then hollow them out with an adze. One part serves as the coffin, the other as the lid ; the body is placed within, and the two are secured together by means of strips of pliable canes bound round them.

After the coffin is lowered into the grave, many things belonging to the deceased are cast in, together with rice, tobacco, and betel nut, as they believe they may prove useful in the other world, or as it is called by them Sabayan.

It was an old custom, but now perhaps falling somewhat into disuse, to place money, gold and silver ornaments, clothes, and various china and brass utensils in the grave; but these treasures were too great temptations to those Malays who were addicted to gambling; and the rifling of the place of interment has often given great and deserved offence to the relations. As it is almost impossible to discover the offenders, it is now the practice to break in pieces all the utensils placed in the grave, and to conceal as carefully as possible the valuable ornaments. The whole tribe of the Lundu Sibuyaus was thrown into a great state of excited indignation on finding that some Malays had opened the place of interment of the old Orang Kaya Tumanggong of Lundu, and stolen the valuable property. This was the chief who was so firm a friend of the Europeans, and whose name is so often mentioned in former works on Borneo.

The relatives and bearers of the corpse must return direct to the house from which they started before entering another, as it is unlawful or unlucky to stop, whatever may be the distance to be traversed.

They are often very particular about the dress in which they are to be buried. Many of the old Sakarang women have asked Mr. Johnson for handsome jackets to be used after their death for this purpose, saying that when they arrived in the other world, they would mention his name with respect and gratitude on account of the kindness shown to them in this.

The Dayaks who have fallen in battle are seldom interred, but a paling is put round them to keep away the pigs, and they are left there. Those who commit suicide are buried in different places from others, as it is supposed that they will not be allowed to mix in the seven-storied Sabayan with such of their fellow-countrymen as come by their death in a natural manner or from the influences of the spirits.

It is very satisfactory to be able to state that the Sea Dayaks have a clear idea of one Omnipotent Being who created and now rules over the world. They call him Batara; beneath him are many good and innumerable bad spirits, and the fear of the latter causes them to make greater offerings to them than to the good spirits. The awe with which many of them are named has induced a few, among others, Mr. Chambers, to imagine that their religion is a species of polytheism. But that is, I think, clearly a mistake: as well might a Mahomedan declare that

Christians were Polytheists, because Roman Catholics
believe in the interposition of the Virgin and of the
saints, and because members of all sects fear the wiles
of Satan.   It is a common saying among the Dayaks,
With " God's blessing we shall have a good harvest
next year."

Mr. Gomez, who has lived nine years among the
Sibuyaus, and Mr. Johnson, who has mixed with all
sections of the Sea Dayaks still longer, take my
view.   There are evil spirits of various kinds who
reside in the jungles, or the mountains, or the earth :
all sicknesses, misfortunes, or death, proceed from
them, while to Batara is attributed every blessing.

But when they make offerings, both are propitiated,
and, as usual, the wicked have the larger share.
The priests offer a long prayer, and supplicate them
to depart from the afflicted house, or from the sick
man.   Of the seven platefuls of food, four are given
to the evil spirits, and cast forth or exposed in the
forests, while the others are offered to the good spirits,
who are implored to protect and bless them.   The
food offered to the latter is not considered to be interdicted, but may be, and is always, eaten.

The Lingga Dayaks, besides Batara, have various
good spirits—as Stampandei, who superintends the
propagation of mankind ; Pulang Ganah, who inhabits
the earth and gives fertility to it, and to him are
addressed the offerings at the feasts given whilst
preparing the rice cultivation ; Singallong Burong, the
god of war, excites their utmost reverence, and to
him are offered the head feasts.   On those occasions,
he comes down and hovers in the form of a kite over
the house, and guns are fired and gongs are beaten

in his honour: his brave followers married to his
daughters appear in the form of their omen birds.
No wonder he is honoured: he gives success in war,
and delights in their acquisition of the heads of their
enemies. Nattiang inhabits the summits of the hills,
and is one of their demigods. The Linggas tell
many stories of his exploits: the most famous was
his expedition to the skies to recover his wife, who
had been caught in a noose and hoisted up there
by his old enemy, Apei Sabit Berkait. To dream of
him is to receive the gift of bravery. Mr. Chambers
would add much to our knowledge of these people
if he would make a collection of their stories and
ballads.

Among the Sakarangs the belief in one Supreme
Being is clear, and they do not appear to have any
inferior deities who approach him in attributes: they
have demigods, good and bad spirits, but no sharer
of God's throne. They believe that the good and
bad spirits have the power to prevent, or to enable
them to succeed in any object they may have in view.
They, therefore, make offerings to them, particularly
when any of their family are suffering from illness.

When the small-pox was committing sad havoc
among those villagers who would not allow themselves
to be inoculated, they ran into the jungle in every
direction, caring for no one but themselves, leaving
the houses empty, and dwelling far away in the most
silent spots, in parties of two and three, and sheltered
only by a few leaves. When these calamities come
upon them, they utterly lose all command over themselves, and become as most timid children. Those
seized with the complaint are abandoned: all they

do is to take care that a bundle of firewood, a cooking-pot, and some rice, are placed within their reach. On account of this practice, few recover, as in the delirium they roll on the ground and die.

When the fugitives become short of provisions, a few of the old men who have already had the complaint creep back to the houses at night and take a supply of rice. In the daytime they do not dare to stir or to speak above a whisper for fear the spirits should see or hear them. They do not call the small-pox by its name, but are in the habit of saying, "Has he yet left you?" at other times, they call it jungle leaves or fruit; and at other places the datu or the chief. Those tribes who inoculate suffer very little.

Their priests frequently use the names of the invisible spirits, and are supposed to be able to interpret their language, as well as to hold communion with them; and in ordinary times they pretend to work the cure of the sick by means of incantations, and after blinding the patient's eyes, pretend by the aid of the spirits to draw the bones of fish or fowls out of their flesh. When the Dayaks are questioned as to their belief in these easily-exposed deceits, they say no; but the custom has descended to them from their ancestors, and they still pay these priests heavy sums to perform the ancient rites.

Though these priests are of course men, yet some pretend to be women, or rather dress as such, and like to be treated as females. In Lingga, however, out of thirty, only one has given up man's attire. Many of the priests are the blind and maimed for life, who by following this profession are enabled to earn a livelihood.

If a Dayak lose his wife, he gives a feast, which is really an offering to the departed spirit. After the death of relatives, they seek for the heads of enemies, and until one is brought in they consider themselves to be in mourning, wearing no fine clothes, striking no gongs, nor is laughing or merry-making in the house allowed; but they have a steady desire to grieve for the one lost to them, and to seek a head of an enemy, as a means of consoling themselves for the death of the departed.

At the launching of a new boat, preparatory to head-hunting, the spirits presiding over it are appeased and fed, and the women collect in and about it, and chant monotonous tunes; invoking the heavenly spirits to grant their lovers and husbands success in finding heads, by which they may remove their mourning and obtain a plentiful supply of the luxuries and necessaries of life.

The principal sacrifice of the Sakarang Dayaks is killing a pig and examining its heart, which is supposed to foretel events with the utmost certainty. As an instance: should they find a dead animal on land prepared for a farm, according to their established custom, they should give it up, and commence a new one; but if the season for burning the jungle be passed, they endeavour to avert this loss by consulting the heart of a pig. The animal is sacrificed, and the greatest attention is given to the signs discovered upon his heart: if they be satisfactory, the farm land may be used; if not, it is completely abandoned.

After their great head feasts, they also examine

the hearts of pigs, and their gray-headed leaders
surround and look extremely grave over the bleeding
spectacle which they one by one turn over with the
point of a stick to examine the run and position of
the veins; each as he does it offers some sapient
remark; and the result generally is, that there are
still numerous enemies, but far away: but however
powerful these may be, they themselves are more
powerful, and in the end will overcome them.

Not many years ago, Rentap, the pirate chief, who
formerly resided in a stronghold on the summit of the
Sadok mountain, took a Sakarang lad prisoner.
Although one of his own race, he determined on
putting him to death, remarking—"It has been our
custom heretofore to examine the heart of a pig, but
now we will examine a human one." The unfortunate
boy was dragged about for some time by the hair
of his head, and then put to death and his heart
examined.

It is reported that many years ago a Sibuyau chief
sacrificed some prisoners on the graves of two of his
sons, who, in the same expedition, had been killed by
his enemies.

To hear the cry of a deer is at all times considered
unlucky; and to prevent the sound reaching their
ears during a marriage procession gongs and drums
are loudly beaten. On the way to their farms,
should the unlucky omen be heard, they will return
home and do no work for a day.

It is a very curious custom also, that if two men
who have been at deadly feud, meet in a house, they
refuse to cast their eyes upon each other till a fowl has
been killed and the blood sprinkled over them; and,

as already fully described, when two tribes make peace, after solemn engagements are concluded, a pig is killed, the blood of which is supposed to cement the bond of friendship.

They believe in a future state—considering that the Simañgat, or spiritual part of man, lives for ever, that they awake shortly after death in Sabayan or the future abode, and that there they find those of their relatives and friends who have departed before them. The Sibuyaus divide their Sabayan into seven distinct stories, which are occupied by the souls of the departed according to their rank and position in life. The really wicked occupy the lowest; but, whether happy or miserable, they acknowledge ignorance.

The Dayaks are very litigious, and few would have the patience to investigate one of their cases. The amateur lawyers of a tribe are acute in inquiry, quick in making retorts, and gifted with wonderful memories, generally referring to precedents of the customs of their forefathers in the settlement of fresh cases.

A head feast consists in a general meeting of the tribe in the man's house who gives the entertainment. He prepares for it two or three months before it takes place, collecting fish, fowls, eggs, plantains, and other fruits, and in manufacturing an intoxicating drink from rice. When all these things are ready, poles are cut of various lengths, one for each of the heads that may be there to be rejoiced over; there are also fantastically-shaped wooden birds, which undergo various evolutions in the house; and, after the feast is over, are placed on the top of the before-mentioned poles, with their heads turned in the direction of the enemies' country. The people, dressed in their best clothes, collect in the house, and commence the feast by all the youthful portion of the community engaging in cock-fighting —real cock-fights, too often with very formidable steel spurs. They are very partial to this amusement, and will go far and pay much for a good bird, and will bet heavily on a well-known cock.

After some hours engaged in this amusement, they commence drinking and eating, a part of the ceremony which does not entice the European stranger, nor can the peculiar smell increase his appetite. It is an extraordinary accumulation of food: fowls roasted with their feathers on, and then torn joint from joint; eggs black from age, decayed fruit, rice of all colours and kinds, strong-smelling fish, almost approaching a state of rottenness; and their drink having the appearance and the thickness of curds, in which they mix pepper and other ingredients. It has a sickening effect upon them, and they swallow it more as a duty than because they relish it. Before they have added any extraneous matter it is not unpleasant, having something of the taste of spruce beer.

They have then several processions, each headed by chiefs marching with grave countenances, and followed by a youthful crowd. Their movements are not graceful while parading about a house, as they put their bodies into the stiffest postures. The women also, adorned with trappings and beads of every colour, walk up and down, scattering yellow rice about the house and on the heads of the men. The feast lasts three days and nights, and winds up by their becoming amicably intoxicated, always excepting the women, who do not drink, but take care of their drunken husbands and relatives. This feast is intended as an offering to Batara, on account of their success against enemies, and as a thanksgiving for a plentiful harvest. To fail in this testimony of gratitude would be grievous in their eyes. The Sea Dayaks follow the custom of Pamali, or taboo, and believe in omens.*

*Head-hunting.*—This practice has no doubt obtained among the Dayaks from the earliest times, and when carried on by the interior tribes very few lives were lost; but it much retarded the progress of the country, as it rendered life and property insecure. The Sakarang and Seribas, within the memory of living men, were a quiet, inoffensive people, paying taxes to their Malay chiefs, and suffering much from their oppressive practices,—even their children being seized and sold into slavery. When the Malay communities quarrelled they summoned their Dayak followers around them, and led them on expeditions against each other. This accustomed the aborigines to the sea; and being found hard-working and willing men, the Malays and Lanun pirates took them out in their marauding expeditions, dividing the plunder—the heads of the killed for the Dayaks, the goods and captives for themselves.

Gradually they began to feel their own strength and superiority of numbers. In their later expeditions the Malays have followed rather than led. The longing these Dayaks have acquired for head-hunting is surprising. They say, " The white men read books, we hunt for heads instead." Until the

* See chapters on the " Social Life of the Land Dayaks."

Sarawak Government curbed their proceedings they were known to coast down as far as Pontianak, and occasionally they had been met forty miles out at sea in their rattan-tied boats, some of them seventy feet in length. In rough weather most of the crew jump overboard and hold on to the sides while the rest bale the boat out. They say, when this occurs in places suspected to be frequented by sharks, they each tie a bundle of the tuba plant round their ancles to drive the devouring fish away. The juice of the tuba is the one used to intoxicate fish.

About thirteen years ago, I heard the Natuna people give an account of a horrible transaction that took place in one of their islands. A party of Seribas Dayaks were cruising about among the little isles near, and had destroyed several women and many fishermen, when they were observed, towards evening, creeping into a deep and narrow inlet to remain during the night. The islanders quietly assembled and surprised their enemies, killing all but seven, who were taken prisoners—six men and one lad. The former they roasted over a slow fire, and they declared that the bold fellows died without uttering a cry of pain, but defying them to the last; the lad, who stood trembling by, uncertain of his fate, was sent back to the coast with a message to his country-men, that if they ever came there again, they would be all treated in the same way. This fearful warning was sufficient to deter their seeking heads again in that direction.

Parties of two and three sometimes went away for months on an inland incursion, taking nothing with them but salt wrapped up in their waist-cloths, with which they seasoned the young shoots, and leaves, and palm cabbages, found in the forests; and when they returned home, they were as thin as scarecrows. It is this kind of cat-like warfare which causes them to be formidable enemies both to the Chinese and the Malays, who never feel themselves safe from a Dayak enemy. They have been known to keep watch in a well up to their chins in water, with a covering of a few leaves over their heads to endeavour to cut off the first person who might come to draw water. At night they would drift down on a log, and cut the rattan cable of trading prahus, while others of their party would keep watch on the bank, knowing well where the stream would take the boat ashore; and when aground they kill the men and plunder the goods.

An atrocious case happened many years ago up the Batang Lupar, where a young man started on an expedition by himself to seek for a head from a neighbouring tribe. In a few days he came back with the desired prize. His relatives questioned him how it was he had been away so few days, as they had never been able to do the same journey in double the time. He replied gravely that the spirits of the woods had assisted him.

About a month afterwards a headless trunk was discovered near one of their farms, and on inquiry being made, it was found to be the body of an old woman of their own tribe, not very distantly related to the young fellow himself. He was only fined by the chief of the tribe, and the head taken from him and buried.

If a large party intended starting under a leader of

any note, they waited till he had first built a hut not far from the village, and listened for an omen from the cry of the birds. As soon as a good one was heard, they started ; and when a certain distance from home, stopped and held a consultation, in which they decided on the mode of attack, and how the heads, captives, and plunder should be divided. Large rivers intervening did not deter them, as they could always build boats, tying them together with rattans, each being capable of holding about thirty men. On their return they hid the planks in the jungle, to be used on a future occasion.

Their war boats are well constructed and good models, and very fast; some will hold as many as sixty or seventy men, with two months' provisions. The keel is flat, with a curve or sheer of hard wood. A long one does not exceed six fathoms, and upon it they will build a boat of eleven fathoms over all. The extra length of planks, which overlap, is brought up with a sheer. They caulk the seams with a bark which is plentiful in the jungle. No other fastenings but rattans are used.

They paint their boats red and white,—the former is generally an ochre, but occasionally they use a kind of red seed pounded; the white is simply lime, made from sea shells. In their boat expeditions they always take a supply of red ochre to eat, in case of becoming short of other provisions ; and we once found in some deserted Seribas' prahus many packets of a white oleaginous clay used for the same purpose. The bark they employ for caulking is very tough, and beaten out, serves to make useful and comfortable coverlets, as well as waist-cloths and head-dresses.

I have mentioned that the possession of a head is necessary to enable the Dayaks to leave off mourning. I once met the Orang Kaya Pamancha of Seribas, the most influential chief in the country. He was dressed in nothing but a dirty rag round his loins, and thus he intended to remain until the mourning for his wife ceased by securing a head. Until this happens they cannot marry again, or appease the spirit of the departed, which continues to haunt the house and make its presence known by certain ghostly rappings. They endeavour to mollify its anger by the nearest relative throwing a packet of rice to it under the house every day, until the spirit is laid to rest by their being able to celebrate a head feast: then the Dayaks forget their dead, and the ghosts of the dead forget them. When passing a burial-ground, however, they throw on it something they consider acceptable to the departed.

In writing about head-hunting, I should more frequently employ the past tense, as all those portions of these tribes, which have been brought under English influence, are rapidly losing these customs; and could any profitable agricultural industry be introduced among them, they would soon expend their energies in money-making.

The Dayaks are exceedingly quick in commercial transactions; and most of them who did not know the value of a piece of money six years ago are now active traders. They are said to be more acute than Malays, so that even the Chinese find they cannot cheat them after the first year. They are hoarding, though liberal according to custom; but generally they are much disposed to be avaricious and close-

fisted.   The Malays sometimes make good bargains
with them by using soft and flattering language, but
the Dayaks often repent of being so wheedled, and
will claim justice before the courts.

The Sea Dayaks, contrary to ancient custom, have
the habit of keeping a few slaves, and are generally
kind masters;   but the system has been a very
bad one, as many unfortunate people have become so
in consequence of the debts or the crimes of their
parents or grand-parents.   It is scarcely right to
give the name of slaves to these people, as on the
payment of the original debt or fine they become
free.

They have no graven images, nor do they practise
any outward or visible signs of idolatry, nor have
they any mode of religious worship further than a
solemn attention to superstitious practices and observances.  Several Dayaks have an objection to eating
the flesh of pigs, deer, and other animals; but it is
because they are afraid of getting certain complaints,
as skin diseases, and the custom becomes hereditary,
as many families are subject to them; or it arises
from the fear of going mad;  or as some married
women tremble to touch deer's flesh previously to the
birth of their firstborn; or because they have received
warning in dreams not to touch a particular kind of
food.   Their religious opinions do not forbid them to
eat any kind of animals.

The Sea Dayaks, however, would not intentionally
kill a cobra, one species of the lizard, or owls, or any
of their birds of omen.   There are, also, certain
animals and other birds which many families abstain
from injuring;  in some cases, owing to a dream;

in others, to help traditionally received from them by an ancestor. In others, it is forbidden to kill a civet cat, an orang-utan, or an alligator; and they give such reasons as the following:—" One of my ancestors, a clever man, cured a sick alligator, and then they made an agreement that neither should injure the other." Another said, when his great-grandfather first settled at the hill of Banting, the orang-utan abounded there. Their enemies once came to attack the place, but were repulsed by the assistance of the orang-utans, who crowded to the edge of the fruit groves to glare on the strangers, and were probably mistaken for men. As a reason for not destroying the cobra, they say, " It has always been forbidden, those who dream of them are lucky, and often do the great spirits put on the forms of snakes."

They sometimes change their names after severe sickness, when their priests recommend it on the restoration of health. And, also, in the event of a slave becoming free, his late master gives a feast upon the occasion of manumitting him, and proclaims his freedom in public. They often present a spear upon the occasion, the meaning of which is that, if he be again claimed as a slave, the spear may be used to put to death his former master.

It is contrary to custom for a man to marry a first cousin, as they look upon them as sisters. No marriage is allowed with aunt or niece, and some objection is made in a few of the communities to a man marrying a deceased wife's sister, or a woman taking her husband's brother; but these customs are not always followed, and I have heard of uncles marrying

nieces, and a marriage with a deceased wife's sister is
also permitted, provided her parents approve of the
man; and it is then often encouraged by them in
order to bring up the children as one family.

Their priests have little or no knowledge of medicine, but trust, in most cases, to their occult sciences.
In ordinary sickness the relatives are attentive, but
not so, as I have said, when there is a sweeping
epidemic, as small-pox; in such cases they think it
to be useless striving against so formidable a spirit.
When cholera was in the country, the Dayaks lost
comparatively few, as they healed those taken with it
by rubbing and warmth; but the Malays appeared to
have done everything they should not have done—
drinking, when in health, nothing but hot water,
taking no exercise, and only eating a little rice; the
consequence was they were too weak to strive against
the complaint when seized.    The most successful
system practised by the natives appears to be to rub
the stomach and limbs with cajput oil (kayu putih
oil), and administer a strong dose of spirits immediately the first symptoms are perceived.    It is said
a few drops of the oil are also given with success.
When the cholera, after committing great ravages in
the capital, appeared among the Muruts and Bisayas
of Limbang, they all fled from their villages, retiring
to the hills and the depths of the forest; their loss
was very slight.

The women manufacture a coarse cloth; making
and dyeing their own yarn, beating out the cotton
with small sticks, and, by means of a spinning-wheel,
running it off very quickly.   The yarn is not so fine
as what they can buy of English manufacture, but it

is stronger, and keeps its colour remarkably well; and no cloth wears better than Dayak cloth.

Their agricultural pursuits are limited in number, and with little labour the soil yields sufficient crops to supply their wants. They plant rice once a year; those who live on dry and high land have also cotton and tobacco. They grow enough sugar-cane for their own eating, not for making sugar; and they are so eager for gain, that it would not be difficult to induce them to plant crops requiring only ordinary superintendence. They sow the cotton-seed after the rice harvest. Their agricultural instruments are strong swords, made by themselves from imported iron, used for cutting grass or young jungle; and a kind of small axe and adze in one, by turning the iron in its socket. This instrument they use in shaping out planks for boats, and for felling the larger trees; and, in their hands, it brings down the timber as fast as an English axe would in the hands of a backwoodsman. One method they adopt for getting rid of old jungle is this:—first of all, they clear away the underwood and the branches near the ground, then with their axes they cut the larger trees more than half through; at last, choosing some giant of the forest, they fell it completely: in its fall it drags all the others after it, as they are connected together by twining creepers of great size and strength. It is a dangerous practice, and requires care to avoid the wide-spread fall, that comes to the earth with an awful crash.

They obtain bees'-wax from the nests built on the tapang tree, and climb the loftiest heights in search of it, upon small sticks, which they drive as they advance up the noble stem that rises above a hundred

feet free of branches, and whose girth varies from
fifteen to five-and-twenty feet.  Once these pegs are
driven in, their outer ends are connected by a
stout rattan, which, with the tree, forms a kind of
ladder.

It requires cool and deliberate courage to take a
bee-hive at so great an elevation, where, in case of
being attacked by the bees, the almost naked man
would fall and be dashed to atoms.  They depend upon
the flambeaux they carry up with them, as, when the
man disturbs the hive, the sparks falling from it
cause, it is said, the bees to fly down in chase of
them, instead of attacking their real enemy, who then
takes the hive and lowers it down by a rattan string.
The bees escape unhurt.  This plan does not appear
to be as safe as that pursued by the Pakatan Dayaks,
who kindle a large fire under the trees, and, throwing
green branches upon it, raise so stifling a smoke that
the bees rush forth, and the man ascending takes their
nest in safety.  Both these operations are generally
conducted at night, although the second might be, I
imagine, practised in safety during the day.

There is a custom existing among the Dayaks of
the Batang Lupar which I have not heard of elsewhere.
Beside one of the paths in the Undup district there
are several heaps of sticks ; and in other places, of
stones, called " tambun bula," or lying heaps.   Each
heap is in remembrance of some man who has told a
stupendous lie, or disgracefully failed in carrying out
an engagement; and every passer-by takes a stick or
a stone to add to the accumulation, saying, at the
time he does it, " For So-and-so's lying heap."   It
goes on for generations, until they sometimes forget

who it was that told the lie; but, notwithstanding that, they continue throwing the stone.

At another place, near many cross roads, there is a tree on which are hung innumerable pieces of rag; each person passing tears a little bit of cloth from his costume and sticks it there. They have forgotten the origin of this practice, but fear for their health if they neglect it. One Dayak observed, " It is like that custom of some European nations giving passports to those who enter or leave their country." If this be a true explanation, it is, perhaps, to give the spirits of the woods notice who have passed that way, and the Dayak's observation shows how quick they are, and how well they remember what they have heard.

They practise various ordeals; among others, two pieces of native salt, of equal weight, are placed in water; that appertaining to the guilty party melts immediately; the other, they affirm, keeps its form; but, in fact, the one that disappears first proves the owner to be in the wrong. Another is with two land shells, which are put on a plate and lime-juice squeezed upon them, and the one that moves first shows the guilt or innocence of the owner, according as they have settled previously whether motion or rest is to prove the case. They talk of another, where the hand is dipped into boiling water or oil, and innocence is proved by no injury resulting. The favourite ordeal, however, is the dipping the head under water, and the first who puts up his face to breathe loses the case.

I need only observe, concerning their language, that the Sibuyaus, the Balaus, the Undups, the

Batang Lupars, the Sakarangs, Seribas, and those inhabitants of the Rejang living on the Kanowit and Katibas branches, all speak the same language, with no greater modifications than exist between the English spoken in London and Somersetshire. They are, in fact, but divisions of the same tribe; and the differences that are gradually growing up between them principally arise from those who frequent the towns and engage in trade, using much Malay in their conversations, and allowing their own words to fall into disuse. The agricultural inhabitants of the farther interior are much more slowly influenced.

# CHAPTER III.

## THE KAYANS OF BARAM.

IN April, 1851, the steamer *Pluto*, Acting Commander Brett, arrived in Sarawak with directions to
take me on an official visit to Brunei and Baram.
Sarawak was at that time suffering from one of those
unaccountable panics which sometimes seize on both
large and small communities. The report was that a

French fleet was outside preparing to attack the place. People packed up their valuables, and some even carried them off to the forest. The only way we could account for it was the news of the recent destruction of the capital of Sulu by the Spaniards having by this time spread over the Archipelago, and been distorted in various ways.

Starting from Sarawak, we steered our course to the island of Labuan. One evening on a bright, starlight night, we were all sitting on the bridge of the vessel, when we were startled by the cry of a " man overboard." To stop the steamer, pull the trigger that disengaged the flaming life-buoy, and to let down the boats, did not take many minutes, and they soon pushed off from the sides. While we stood on the deck with strained attention, a sharp cry was heard; then there was a dead silence, followed immediately by the sound of the oars in the rowlocks as the men gave way towards the life-buoy that was seen floating astern like a bright torch dancing on the waves. We thought we heard another fainter cry, but the mind in great tension will imagine these things. We could distinguish amid the sound of splashing water the distant shouts of the men as the crews hailed each other, but no answer was given to our captain's eager inquiries, as the rustling of the wind in our rigging, and those varied sounds that ever will arise around a ship laying to, drowned his voice. The anxiety of all was intense as the boats pulled back, and a sickening feeling came over us all when we found that their search had been unavailing. Either strength had failed the man, or a shark had seized him before he could reach the life-buoy. The passionate grief of the son of the drowned Portuguese now struck painfully on our ears, and I was not sorry to gain the refuge of the inner cabin.

In sailing along this coast fine fish and small sharks are often caught by hook and line trailing out far behind the vessels. The Tañgiri fish is perhaps the finest: the usual size obtained varies from three to five feet, and it has something of the look of a salmon, without its richness of flavour. We have caught also many young sharks, but all under five feet; in fact, anything larger would carry away the bait, hook, and all. Young shark is often eaten, both by Malays and Chinese. I have tasted it, and thought it very coarse; but at sea even that change is palatable.

The coast line between Sarawak and Baram point is the least beautiful of the north-west coast. Scarcely any but hills far in the interior are seen, and the land is either flat or gently undulating hill and dale, but with few distinctive features. However, in the depth of the great bay that lies between Points Sirik and Baràm, near the river of Bintulu, there are some fine mountains; and once, during a very clear day, I thought I saw a far distant peak, which might be that of Tilong, according to native report, higher than Kina Balu. Bintulu is now the northern boundary of the territories of Sarawak.

Although I have said the appearance of this coast is not picturesque, yet in the eye of one who looks to the commercial and agricultural advantages, it is satisfactory. Broad plains of alluvial soil, as rich, perhaps, as any in the world, and a fine succession of swelling hill and dale afford some compensation to one who, as I do, looks upon this coast as capable of as much development as a similar space in Java.

Between Bintulu and Baram there are two remarkable serrated mountains—Silungan and Lambir; but in this ninety miles of coast one small village only is to found, and unless you penetrate far into the interior, there are but a few wandering Punans and others who inhabit it.

Baram is a dangerous point to ships, as it lies low and the sea shoals rapidly. Here in the rainy season the fresh water rushes out with so much force, as to carry it unmixed four or five miles from land, where native prahus often take in their supplies. Large trunks of trees are continually floating about, which are brought down from the interior, and are very dangerous to small vessels, and many a Malay trader has owed to them his ruin. Off Sirik Point a prahu struck and immediately sunk. Her captain reported a rock, but as the coast near was simply alluvial deposit, and the fishermen who frequent this spot have never found it, it is generally thought that he suffered from a submerged tree.

I was once a passenger on board a frigate while she sailed by this point. We were sitting below, and heard her distinctly strike, and a grating sound as of crushed coral was audible. "On shore again," was the general observation: we went on deck, to find her running before the wind at ten knots an hour. We had, I believe, simply passed over one of these huge trunks. I have mentioned elsewhere the mass of floating weeds and trees that continually gyrates in a circle about fifteen miles off this point.

Although my object was to visit the Baram river, yet I was obliged to pass on to Labuan and Brunei to obtain interpreters and guides. As we approached our little English colony we found our coal was all used, and we could scarcely reach the harbour, although we burnt a horse-box and everything available on board.

The coast line between Baram and Brunei is very pretty. As we approach the capital, the interminable jungle gives way to grassy hills, with a park-like distribution of timber. Curling wreaths of smoke rising from the shaded valleys, told us that the inhabitants were numerous. In the far distance we could see the great mountain of Molu, the loftiest known, except Kina Balu: the latter was visible to-day, although about 120 miles off; it looked like a huge table mountain rising from the sea, all intervening ground being lost in the distance.

We reached Labuan the day before the Queen's birthday, in time to be present at the official dinner given by Governor Scott. I shall take another opportunity to notice this island.

We heard on our arrival that Mr. Low, the Colonial treasurer, had made an attempt to reach the summit of Kina Balu. It was generally said he had failed; but many years after, I was able to prove that he had reached to within a few hundred feet of the very highest peaks.

After some days' stay to coal, we started for the capital, which lies about thirty-three miles to the S.S.W. The bay opposite Labuan is one of the most striking on the coast. The mountains commence within a few miles of the shore, and tower in suc-

6—2

cessive ranges to Brayong, and Si Guntang, about
8,000 feet in height.

By naval men this is called Thunder-and-Lightning
Bay, and it well deserves the name, as scarcely a day
passes without some heavy squall sweeping down from
the mountains, while the brightest lightning flashes,
and the thunder rolls and re-echoes among the hills.

The entrance to the inner bay, into which so many
rivers pour their waters, is five fathoms, and with a
little care as to the known marks, of easy entrance.
To the right is the low island of Muara, reputed
deadly; but I have stayed there many times, and
none of my people suffered. Keeping along the
southern shore of the island, the channel is reached,
and as we approach the true entrance of the Brunci
river the scenery becomes lovely.

To the right is the island of Iñgaran, with its
remains of Spanish batteries; to the left, picturesque
Chermin. No ship of any size can enter the river,
as eight feet at low water, and fourteen at high, is
what the bar affords, which is also rendered more
difficult by a long artificial dam of stones thrown
across the stream in former times to prevent the
approach of hostile squadrons. The water, however,
has forced an angular passage to the right, through
which vessels are obliged to pass. It is one of the
worst rivers for commercial purposes in Borneo.

Beautiful hills rise sharply from the banks; some
are wooded, with clumps of lofty palms pushing their
way up through the jungle, while others are cleared,
presenting swelling grassy summits and green slopes.
Before us the honoured hill of Sei rises, and forms,
as it were, an abrupt termination of the river. The

Borneans take a pride in this hill that overshadows their town, although its elevation is but 700 feet.

Turning sharply to the right, we saw the first houses of the capital of Borneo, by the natives called Dar'u'salam, or the Abode of Peace, and which has been truly described as the " Venice of hovels." The salt-water creek or river here expands to a small lake, and on mud-banks are the houses, built on the slenderest of piles—mere palms, that rot in three years. Slow, sluggish, and muddy, the water passes underneath, to leave, at ebb tide, exposed banks emitting the most offensive effluvia, which turns the gold and silver of uniforms to the colour of dirt.

As soon as we had anchored, the steamer was surrounded by a crowd of canoes, some so small as scarcely to float a child of five years of age—in fact, but a hollowed log. Mothers do not fear to trust their children in them, as they swim like fishes. It is a saying in Siam, that their children can do three things at a tender age—swim, smoke, and suck. I once saw a child at the breast, but with one eye fixed on his brothers paddling in the water; presently it gave a crow of delight, and leaving its mother's arms, sprang into the river to enjoy the fun. He was not more than three years old.

The whole town appeared to be interested in our arrival, for, as we passed up the broad and deep river between the lines of houses, crowds of men, women, and children thronged the verandahs.

The floating market mentioned by Forrest was there also—several hundred canoes, each containing one or two women, covered over with mat hats a yard in diameter, floated up and down about the town, pulling through the water lanes and resting for a while in the slack tide at the back of the houses. These women, generally ill-favoured old slaves, frequent this migratory assemblage every day, and buy and sell fowls, vegetables, fish, and fruit.

The supply of food for this population of five-and-twenty thousand requires some arrangement: so every morning a market is held at various points, where the hill people assemble and exchange their agricultural produce for salt, fish, iron, and clothes. The old women are diligent frequenters of these places, and buy here to retail in the capital.

I have often come across these extemporized markets: some held under groves of fruit-trees; others on grassy fields, but, by choice or accident, always in a lovely spot.

We had not long been anchored when the Sultan and ministers sent messengers on board, to inquire the news and invite me to a meeting. They are very anxious about the result of my visit to the Kayans, as there is little doubt that this slave-acquiring and head-hunting people are destroying the interior population.

To-day they had received news that three long war-boats of their enemies had been dragged over into the waters of the upper Limbaug; that they had attacked a party of the Sultan's Murut subjects, and killed six, after which they had immediately returned to their own country. It is evident that the Borneans are in great fear of the ultimate result of these forays. The old Sultan being ill, I did not see him, but spent the evening with Pañgeran Mumein, the prime minister (and present Sultan).

He is an amiable man, and bears a better character than the rest; his great fault is grasping. He is always telling the story of his fight with the Kayans, which exemplifies how easily these men were defeated by the use of musketry. Some years since, Pañgeran Mumein hearing that the district of Tamburong was invaded by the people of Baram, collected his followers and guns, and proceeded thither. When they came in sight of the Kayans crowded round a village, the Malays became alarmed, and wished to retreat; but their leader sprang forward and fired a brass swivel at the enemy; it fortunately took effect on one, and the crowd dispersed. Recovering from their fright, the Borneans fired volley after volley into the jungle, and celebrated their victory by loud beatings of gongs and drums. The Kayans, still more frightened, fled in all directions.

Pañgeran Mumein justly observed, that as long as the Kayans were unacquainted with the use of fire-arms, it was easy to defend the country; but that now the Bornean traders were supplying them with brass swivels and double-barrel guns, he thought that the ruin of Brunei was at hand. But the fact is, that though the Kayans are now less frightened at the noise of heavy guns and muskets than they were, they seldom employ them in their expeditions in the jungle, as they cannot keep them in working order.

With the assistance of his followers' memories, Mumein repeated the names of forty villages that had been destroyed within the last ten years, and the majority of the inhabitants captured or killed.

Several of the respectable Malay traders of the place have agreed to go with me as guides and inter-

preters; among the rest are Gadore, Abdul Ajak,
and Bakir, the principal dealers with Baram.   Bakir
had but just arrived from that country, and he says
that the Kayans are anxiously awaiting my arrival,
having heard that I was ready for the steamer.   As
he appears a very intelligent fellow, I will note down
some of the information he gave me about the people.
Their customs appear much the same as those of the
Sea Dayaks: he began, oddly enough, with their
funerals.   When a man dies, they wrap him up in
cloths and place him in a kind of box on top of four
upright poles, and leave him there with some of his
worldly goods—in the case of chiefs, a very large
amount.   Their marriages are simple.   When two
young people take a fancy to each other, their intercourse is unrestrained: should the girl prove with
child, a marriage takes place; their great anxiety for
children makes them take this precaution against
sterility.

We pulled in the evening to visit the fine upas-
tree growing at the end of the reach below the town.
We landed at a Mahomedan burying-place, and there
met a Malay, who warned us not to approach this
deadly tree, but we smilingly thanked him and continued our course, forcing our way through the
tangled bushes at its base: it has a noble stem, some
five-and-thirty feet without a branch, and eighteen
feet in circumference; the colour of its bark is a
light brown.   The tree is a very handsome and
spreading one, and its bright rich green contrasted
well with the dark foliage beyond.

Leaving the burying-ground, we fell down the
river a hundred yards, and then walked up a path

leading over the hills, where a dip rendered the passage easier. Arriving at the summit, we saw the town spread out, map-like, before us, and it is one of the loveliest scenes I have ever witnessed. The sun was just setting amid a broken heap of clouds, and threw its dimmed rays on everything around. The river, slowly meandering through the town and country, flowed past our feet, its rippled waters faintly tinged with purple; while around, till hidden by the now rapidly-approaching darkness, we could perceive a succession of hills, gilded here and there, and generally clothed with trees to the very summit; but, that the eye might not be wearied, many an eminence was grass-covered. A cool breeze blew gently down the river, and was pleasantly refreshing after the hot day.

Before darkness had quite enveloped us, we visited those little grottos whence the Borneans obtain their supplies of drinking water. Rills are led through bamboo-pipes, and brought conveniently to fill the jars that crowd the numerous boats, each waiting its turn. Brunei water is famous; it runs through a sandstone district, and is very clear and tasteless. One of these places is called to this day "The Factor's Fountain," and brings back to one's mind the time, when the East India Company had a factory here and traded in pepper.

Having collected our Bornean guides, who vainly endeavoured to load the steamer with their trading goods, we bade adieu to the authorities and started for Labuan. We stayed there but a few hours, and then steamed away for the Baram.

Next morning we arrived off the mouth, and, by

not steering towards land till the northern point of
the river bore due east, came in with one-and-
a-half fathom water.   The natives say there is a
deeper channel to be found by keeping close in to
the northern shore, but it has not yet been completely
surveyed.   A fresh breeze was blowing, which curled
the waves and dashed them in breakers on the sand-
bank; so that our passage was made in a sea of foam.
This obstruction renders the river comparatively useless, and is greatly to be regretted, as immediately
the bar is passed the water deepens to four and five
fathoms; occasionally we found no bottom with a ten-
fathom line.

At the mouth, the width of the Baram is about
half a mile; it gradually narrows, and then varies in
breadth from 300 to 500 yards.   Casuarians line the
entrance, then nipa palms, and the usual jungle pressing closely to the water's edge.   A few miles more,
and patches of rich, short grass ornament the banks,
increasing in number as we advanced.   The jungle
presented few varied tints, but pretty creepers and
white and red flowers occasionally showed themselves
among the dark leaves.

About twenty miles up the river was a landing-
place on the right bank, leading to the Blait country,
inhabited by Muruts, who have suffered heavily by
the attacks of the Kayans.

Makota, the Malay noble so often mentioned in
Keppel's *Voyage of the Dido*, as the chief opponent
of European influence in Borneo, and certainly the
ablest and most unscrupulous man, and yet the most
agreeable companion I have found among the Malays,
told me how the Kayans had managed to obtain a

village of Muruts in the Blait country. It had often been attacked, but, as a strong stockade had been built round it, they had defied the enemy.

One day, a fugitive party of three men and several women and children were seen flying from the jungle towards the Murut village. Some armed men went out to meet them, and they said that they had run away from the Kayans, and were now escaping pursuit. They proved to be Muruts of a distant river, who had been captured and held in slavery by the Kayans. The Blaits received them with hospitality, and offered them room in their long village houses that contained 150 families. The fugitives, however, said they preferred keeping their party together, and asked leave to build up a temporary hut against the inner side of the stockade. Permission was granted, and they lived there six months, working at a farm with their hosts.

One of these men, after the gathering in of the harvest, stayed out till sunset, and explained it by saying he had been hunting, and that the chase had led him farther than he intended. It was a dark night that followed; and, about four in the morning, a large party of Kayans crawled quietly up to the stockade, and found an entrance prepared for them. The posts had been removed by the stranger Muruts, who had gradually cut through the wood that formed the inner wall of their temporary shed. When sufficient were within the defences, a loud shout was raised, and fire applied to the leaf houses. The villagers rushed out to be cut down or captured. In the confusion and the darkness, however, the larger portion escaped, but left about a hundred and fifty

bodies and captives in the hands of the Kayans; and
I am not sorry to add, among the former were the
three treacherous men who had caused this awful
scene. Some of the attacking party not obtaining
heads, quietly possessed themselves of those of their
three allies.

Kum Lia planned and led this foray. I had
some doubts of the truth of this circumstantially told
story; and many years after, meeting Kum Lia in
daily intercourse, I asked him about it. He was
proud to acknowledge that he was the author of the
able stratagem, but was not clear as to whether they
had also slain their allies, but thought it very possible
that his followers had done so.

At sunset we passed the island of Bakong, divided
by narrow waters from the shore, and along the banks
grass grew luxuriantly. We were struck by the
appearance of dark objects; and, seeing them move,
telescopes were pointed, and they proved to be a herd
of Tambadau, or wild cattle, and at the edge of the
jungle was a group of deer.

We anchored at the entrance of the Bakong stream,
about thirty-five miles from the mouth of the Baram.
During the night careful observations were made, and
it was found that at the height of the flood the river
rose only three feet, and the strength of the current
averaged only one mile per hour.

Started before sunrise; the stream continues much
the same. At first there were more open glades, with
rich soft-looking grass like our English meadows;
traces of wild cattle and deer were constantly to be
observed. The river was seldom over four hundred
yards in breadth, but never less than two; the sound-

ings changed from three fathoms to no bottom with
the usual line, but this great variation was caused by
our not always being able to keep in the deepest part
of the stream.

A glance at the map will show how very abrupt are
the turnings, and how the stream doubles on itself,
rendering it a very difficult matter to steer. Occasionally the current would catch the bow of the
steamer, and force it on the shore; but immediately
the stern felt the same force, it was pressed also
towards the bank, and the stem again would point up
stream. It was at last found the easiest and safest
way to turn the sharp points.

To-day we steamed by several Malay trading prahus
pulling up the stream, and observed one enormous
Tapang tree that rose close to the water's edge.

Early in the afternoon we passed the embouchure of
the Tingjir on the left bank; it was about a third
of the size of the Baram, and is said to be shallow: it
is well inhabited by a tribe of people called Sububs,
with whom the Kayans are interspersed. A couple
of hours after, we reached the Tutu on the right bank;
up this the Kayans proceed when intent on a foray in
the Upper Limbang country.

Saw the first Kayans near this spot. Two canoes
were coming down the river; directly they perceived
the moving monster approaching, they turned and
fled; but as they found we were overtaking them,
they deserted their canoes and dashed ashore. Three,
however, remained at the edge of the jungle, and we
reassured them by waving our handkerchiefs. It
was a pardonable fear, they had never before seen
anything larger than their own war boats. They

looked very much like the Kanowit Dayaks before described.

We had one fine view of the peak of Molu and of its surrounding ranges; occasionally the banks are becoming steep.

Anchored after sunset, above one hundred miles from the mouth; we are now far beyond the influence of the tides, yet the current averaged but a mile and a half.

Again started before sunrise; the river continued its winding course with a few patches of greensward; our guides say there are no more wild cattle, but many deer in this neighbourhood. We passed the sites of numerous deserted plantations and of a few new ones: we startled the people at a farmhouse by running our bowsprit into their verandah: no wonder the women and children fled shrieking to the jungle.

Most of these habitations are built on high posts, and are very neatly constructed. Generally, the people showed little fear, but crowded the verandahs to look at us, some rushing to their boats to follow. We again found a little difficulty in rounding the sharp points, and were constantly striking the banks, but no damage was done, although we were often among the overhanging branches of the jungle.

We touched once, while near the centre of the stream, on what I do not know, probably a rock or a stump of a tree—the snags of the American rivers. But just above this spot was the abrupt hill of Gading, that rises perpendicularly from the banks, and is brightly white, with deep fissures, and is celebrated for its birds'-nest caves. I am sorry we did not stop to examine this, as many years after I found among the Muruts of the centre of Northern Borneo, a small slab of white marble, that I could only trace as having been brought from the Baram river. The Malays called it Batu Gading, or ivory-stone : it was pure white.

Among our Malays was one who had frequently traded with the north-east coast, and the mention of Gading (ivory) brought to his recollection that elephants exist in the districts about the river Kina Batañgan. I have seen many tusks brought to Labuan for sale, but never measured one longer than six feet two inches, including the part set in the head.

I have met dozens of men who have seen the elephants there, but my own experience has been limited to finding their traces near the sea-beach. It is generally believed that above a hundred years ago the East India Company sent to the Sultan of Sulu a present of these animals ; that the Sultan said these great creatures would certainly eat up the whole produce of his own little island, and asked the donors to land them at Cape Unsang, on the north-east coast of Borneo, where his people would take care of them. But it is contrary to their nature to take care of any animal that requires much trouble, so the elephants sought their own food in the woods, and soon became wild.

Hundreds now wander about, and constantly break into the plantations, doing much damage ; but the natives sally out with huge flaming torches, and drive the startled beasts back to the woods.

The ivory of Bornean commerce is generally procured from the dead bodies found in the forests, but there is now living, one man who drives a profitable trade in fresh ivory. He sallies out on dark nights, with simply a waistcloth and a short, sharp spear : he crawls up to a herd of elephants, and selecting a large one, drives his spear into the animal's belly. In a moment, the whole herd is on the move, frightened by the bellowing of their wounded companion, who rushes to and fro, until the panic spreads, and they tear headlong through the jungle, crushing before them all smaller vegetation. The hunter's peril at that moment is great, but fortune has favoured him yet, as he has escaped being trampled to death.

In the morning he follows the traces of the herd, and, carefully examining the soil, detects the spots of blood that have fallen from the wounded elephant. He often finds him, so weakened by loss of blood as to be unable to keep up with the rest of the herd, and a new wound is soon inflicted. Patiently pursuing this practice, the hunter has secured many of these princes of the forest.

One can easily understand how startled a man unused to an animal larger than a pony would feel on suddenly finding himself face to face with a huge elephant. My favourite follower, Musa, has often made his audience laugh by an account of the feelings he experienced, when, pulling up the great river of Kina Batañgan, he steered close in-shore to avoid the strength of the current, and, looking up to find what was moving near, saw a noble tusked elephant above him, with his proboscis stretched over the boat to pick fruit beyond—" The paddle dropped from my hand, life left me, but the canoe drifted back out of danger."

The banks of the Baram gradually became higher,
and topped by neat farmhouses, increased in beauty;
but I think the first view of the Kayan town of
Langusin was one of the most picturesque I have
ever witnessed. Long houses, built on lofty posts,
on hills of various heights, yet appearing to be
clustered together, while near were numerous little
rice stores, neatly whitewashed. I never saw a
prettier-looking place. We steered on, until wo
reached a long village-house, still building, opposite
which we anchored. Crowds immediately assembled
on the banks, and the Bornean traders came off to
give and receive news.

The chief, Tamawun, now sent to know how the
salutes were to be arranged, and we agreed that as
usual we should salute his flag first, and that he
should return it. We were rather surprised to find
an English ensign hoisted, but he had received it
from a trader, and said he would never change it, as
it showed his good feeling towards us.

Among the guns fired was the pivot 32-pounder,
and the sound echoed and re-echoed among the
neighbouring hills, startling the whole population,
who had never before heard anything louder than
a brass swivel. The salute was returned by an
irregular firing, that continued for about an hour—
the greater number of guns the greater honour.

My Malay followers were very desirous that I
should show the utmost dignity, and require the
chiefs of the river to make the first visit; but on that
I declined insisting, and left it to the Kayans to
settle; and, thinking it would show more confidence,
I went on shore while these preliminaries were dis-

cussing, and walked to the spot where all the principal men were assembled under a temporary shed.
Two chairs and two boxes covered with English rugs
were arranged at one end. Before taking my seat,
I shook hands with all around. This was a formal
meeting, and I explained to them the object of our
coming, which was to cement the friendship of the
English with the Kayans. Having just arrived from
the Kanowit, I was enabled to give them some intelligence from their friends and relations. In fact, I
found Kum Nipa's son here, and also Diñgun,
Belabun's brother, and I had the unpleasant task of
informing them that small-pox had broken out on the
Rejang, and was committing fearful ravages. I did
not tell the latter of the death of his younger brother
by Kayan hands, as it might prove disagreeable to
be informed of it publicly.

I did not stay long, as they appeared to be uneasy,
but with general assurances of friendship left them.

It is difficult to describe the outward appearance
of these people, and say anything different from what
I have already said in describing the Sea Dayaks.
They are much like the Sakarangs, except that they
are slightly tatooed with a few stars and other marks;
however, I have not as yet seen much of them.

Along the banks of the river, we observed many
Kayan graves: the body is wrapped up, enclosed
within a hollowed coffin, and raised on two thick,
carved posts, with roughly carved woodwork extending
out from each corner, like those seen on the roofs
of Budhist temples. In one they put so many goods
that the Bornean traders were tempted to rob them;
and had not the Kayans discovered who were the

culprits, the rest would have suffered heavily. The
Bornean thieves escaped, but they and all their con-
nections are for ever precluded from trading with this
district.

Diñgun came on board to hear more particular news
of his family, and was shocked on being informed of
the death of his brother: he told me he should return
home in about five months. Two years ago, he and
a party of thirty started from Kanowit, and proceeded
up the Rejang, amusing themselves with the Kayans;
they then pushed on and crossed over to Baram,
where they had remained guests of the principal
chiefs. He and his companions were easily distin-
guished from their neighbours by their profuse
tatooing. I was enabled to give him some information
about his father, his brothers, and his four children;
about his wife, I do not remember that he inquired.

The Baram is said to abound in alligators, but
they are evidently not very dangerous, as the women
and children bathed daily opposite the ship. Strength
of current, two knots per hour.

Next morning, the chiefs came on board. I will
give their names as a curiosity:—Tamawan, Siñgauding, Kum Lia, the hero of the Blait surprise, Si
Matau, Longapan, and Longkiput, with some
hundreds of followers. They were charmed to be
allowed freely to inspect the vessel. Tamawan looks
a savage, and doubtless is one: he had on but little
dress—a waistcloth of about two fathoms of gray
shirting, a handkerchief tossed over his shoulder,
and a head-dress of dark cloth. He is but slightly
tatooed, having a couple of angles on his breast, a few
stars on his arms, his hands as far as the joints of his

fingers, and a few fanciful touches about his elbows;
his ears were bored and then drawn down by leaden
weights, as is the fashion among the Kanowits; the
tops of his ears were also bored, and the long teeth
of the tiger-cat stuck through them like a pair
of turn-down horns. And such was the dress and
appearance of nearly all but a few young men,
who wore jackets of a variety of colours, with an
equal variety of trimmings. Tamawan was a small
man, but Simatau and Siñgauding were hulking
fellows; they were all strong or wiry-looking men,
capable of much fatigue; their countenances, on the
whole, were pleasant. I took them down to inspect
the machinery, and my Bornean followers were their
guides to show them all the other wonders on board,
particularly the large thirty-two pounder gun, which
greatly excited their respect. Kum Lia, who is the
son-in-law of Kum Nipa, of Rejang, whom I have
mentioned as the chief we intended to visit, when we
were stopped by the small-pox having broken out in
his country, stayed after the others to inquire about
his family. He remembered the name of Niblett,
who commanded the *Phlegethon* when it called at
Bintulu in 1847.

In the evening I visited Siñgauding at his house.
I should like to have taken up my residence on shore,
but they were desirous to make so many preparations
that I gave up the idea, as our stay would necessarily
be short, although I was anxious to observe them
more closely.

Our talk was at first about steamers, balloons, and
rockets, of which they had heard much from the
Borneans. They particularly wished to know if we

had a telescope that could discover the hidden treasures of the earth, as they had heard we possessed one that showed mountains in the moon.

I was unfortunate in the medium through which I obtained my information. The Bornean interpreters are only anxious on the subject of trade; and being Mahomedans always laugh at the superstitions of the wild tribes. I therefore give, with some hesitation, what they told me concerning their religion. They said the name of their god was Totaduñgan, and he was the supreme ruler who created, and now reigned over all; that he had a wife, but no children; beneath him were many other inferior powers. They believed in a future life, with separate places for the souls of the good and of the bad; that their heaven and hell were divided into many distinct residences; that those who died from wounds, from sickness, or were drowned, went each to separate places. If a woman died before her husband, she went to the other world and married. On the death of her husband, if he came to the same world, she repudiated her ghostly partner and returned to him who had possessed her on earth.

Siñgauding's house was of a similar construction to those of the Sea Dayaks, very long, with a broad, covered verandah, as a public room, and a sleeping-place for the bachelors, while off it were separate apartments for the married people, the young girls, and children. The roof was of shingle, the posts of heavy wood, the flooring of long and broad rough planks, the partitions of the same material, with small doors about two feet above the floor, leading into the inner rooms.

Every Kayan chief of consideration possesses a kind of seat formed from the Tapang tree. It is, in fact, a huge slab, cut out of the buttress of that lofty tree ; and this seat descends from father to son, till it is polished and black with age. Siñgauding gave me one, measuring ten feet six inches by six feet six inches. It was made into a very handsome dining-table, but was unfortunately burnt during the Chinese insurrection of 1857. When Siñgauding heard of this, he determined to send me another that should throw the former into the shade ; and I heard that the one selected was fifteen feet by nine. Up to August, 1861, it had not reached me, as all the Malay traders declared their boats were too small to receive it.

Near the spot where we sat conversing were open baskets, hung near the fire-places, containing the human heads they had captured. The house certainly did not look cheerful ; but I saw it under unfavourable circumstances—a dark evening with constant drizzling rain.

As yet, I have seen but the few women who bathe opposite to the ship. They are generally tatooed from the knee to the waist, and wear but a cloth like a handkerchief hung round the body, and tucked in at one side above the hip, leaving a portion of the thigh visible. When bathing, their tatooing makes them look as if they were all wearing black breeches. They are tolerable-looking women ; and I saw a few pleasant countenances.

The visit of the steamer was not timed very fortunately, as Tamadin, an influential chief, with a large party, was away head-hunting ; and a rumour had arrived of a very severe loss having been suffered by a force that started for the interior of the Limbang and Trusan rivers. If we could stay twenty days we should see all the population ; but I have had a hint that the provisions are running short, and nothing can be procured here but a few pigs, fowls, and goats, all very dear.

I have calculated the population of this town, called Lañgusin, at 2,500 souls, and this is perhaps under the mark. From my inquiries, however, the interior must be tolerably well peopled.

At ten o'clock at night, the shouts and yells of the Kayans on shore were borne to us, as they were working with might and main to finish the long village-house of Tamawan. He gave them some drink, and they worked half the night.

They showed me some very pretty mats to-day made by the wandering tribe of Punans, who live on jungle produce, and collect honey and wax.

Next day I sent some presents to Siñgauding and Tamawan, and at their special invitation went ashore to meet them. A large temporary shed sheltered us from the sun. There was no inconvenient crowding, not more than a hundred men being assembled, and about twenty women, the wives and daughters of their chiefs. Among them there were some interesting girls. They wore their long black hair quite loose, only white fillets being bound round the forehead, so as to cast the hair in heavy masses over their ears and down their backs. Their countenances were open, bright dark eyes, smooth foreheads, depressed noses, clear skin, but indifferent mouths. They had good

figures and well set up busts.    I have as yet seen no
old women and men in the tribe.

One of the objects of my visit was to inquire into
the alleged bad conduct of an English trader and of
a Sarawak Malay.    I spent two hours in this investigation.    When this was over, native arrack and
some of my French brandy was introduced.    About a
third of a tumbler of the former was handed to me.
As I raised it to my lips, the whole assembly burst out
into what appeared a drinking chorus ; and this they
did when any man of note drank.    A little spirit getting into them, they became more cheerful and amusing ; and we talked about their head-hunting propen-
sities.    The wholesome advice I felt compelled to
give them on this subject made them feel thirsty, and
Tamawan seizing a bottle, filled two tumblers two-
thirds full of raw spirit and handed it to me, and
asked me to drink with him to the friendship of the
two nations.    Could I refuse? No.    I raised the
tumbler to my lips, and amid a very excited chorus
allowed the liquor to flow down.

When this was finished, Tamawan jumped up, and
while standing burst out into an extempore song, in
which Sir James Brooke and myself, and last, not
least, the wonderful steamer, was mentioned with
warm eulogies, and every now and then the whole
assembly joined in chorus with great delight.

Tamawan now sat down and talked about head-
hunting again.    He said that when the Kayans
attacked a village, they only killed those who resisted or attempted to escape ; the rest they brought
home with them, turning them in fact into field slaves.
He declared, however, that his great village, and

twenty-one others, were averse to the practice of head-hunting; but that over the twenty-eight other villages he had no influence. The above forty-nine villages he went over by name, and mentioned likewise the principal chief in each. They assert that a village was considered small that had only a hundred families, while a large one contained four hundred. If we may judge from the account he gave of the town opposite which we are anchored, he must have underrated considerably. He said this contained two hundred families; but after going over the numbers in each village-house, we came to the conclusion that there were at least five hundred families in Langusin. But as long as head-hunting is considered an honourable pursuit, and the acquisition of Murut slaves enables the chiefs to live without labour, it will be impossible to put a stop to their forays.

Tamawan had excited himself on this subject, and again feeling very thirsty after all the information he had given me, now looked about for something to drink. I was beginning to congratulate myself on its being finished, when he spoke to a very pretty girl who was standing near, and she instantly disappeared to return with a couple of bottles of brandy in her hands. The two tumblers were again filled more than half-full—one for me, the other for himself. I remembered what Sydney Smith said of the little effect spirit often has on the temperate man, and joined him in this last pledge. I pitied the poor Malays, who had never been accustomed to anything stronger than tea, being forced to follow our example; and yet it was ridiculous to watch their contortions

and wry faces, as their inexorable hosts forced them to
swallow their allowance.

Now came a ceremony new to me: a young pig was
brought in by the pretty waiting-maid and handed over
to one of the men present, who bound its legs, and
carrying it out opposite to where the *Pluto* was
anchored, placed it on the ground. Mats were laid
around, and a chair was provided for me. Tamawan
now came forward and commenced an oration. His
voice was at first thick from the potency of his previous draughts; but warming on his subject, he
entered at large on the feelings of friendship with
which he regarded the English; spoke of the wonderful vessel that came with oars of fire; seized my
hand, and gesticulated excitedly with the other; then
pointing to the pig, he entered on what appeared to
be a prayer, as he seemed appealing to something
beyond him; he took a knife, and cut the pig's throat;
the body was then opened, and the heart and liver
taken out and placed on two leaves, and closely
examined, to judge from their appearance whether
our visit would be fortunate for the Kayan nation.
Every chief present felt their different proportions,
and Tamawan pointed out to me the various indica-
tions. Luckily for our friendship, they found that
every portion portended good fortune. With his
bloody hand Tamawan grasped mine, and expressed
his delight at the happy augury. Throwing away
the auricle of the heart, they cut up the rest to eat,
and placed the pieces over the fire, using a bambu as
a cooking vessel.

I now took my leave, rather tired with my four
hours' exertions, and returned on board. The cere-

mony of examining the heart and liver of the pig
was too classical not to merit particular notice, though
I have already mentioned that the Sakarang Dayaks
practise the same.

Next day being Sunday, the Malays kept the
Kayans from coming on board. I inquired particularly as to the meaning of Tamawan's address
yesterday, and I hear that it was an invocation to
the spirits of good and evil to allow him to discover
from the heart of the sacrifice whether our visit was
to prove fortunate or not to the Kayan nation.

Siñgauding sent on board to request me to become
his brother by going through the sacred custom of
imbibing each other's blood. I say imbibing, because
it is either mixed with water and drunk, or else it is
placed within a native cigar and drawn in with the
smoke. I agreed to do so, and the following day was
fixed for the ceremony. It is called Berbiang by the
Kayans; Bersabibah by the Borneans. I landed with
our party of Malays, and after a preliminary talk, to
give time for the population to assemble, the affair
commenced. We sat in the broad verandah of a long
house, surrounded by hundreds of men, women, and
children, all looking eagerly at the white stranger
who was about to enter their tribe. Stripping my
left arm, Kum Lia took a small piece of wood, shaped
like a knife-blade, and slightly piercing the skin,
brought blood to the surface; this he carefully scraped
off: then one of my Malays drew blood in the same
way from Siñgauding, and a small cigarette being
produced, the blood on the wooden blades was spread
on the tobacco. A chief then arose, and walking to
an open place, looked forth upon the river and in-

voked their god and all the spirits of good and evil
to be witness of this tie of brotherhood. The cigarette
was then lighted, and each of us took several puffs,
and the ceremony was concluded. I was glad to
find that they had chosen the form of inhaling the
blood in smoke, as to have swallowed even a drop
would have been unpleasant, though the disgust
would only arise from the imagination. They sometimes vary the custom, though the variation may be
confined to the Kiniahs, who live farther up the
river, and are intermarried with the Kayans. There
a pig is brought and placed between the two who are
to be joined in brotherhood. A chief offers an invo-  •
cation to the gods, and marks with a lighted brand
the pig's shoulder. The beast is then killed, and
after an exchange of jackets, a sword is thrust into
the wound, and the two are marked with the blood of
the pig.

I hear that I am in very high favour with the
Kayans, from my joining their drinking party and
now entering their tribe, and binding myself to them
by a tie which they look on as sacred. We had a
long talk about the advantage which would accrue to
trade if the Kayans establish their town nearer the
mouth of the river; as at present it takes a Malay
boat sixteen days to reach it in the fine season, and
thirty in the wet. I found they had tried it once, by
removing to the mouth of the Tingjir; but building
their houses over the freshly-cleared jungle they lost
a great many men by fever. They accounted for this
by saying they had accidentally fallen upon a spot that
was much frequented by evil spirits, and so had returned to their original site.

To close this meeting merrily, a large jar of arrack was introduced, and subsequently a bottle of brandy. Excited by this, Si-Matau clothed himself in full war costume and commenced a sword dance. He was a fine, strong fellow, and with his dress of black bear-skin ornamented with feathers, his sword in hand, and shield adorned with many-coloured hair, said to be human, he looked truly formidable. His dancing expressed the character of the people—quick and vigorous motions, showing to advantage the development of his muscles. He was accompanied by the music of a two-stringed instrument, resembling a rough guitar: the body was shaped like a decked Malay trading prahu, with a small hole an inch in diameter in the centre; the strings were the fine threads of rattan twisted and drawn up tightly by means of tuning-keys; however, the sound produced was not very different from that of a tightly-drawn string. Some of the lookers-on were young girls with regular features, light skins, and good figures, and with a pleasing, pensive expression.

I looked about the house to-day, and though it is boarded all through, and, therefore, more substantial than those of the Sea Dayaks, yet it did not appear so bright and cheerful as the light yellow matted walls of the latter. I never saw so much firewood collected together as in these houses: on a fine framework spreading partly over the verandah and partly over their rooms, many months' supplies are piled even to the roof;—of course it is a great advantage to have dry materials in all weathers, and it is a provision against times of sickness or busy harvest-work.

Last night there arrived overland the news I had previously given them of the small-pox having broken out among the Kayans of Rejang, and to-day it formed the subject of conversation. They were anxious to have that medicine which the white men put into the arm, and which they were told came from the belly of a snake.

Tamawan, who was on board this morning, was greatly pleased at witnessing the musket exercise, and when he came on shore, went through it again to the admiration of his followers.

As the Kayans believed some misfortune would happen to us if I went anywhere but straight on board the ship, or if Siñgauding left his house during the day, I remained quiet, and talked over affairs with the Malays.

I find that, as among the Kanowits and other Dayaks, after the death of a relative they go out head-hunting, but do not kill the first person met; but each one they pass must make them a trifling present, which is no doubt quickly given, to get rid of such unpleasant neighbours.

Nakodah Abdullah, who has traded with this country since he was a boy, and Nakodah Jalil, another experienced man, came to spend the afternoon with me. They say the origin of the Kayans coming to the Baram was this : About twenty-five or thirty years ago, there were three powerful chiefs living in the Balui country—as the interiors of the Rejang and Bintulu rivers are called—Kum Nipa, Kum Laksa, and the father of my brother Siñgauding ; that Kum Laksa quarrelled with the last, and being joined by Kum Nipa, a feud arose, in the

course of which the father of Siñgauding was killed.
The relatives, to save the infant son, fled to the
Baram with all those who were well affected to the
family : some thousands came over, and singularly
enough, they were well received by the Kiniahs, the
original inhabitants of the country. Though they
are said to speak distinct languages, they soon commenced intermarrying, and are gradually becoming
one people. I am inclined to think, from their own
remarks, that they must originally have come from
the same part of Borneo, and that the difference of
language is not greater than that which exists among
the various branches of the Sea Dayaks. The other
inhabitants of the river are the Sububs, on the Tingjir, and the numerous Murut slaves captured in their
forays. Si-Matau, who danced so vigorously this
morning, was a Subub.

I tried, by the aid of the Malay traders, to draw
up a vocabulary of the language, but found that the
ignorance of these men was too great to enable me to
make one entitled to any confidence. I noticed that
half their conversation with the natives was carried
on in corrupt Malay words, and these they gave me
as true Kayan expressions.

Before the arrival of the Kayans, the trade to this
river was merely nominal; but they, knowing the
value of the edible birds'-nests, soon changed the
face of matters, as they discovered caves plentifully
supplied with this article of Chinese luxury. Their
houses are now built in the neighbourhood of the
resort of this wealth-creating bird. Quite lately,
however, they wantonly injured their own interests
by taking the nests five times a year, and never allow-

ing the birds a chance of hatching an egg; the consequence has been, that they are seeking more secluded
spots, and are reported to be resorting to the numerous caves found in the mountain of Molu. The
other articles of trade are camphor, wax, gutta-
percha, and, lately, a little india-rubber.

They principally import gray shirtings and chintzes;
the Malays, vying with each other, took one year, it
is said, 50,000 pieces, and allowed the Kayans to
have them on credit. Since then everything has
gone wrong—debts are not paid, quarrels arise, and
the caves are ruined by endeavouring to obtain the
means of purchasing more articles.

In some respects, the Kayans differ in their customs
from the other aboriginal tribes of Borneo. At the
birth of a chief's child there are great rejoicings; a
feast is given, pigs, and fowls, and goats being freely
sacrificed. Jars of arrack are brought forward, and
all the neighbours are called upon to rejoice with
their leader. They say that on this occasion a name
is given if the omen be good. A feather is inserted
up the child's nostril, to tickle it; if it sneeze it is a
good sign, but if not, the ceremony is put off to
another day. I may mention one inhuman custom,
which is, that women who appear to be dying in
childbirth, are taken to the woods and placed in a
hastily-constructed hut; they are looked upon as
interdicted, and none but the meanest slaves may
approach them, either to give them food or to attend
to them.

Marriages are celebrated with great pomp; many
men have ruined themselves by their extravagance on
this occasion. Tamading, with princely munificence,

gave away or spent the whole of his property on his wedding-day.

As among the Sea Dayaks, the young people have almost unrestrained intercourse; but if the girl prove with child, a marriage immediately takes place, the bridegroom making the richest presents he can to her relatives. The men, even the greatest chief, take but one wife, and, it is said, consider it shameful to mix their blood, and never, therefore, have any intercourse with the inferior women or slaves.

I have already mentioned the coffins elevated on posts; this, doubtless, extends only to the rich, the poor being simply buried.

There is another practice of the Kayans, which was mentioned by Dalton * as existing among those he met on the Koti river; it was disbelieved by many at the time, but it is undoubtedly true: the rich men using gold, the poorer silver, bones of birds, and even hard wood. The doctor of the *Semiramis* steamer carefully examined a great number of Kayans, and expressed his astonishment that no injury resulted from this extraordinary practice. A German missionary has accused the Southern Kayans of certain gross usages; but I heard nothing of them, and do not credit his account—his mistakes arising, most probably, from his want of knowledge of the language.

I procured to-day a packet of the iron they use in smelting; it appeared like a mass of rough, twisted ropes, and is, I think, called meteoric iron-stone. They use, also, two other kinds, of which I did not obtain specimens. We found a little coal in the black shale

* See Dalton's *Koti;* Hunt's *Notices of the Indian Archipelago.*

on which the town is built, and they spoke of golden
pebbles, most likely iron pyrites.

We had heavy rain every night; the current became stronger, and the river rapidly rose.

We went next day to visit the caves whence they
get the edible birds'-nests. We pulled down in the
steamer's cutter for about a mile, and then up a
narrow stream, till we could force her along no
farther. We now landed to walk the rest of the
way. Among our party were some who had not been
accustomed to forest work, and they came arrayed in
uniform and patent leather boots, thinking there was
a dry and open road. Their surprise was great and
not agreeable when they found muddy ground and
the bed of a mountain torrent had to be traversed.
Our guide struck into the stream directly, and our
party broke up, some following him, while others
sought a dryer way. From the stream we entered a
thick wood of young trees; then again across the
stream, up the bed of a mountain torrent, now partly
dry; steep, slippery stones, some overgrown with
moss, others worn to a smooth surface; up again,
climbing the hill, over fallen trees, down deep ravines,
across little streams, jumping from rock to rock, until
after an hour's hard work we arrived at a little house
on the top of a hill—the neatest little house imagi-
nable, walls and floor of well-trimmed planks, and
roof of bright red shingle; it was perfectly new, and
was the residence of the guardian of the cave.

I looked vainly about me for the entrance, and on
asking, they pointed to a deep gully, but I could see
nothing but bushes and grass; but on descending a
short distance, I saw the bottom of the gully suddenly

divide, leaving a rocky chasm some thirty feet in depth. A slight framework of ironwood enabled us to get down over the slippery rocks, and we soon saw that the cave extended back under the little house, and looked gloomy and deep. Our guide now lit a large wax taper, very inferior for this purpose to the torches used by the Land Dayaks in Sarawak, and led the way. The cave gradually enlarged, but by the imperfect light we could only distinguish masses of uneven rock on either side. As we advanced towards those parts where the finest white nests are found, the ground became covered many feet deep with the guano of the swallow, which emitted scarcely any smell. We advanced nearly two hundred yards without seeing a single nest, Siñgauding's men having completely cleared the cave the day before : it was very vexing, as we desired to see the nests as they were fixed to the rocks. The cave gradually became narrower and lower, but we continued our advance till we were stopped by its termination in this direction. Our guides observing our disappointment in not finding any nests, told us that there were a few in another branch. So we retraced our steps till we reached a passage on our left, and presently arrived at a spot where we descended abruptly some twelve feet ; it was pitch dark, as the guide had gone rapidly ahead. On reaching the bottom, I put my foot cautiously down, and could find nothing : the passage being very narrow I was enabled to support myself with my hands on either side while feeling with my feet for standing ground. There was none in front, but on either edge there was just resting room for the foot ; so this chasm was passed in safety.

I shouted out to my companions to take care, and the guide returning, we examined what we had escaped: it was a black hole, into which we threw stones, and calculating the number of seconds they took in reaching the first obstruction, we found it about three hundred feet deep. The stones bounded on the rocks below, and we could hear them strike and strike again, till they either reached the bottom, or till the sound was lost in the distance.

We then advanced to a large hall, apparently supported in the middle by a massive pillar, which was in fact but a huge stalactite. From above fell a continued shower of cold water, which doubtless was the cause of those innumerable stalactites that adorned the roof.

We continued advancing for about seventy or eighty yards farther, the cave getting narrower and narrower till two could not move abreast. Except where the guano lay, the walking was difficult, as the rocks were wet and excessively slippery, and open chasms were not rare. In the farther end we were shown the places where the best nests were obtained: the dryest portion of the sides of the cave are chosen by the birds, and these appeared seldom to occur—I found but one inferior nest remaining. Disturbed by our movements and by yesterday's havoc, the swallows were in great commotion, and flew round and round, and darted so near our solitary light that we were in great fear for its existence.

The natives say that in these caves there are two species of birds—the one that builds the edible nest, and another that takes up its quarters near the entrance, and disturbs, and even attacks the more

valuable tenants. The Kayans endeavour to destroy
these, and while we were there knocked down some
nests constructed of moss, and adhering to the rock
by a glutinous but coarse substance. The fine edible
one looks like pure isinglass, with some amount of
roughness on its surface. The best I have seen
are four inches round the upper edge, and appear
like a portion of a whitish cup stuck against a
wall.

On examining the construction of the mountain,
one's first impression is, that all these huge rocks
were thrown in heaps together; but, doubtless, water
is the agent in forming these caves and the deep
fissures that penetrate to the water-line in these limestone mountains.

I believe the guides took us to the smallest cave,
as I am sure, from the produce of the district, that
there must be many more better adapted for the
swallows, or else that they must be very numerous.
In fact, the guides told us that Siṅgauding had
several others, and that Tamawan in right of his
wife had the best. As they showed no inclination
to take us to the uncleared caves, we did not press
them.

The person who is employed to guard this place is
a singular-looking old man; they say they captured
him in the distant mountains during one of their
expeditions. He speaks a language unknown to
them, but is now learning a little Kayan; he looks
very contented, and has certainly the neatest house I
have seen in Borneo for his dwelling.

On our return it rained a little, and we had, in
many places, to sit and slide down the slippery

rocks; we all looked, on our return from our expedition, in a very different condition from that in
which we started.

Siñgauding came in the afternoon to pay me a visit,
and brought with him Si Awang Lawi, the principal
chief among the Kiniahs; he appeared a frank old
man. They stayed for some time with me talking
over various subjects connected with trade. He was
very intelligent, and pressing that I should go and
visit his people; but it was beyond my power. He
told me, also, that a Kayan, one of a party of several
hundred head hunters, had returned half starved, and
reported that he was the only survivor. There was
much mourning in the upper villages.

I may mention that these men have become so very
conceited that they consider themselves superior to
all except ourselves; and, in their pride, they have
actually commenced killing the swallow, that consti-
tutes their wealth, saying it becomes a great chief to
feed on the most valuable things he possesses, regard-
less of the ultimate consequences.

To-morrow being fixed for our departure, I have
been requested to pay Si Obong, Tamawan's wife, a
visit. I found her residing in a temporary house,
awaiting the completion of the great residence that
was rising rapidly, and whose progress we could watch
from the ship.

Si Obong was seated on fine mats, and was surrounded by various cushions. She had passed her
first youth, and had become very stout; in fact, her
limbs were much too large for a woman. She wore
little clothing—a couple of English handkerchiefs,
still in one piece, put round her hips, hanging down,

and tucked in at the side, and over her bosom she
occasionally threw a loose black cloth.   Her face was
round, good-tempered, but rather coarse ; her voice
was gentle, and she wore her long black hair hanging
loose, but kept off her face by fillets of white bark.
The most curious part of her costume is what I must
call a hip-lace of beads, consisting of three strings,
one of yellow beads ; the next of varied colours, more
valuable; and the third of several hundred of those
much-prized ones by the Kayan ladies.   It is difficult
to describe a bead so as to show its peculiarities.   At
my request, she took off her hip-lace and handed it
to me ; the best appeared like a body of black stone,
with four other variegated ones let in around.   It
was only in appearance that they were let in ; the
colours of these four marks were a mixture of green,
yellow, blue, and gray.

Were I to endeavour to estimate the price in produce she and her parents had paid for this hip-lace,
the amount would appear fabulous.   She showed me
one for which they had given eleven pounds' weight
of the finest birds' nests, or, at the Singapore market
price, thirty-five pounds sterling.   She had many of
a value nearly equal, and she wore none that had
not cost her nine shillings.

She was the only daughter of a chief of the highest
extraction, and Tamawan owed the principal share
of his influence, and perhaps all his wealth, to her.
The caves he possessed were hers, and she had been
won by the fame of his warlike expeditions and the
number of heads that were suspended around his
house.   There is no doubt that the Baram Kayans
are less desirous of heads than they were, and prefer

slaves who can cultivate their farms, and thus increase their fortune and consideration.

Tamawan complained bitterly that his strength was leaving him, that his body was becoming of no use, and that I must give him medicine to restore him. I promised him a few tonics, at the same time pointed out to him that he was suffering from rheumatism, caught whilst sleeping in the jungle during his last expedition; recommended him to stay at home, to wear more clothing, to drink less ardent spirit, and not indulge so much in fat pork.

Si Obong offered me refreshments in the shape of arrack and preserved fruit, but of neither did she herself partake. I noticed two of her attendants, who were really pretty, being blessed with well-shaped noses and mouths, a rarity among the natives of Borneo. They both sat silent and did not exchange a word, but were ready to obey the slightest call of their mistress.

Si Obong had her arms much tatooed, and she was also ornamented in that manner from just under the hip joint to three inches below the knee. This could be observed, as her dress opened at the side. She showed me in what way she employed her time; among other things, she had made a rattan seat, covered with fine bead-work, for her expected baby. When the women go out, the child is placed in this, which is slung over the back. The baskets around, which were filled with her clothes, were also her handiwork, and were carefully made, and likewise ornamented with innumerable small Venetian beads. There appeared no want of goods here, as they were heaped in all directions; among other things I noticed were an old English lamp, half-a-dozen tumblers, four bottles of brandy, a brass kettle, and cooking pots.

After sitting there about a couple of hours, I took my leave and returned on board ; and then sent Si Obong what I thought would please her, in the shape of a silver spoon, a silver fruit-knife, some gaudy handkerchiefs, looking-glasses, and other trifles. The silver articles, I heard, greatly delighted her.

The chiefs all came on board to make their farewell visit, and they were eager that I should spend my last evening with them ; they carried me off, and talking was kept up till a musket shot from the ship gave notice that a few fireworks were about to be let off. The whole assemblage of several hundreds hurried to the river's bank, tumbling over each other in their eagerness.

The rockets and blue lights filled them with astonishment and delight ; the former as warlike instruments with which they could defeat their enemies, and the latter because, they said, it turned night into day. I stayed with them till ten, and promised, if possible, to return and spend a few months with them. On no other condition was I to be suffered to depart. They hinted that, united, we could soon possess the neighbouring countries between us.

Siñgauding sent me, to-day, a sword made with his own hands, a war dress of tiger-cat skin, a head-dress of the same material, with a long feather of the Argus pheasant stuck into it. The peculiarity of the Kayan sword is that it is concave on the upper side, and convex below, and is made either right-handed or left-handed. It is a dangerous instrument

in the hands of the inexperienced; for if you cut
down on the left side of a tree with a right-handed
sword, it will fly off in the most eccentric manner;
but, well used, it inflicts very deep wounds, and will
cut through young trees better than any other instrument. I sent, as a return present, a heavy cavalry
sword; in fact, I was nearly exhausted of the means
of making presents.

I may remark that their iron ore appears to be
easily melted. They dig a small pit in the ground;
in the bottom are various holes, through which are
driven currents of air by very primitive bellows.
Charcoal is thrown in; then the ore, well broken up,
is added and covered with charcoal; fresh ore and
fresh fuel, in alternate layers, till the furnace is
filled. A light is then put to the mass through a
hole below, and, the wind being driven in, the process
is soon completed.

To-day we nearly had a serious accident: one of
the quartermasters, in getting into a canoe, fell into
the stream, which, swelled by the heavy rains, was
running swiftly by; he was carried away in a moment,
but the Kayans were instantly after, and brought him
back safe, though half-choked with water.

At sunrise we started on our return. All the inhabitants of the town assembled on the river's bank
to witness our departure. The steamer turned with
ease, and was swept with great speed down the stream.
We took a native trading vessel in tow, which assisted
our steering, and reached the mouth on the following day without the slightest accident.

I hear that the exclamations of the Kayans, when
they first perceived the steamer rounding the point,

were—"Here is a god come among us!" others cried, "It is a mighty spirit!"

The latitude of the town is 3° 30′; the longitude, 114° 40′.

I regret I was never again enabled to visit the Baram River, as, besides the personal gratification derived, there is a great public good done, by a constant friendly surveillance over the aborigines. Many of the Kayans returned my visit to Labuan, but I was absent; it was not, however, material, as they were well treated by the colonial officers.

Whilst in Baram I could hear nothing to confirm the account that any of the Kayans were cannibals. We first heard the charge against them from three Dayaks of the tribe of Sibaru, whose residence is on the Kapuas River, in the district of Santang, under Dutch influence. I was present when they were carefully questioned, and, though their information has already appeared, I will repeat the substance.

They said that their tribe and a party of Kayans attacked, unsuccessfully, a small Malay village; but, in the fright, the body of one of their enemies was secured. Their allies immediately sliced off the flesh and put it away in their side baskets; and in the evening, while all the party were preparing their supper, they brought out the human flesh, and roasted and eat it. They saw it themselves. The Dayaks of Jangkang, on the Skeium, between the districts of the Sarawak and Dutch territories, are universally accused of cannibalism.

I do not remember having heard any other persons actually affirm that they had seen the Kayans eat human flesh, till the subject was brought up last year

before the present Sultan of Borneo and his court;
when Usup, one of the young nobles present, said
that in 1855 some Muka men were executed at Bintulu, and that a few of the Kayans, who had assisted
in their capture, took portions of the bodies of the
criminals, roasted and ate them. This was witnessed by himself and many others who were then
present. The Kayans had not, as a body, joined in
this disgusting feast; but, perhaps, some of the more
ferocious may practise it to strike terror into their
enemies.

The account given by the Malays of the former
system of trade pursued by the Kayans is curious.
They say that when a native merchant arrived at the
landing-place of a village, the chief settled the terms
with him, and all the goods were carried up to the
houses, and placed in a prepared spot, secure from
pilferers. For a week no business was done, but the
stranger and his followers were feasted at the public
expense. After that, the goods were brought out
and spread in the public room, and the prices fixed.
The chief selected what he wanted, and the next in
rank in rotation, till all the villagers were satisfied.
Three months' credit was always given, but at the
appointed day the produce in exchange was ready for
the trader. I imagine the Malays would be glad to
return to the old system.

The Kayans were seldom very welcome guests at
a small village, helping themselves freely to everything that took their fancy; but this only occurred,
as a Malay shrewdly observed, in places where they
were feared.

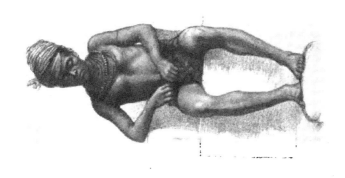

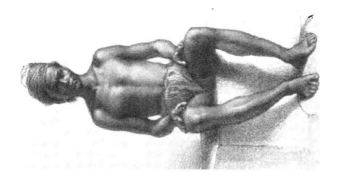

I have already...
but and not...
the Senate...
to accept the... invitation to accompany
him on the tour... sapped is he was absent...
among the Land mocks of the left...
of the Senate... As the
crew was selected to...
with the peculiar
that there is so...

# CHAPTER IV.

## THE LAND DAYAKS.

I HAD already made many visits among the Dayaks,
but had never penetrated to the interior waters of
the Sarawak river. I was, therefore, quite ready
to accept Captain Brooke's invitation to accompany
him on the tour of inspection he was about to make
among the Land Dayaks of the left-hand branch
of the Sarawak. As the stream is full of rapids, our
crew was selected of Sarawak men, well acquainted
with the peculiar navigation. I may here remark
that there is something characteristic about the true
Sarawak man : his look is eminently respectable, his

face is longer and more marked than that of the other Malays, his complexion often darker, his manners quiet and respectful. There is a tradition current in this country, that once upon a time, the capital of Sarawak was at Santubong, the western entrance of the river; that during the absence of the men on an expedition up the country, some marauding Peguans arrived there in their ships, and on finding the defenceless state of the town attacked it, carried it by assault, and made off with their spoils and innumerable female prisoners. The Sarawak men fortunately returned a few hours after, and instantly gave chase. Their fast war boats soon overtook the clumsy Pegu ships. They made short work of it: killed the marauding chiefs and brought back the rest prisoners to Santubong. The Samarahan and some of the Sarawak men are said to be descended from them, and this, if true, may account for the darker complexion.

The Sarawak river is not navigable for ships far above the town, though at the height of the flood a large vessel was once taken fifteen miles above it to a place called Ledah Tanah. This occurred some thirty years ago. A large English ship, laden with sugar, put into the mouth of the Sarawak river for water. The captain and mates were invited to meet the rajahs of the country. They went on shore, where they were informed that their vessel was too leaky to proceed on her voyage, but that they would be provided with a passage to Singapore in one of the native prahus. Resistance was useless. They were surrounded by hundreds of armed men, and were hurried off to sea immediately to be murdered at

the first island. The *Lascar* crew were detained
as slaves. Two of them were still alive when I
first reached Sarawak. Many of the Malays have told
me that sugar never was so plentiful in their houses
either before or since. The banks of the river on
either side continue low, and are adapted in their
present state for rice cultivation, though with a little
drainage, the Chinese can render the soil admirably
suited for sugar-cane and other cultivations. It is a
pretty but monotonous pull, the scenery being only
occasionally varied by views of the surrounding
mountains.

We passed the first night at Ledah Tanah, or
Tongue of Land, the point of junction of the two
branches of the river. Here the Rajah had a cattle
farm, and a pretty cottage surrounded by fruit trees,
principally of magnificent durians. This fruit is the
subject of much controversy. It varies in size from
a six to sixty-eight pounder shot, and looks like an
enormous chestnut, with its prickly outer coating on.
On opening this rough rind, we find five or six rows
of seeds covered with a white or yellow pulpy substance, which tastes and smells like a custard strongly
flavoured with onions, or, to those who delight in it,
it is of a delicious and unapproachable flavour, and,
when perfectly fresh, has a pleasing perfume. These
different opinions are given at the same moment, by
different persons describing the same fruit.

When the people abandoned Santubong, they
retired to Ledah Tanah, where they established their
town; the posts of some of their houses still remain,
being of iron-wood, which may be said practically to
last for ever.

We continued our course up the river, the character of the scenery becoming more interesting every
moment. The stream narrows, the water is clearer,
shallower, and its course is interrupted by rocks and
large stones, over which the stream foams, dashes,
breaks, rendering the passage dangerous for small
boats ; indeed, the name of one of these rapids,
Rhium Bangkei—" The Rapid of the Corpse"—
would seem to prove that fatal accidents do occur.
The swamping of a boat, or the loss of goods, by
inexperienced hands, is not rare.

The first mountain we passed was that of Stat,
which, though not more than 1,500 feet high, is in
many respects remarkable, rising abruptly from the
low country, a real isolated peak that may be distin-
guished even out at sea ; from one view it appears
like the end of a bent finger. In common with most
of the limestone mountains in Borneo, it presents bare,
perpendicular surfaces, with jagged rocks at the edges,
but surrounded by vegetation, and that vegetation
growing where soil can scarcely be supposed to exist ;
in fact, the roots of the trees penetrate far into the
inner portion of the mountain, through deep fissures
and clefts. The other mountains visible during our
progress to-day had the same general features, particularly the two which rise near the village of San
Pro, where we intended to pass the night.

In our evening walk we were much struck with
the remarkable beauty of this place ; the two lofty
and almost perpendicular mountains rise abruptly
on either side of the river, leaving but a strip of
land on the water's edge. One called Sibayat towers
above the village on the left bank ; the other,

Si Bigi, is on the opposite side; the river, now running through limestone, sparkles clear at their feet, undermining the rocks on either side, and forming fantastic little caves, crowned above with noble overhanging trees. Abrupt turns, short reaches, and pebbly beds added to the beauty of the scene, and, just as the last rays of the sun were gilding the summits of the twin peaks, we sat down on the huge trunk of a fallen tree, which the floods of the rainy season had swept down from the interior, and half buried in the sand and pebbles. There we remained till the shades of evening had completely closed in around us, speculating on the probable future of the country, and the words almost rose simultaneously to our lips—were we missionaries, we would fix our houses here. With my own idea of what a missionary should do, there could be no better spot than San Pro to commence operations. The village was not large, but it is better completely to gain over twenty families, than exhaust one's energies merely skimming over the surface of a dozen tribes, leaving no permanent impression. We fixed on the best locality for a house, a trim garden, a diminutive church, and a school. It is a soil that would repay culture.

We were not fortunate in the time of our visit, as most of the people were away preparing their farms. We took up our residence in the head-house, which, however, was destitute of the usual ornaments. It was quite new. All head-houses have the same appearance, being built on high posts above the ground, and in a circular form, with a sharp conical roof. The windows are, in fact, a large portion of the roof, being raised up, like the lid of a desk, during fine weather, and supported by props; but when rain or night comes on, they are removed, and the whole appearance is snug in the extreme, particularly when a bright fire is lit in the centre, and throws a fitful glow on all the surrounding objects. Around the room are rough divans, on which the men usually sit or sleep, but that night, there being a cold wind and a drizzling rain, a good fire was kept up, and the people crowded near. I awoke at about two, and put my head out of my curtains to look at a night-scene : a dozen of the old men were there collected close over the fire, smoking the tobacco we had given them, and discoursing in a low tone about us. The flames occasionally shot up brilliantly and showed me the curious group, and then, as they faded away, nothing but the outlines of the half-naked old men could be seen cowering over the embers, as a ruder blast or a heavier shower brought the cold wind upon them.

Started early in the morning. The limestone rock, undermined in every direction, was worn into very singular shapes. Occasionally the tall trees, finding insufficient support, had broken from the bank, and slipped their roots into the river, to be completely washed away by next flood. At ten, brought up on a pebbly beach for breakfast, opposite a little cave, about which the Dayaks have as usual a story—this time an indelicate one. Continuing our course, we reached the mountain of Rumbang, remarkable for its curious caves. We had brought guides with us from San Pro, and stopping at the nearest point went ashore, and after a walk and climb of a few hundred yards, reached the entrance of the first cave.

Descending over a few rough stones, we found ourselves in the interior, through which a small stream
makes its way.  Having lighted a candle and a torch,
we advanced—now fording the brook, now jumping
over it: the floor is principally pebbly, though occasionally we met with soft sand and slippery rock.  The
cave itself has no remarkable feature, but is never-
theless interesting.  Its height varied between thirty,
forty, and fifty feet—its exit beautiful in rugged feature
in a soft light, which subdued the uncouth shapes
of the rocks, and rendered them striking and pleasing
to the eye.  This we particularly noticed on our
return, when we approached the entrance.  Then the
light played on the surface of the stream, as it
bubbled onward in its course, and the reflection
slightly illuminated the surrounding features, reminding me of a robber's cave in a dissolving view.

To-day we only penetrated through the mountain
and looked at the country beyond, a restricted view,
as the jungle closely hemmed round the cave: afterwards I heard that we need not have returned the
way we came, but that if we did not fear a steep
climb, there was a cavern exactly above the one we
had come through that would lead us back to the
river—in fact, an upper tunnel.  We thought at first
it must be a joke of the Dayaks, but they assured us
of the truth: so we told them to lead the way.  It
was difficult, in fact very difficult, until we came to
an overhanging rock, against which a long pole leant
with an occasional cross-piece; at the top was another
overhanging one, round which it was necessary to
pass by leaning the body over the abyss, and trusting
entirely to our hands and to the strength of the

roots. The Dayak guide led the way, and as we approached this difficulty we observed him smile. It was at an unfortunate boast. When we first proposed to make the ascent, our guide observed—" No one but a Dayak can go up there." I unfortunately answered, " Wherever a Dayak can go, an English-man can follow." Hence his smile. He proceeded cautiously, as these rough ladders are often rotten, and, it is said, occasionally left unfastened to entrap an unwary thief, who may desire to pilfer the edible swallows' nests found in the upper caves. When he had reached the summit, he invited me to follow; there was no help for it, so I tried ; the pole was no great difficulty, but the rounding the overhanging rock with my body leaning over the abyss tested my strength and nerve ; one of the party followed, the other thought it wiser to return by the way he came. It repaid us, however ; the cave, though not lofty, was full of large chambers, of narrow passages, and occasionally of huge chasms penetrating to the depths below. They said the whole mountain was perforated by these galleries. Our return to the boat was difficult, as we had to force our way through the tangled bushes, and over ground unknown even to the Dayaks. We found our companion seated in the boat, discussing some cool claret and water, and as he beheld us coming in tired, hot, covered with dirt, and with clothes half torn from our bodies, I fear he did not envy us.

Our men had now to drop their paddles once at least in every reach, and to seize their poles and force us along up the gradually lengthening rapids; the motion of the boat thus propelled is exceedingly

pleasant; at one spot we noticed a Dayak suspension-
bridge that spanned the river above a dangerous
rapid.   Kasim, a favourite follower, turned to us
and said, "It was here that the Datu Tumanggong
nearly lost his life."   We asked how.   I will let
Kasim relate his story; it is an illustration of
Bornean ways.

The Datu Tumanggong is the chief third in rank
in Sarawak, and was in his early days known as a
successful pirate.   He was also the terror of the
Dayaks.   Many years before Sir James Brooke
arrived, he had for some cause killed a Dayak of the
tribe of Si-Buñgoh, in those days not considered a
deed requiring particular notice ; but on this occasion
the tribe determined to be revenged.   The next time
the Datu was known to be on his way up the river,
the Dayaks assembled in great numbers round the
suspension-bridge, concealing themselves among the
trees.   Unsuspicious of the ambuscade, the chief,
with twenty Malay followers, was endeavouring to
pole up the rapid, when a shower of spears threw
them into confusion; the Datu was principally aimed
at, his umbrella was torn to shreds, and he was
wounded severely about the shoulders.   The men
dropping their poles, allowed the boat to get across
the stream, and she was instantly upset; while they,
unable to see their enemies, scattered themselves in
every direction, and hiding among the rocks shouted
to their chief to fire.   They say he stood his ground
manfully, and fired twice without success at his foes,
who, thus emboldened, drew nearer.   The water was
rushing down with great force and reached over his
knees, which rendered the operation of loading

extremely difficult, but his third shot was fortunate, for bringing down the boldest Dayak, it created a panic among the rest. On collecting his followers, he found two killed and several wounded, among the latter one of our present boatmen. I have often heard the Datu tell the story since with great glee, his voice rising, and going through all his remembered movements with wonderful spirit. "Ah, I was young in those days."

There is a very singular belief prevalent among the Malays—it is this, that men, by going through certain ceremonies, can render themselves invulnerable. The Datu, notwithstanding the many wounds he has received, is still popularly believed to be so. They generally say that these men can never have their skin cut by any sharp instrument, and the offer to test the truth by the application of a razor is not considered polite. The old Datu has often said—"It is as well that the vulgar should believe it, though we know better."

The favourite spot chosen by the novitiates was in the jungle at the back of Sir James Brooke's former house, between two little streams, called the greater and lesser Bedil (a brass gun). The aspirant was required to remain three days alone in the woods without speaking to a soul; to live very sparingly, and not to indulge in the favourite luxuries of tobacco, sirih and betel. If on the third day he dreamt of a beautiful spirit descending to speak to him, he might consider that his work was accomplished. Patah, the Datu's son, a fine, bold and good fellow, told me he had tried twice, but the fairy had never appeared to him.

On reaching the landing-place leading to the
Grung village, we found a large party of Dayaks
assembled, who begged us to remain and visit their
houses; but instead, we promised to return in a few
days, and meet the representatives of the neighbouring tribes at their village. We now pushed on to the
Sibuñgoh Dayaks, who inhabited the river's bank;
but on our stopping at the landing-place, an old man
came down to say that the long house before us was
pamali or tabooed, and that the Orang Kaya was
himself in that unenviable predicament. So we
pulled across the river and took up our quarters near
a pebbly beach; the men making temporary mat huts,
while we stayed in the boat. In the course of the
evening, a number of the elders of the neighbouring
village houses of the same tribe came down to see us,
and promised to provide small canoes and Dayaks to
take us up the stream, as it had become too shallow
to allow of our continuing in the large boat.

At six the Sibuñgoh Dayaks brought the light
canoes with which we were to continue our progress
up the river. We left all our crew behind, taking
with us only our personal servants and Kasim. It
was quite a little procession. Each canoe contained
but two Dayaks and one passenger. We started, and
were poled up at a rapid pace against the stream.
Our canoes were small, drawing but a few inches of
water, and were managed, as I have said, by two
Dayaks, one standing at the stem, the other at the
stern; with long bamboos in their hands, they im-
pelled us forward at a great pace.

The scenery varied much; occasionally we passed
beneath high hills, which rose smilingly above us,

clothed to the summit with vegetation; Bornean hills seldom frown, their clothing is too luxuriant, their aspect generally free from harsh outlines, even their precipices have some softening feature. On we passed, sometimes a long reach stretched before us, completely overshadowed by trees whose branches entwining from bank to bank completely sheltered us from the sun, then reclining on our pillows we could indulge in snatches from the *Quarterly* or *Edinburgh*. Could the authors of some of the articles but imagine the variety of situations in which their effusions would be perused, could they anticipate the delight they inspire in the British traveller who works his way onwards even towards the interior of Borneo, they would, I think, be surprised and gratified. The magazines and reviews are the solaces of educated exiles in all positions. From these soft scenes and pleasant employments, we were constantly aroused by our approach to roaring rapids, which foaming over scattered rocks threatened destruction to our frail canoes; but the skill of the Dayak was never at fault, we passed every obstruction without an accident. At these rapids, as at those before mentioned, boats are often lost.

As we approached the country of the Senah tribe, the banks became more uniform in appearance, and the bamboo constantly formed the principal vegetation: these bamboos are wonderfully useful to the Dayaks, and are turned to many purposes. In height they sometimes exceed sixty feet. During this tour I have seen them used, stretched in lengths, for paths, placed notched for steps up steep ascents, as railings for rice fields and yam gardens, as posts

for houses; split they form the floors, beaten out they
are the walls of many of the dwellings, and neat and
pretty they look; cut into lengths, water is carried in
them; joined together they form aqueducts that stretch
for hundreds of yards; with them the Dayaks can
strike a light; and last, not least, they are used to
cook rice in—they are hard enough to stand the fire
until the food be ready to eat.   They are put to
numerous other uses, but the above enumeration is
sufficient.

The Senah Dayaks plant yams to a great extent;
they grow to a large size, and boiled have an excellent
flavour, whether used as a vegetable or a salad.  These
Dayaks are called rich from the abundance of their
rice, which flourishes in their fertile valleys, but more
is chiefly owing to their industry; we saw many
instances of the latter in their fishing apparatus,
which was often very extensive; while the tribes
lower down, with better opportunities, seemed quite to
neglect their fisheries.   Our men unfortunately have
brought no casting net with them, so we are obliged
to be content to hear from the Malays that the flavour
of the fresh-water fish caught here is excellent.   It is
a curious fact, that far as we are above the influence
of the flood tide, and with so many rapids below us,
yet sharks are found here in the fresh water.   I call
it a fact because native testimony is unanimous.   I
remember hearing Mr. Crookshank say to the Datu
Patinggi, the principal native chief, that he considered
it a very curious thing that a fish, supposed to live
only in the sea, should frequent these interior waters.

"Not at all," answered the Datu, "not more
curious than seeing you Englishmen abandon your

own country to come so far and live among us
Malays."

As a general rule, the sharks and alligators do not
meddle with human beings up here, but confine their
attention to the fish, the dogs, and the numerous
droves of wild pigs constantly passing from one bank
to the other.  During the fruit season the movement
among these last is very remarkable ; Mr. Brereton
told me he once saw at least three hundred in one
drove crossing the river Batang Lupar, where it
was above seven hundred yards broad.  I have often
seen them myself in lesser numbers; on one occasion
I was present when seventeen were killed, which
formed a regular feast for some aborigines who secured
the bodies.  Generally a fine old boar leads the way,
and is followed very closely by the rest.  They grow
to a great size; I have seen one carefully measured,
his height at the shoulder was forty-two inches, and
the length of head was twenty-two.

The Senahs have built many of their farm-houses
in the trees overhanging the stream ; in one was a
whole family engaged in the important operation of
preparing dinner; and it was amusing to observe the
little children coming fearlessly to the very edge of
the platform above the rushing stream to look at us,
standing in positions so dangerous that they would
drive an English mother distracted.

As we approach the interior of the Sarawak river,
the mountains become more lofty, and the stream
takes the character of a torrent ; after heavy rains it
rises suddenly and to a great height.  I have seen
grass left by the receding waters at least forty feet
above our present level.  Even after one heavy shower,

all the fords are impassable, so that to avoid this inconvenience the Senah Dayaks have thrown lofty bridges across, to facilitate their communication between their several villages.

How light and elegant do these suspension-bridges look—one in particular I will attempt to describe. It was a broad part of the stream, and two fine old trees hung over the water opposite each other; long bamboos well lashed together formed the main portion, and were fastened by smaller ones to the branches above; railings on either side were added to give greater strength and security, yet the whole affair appeared so flimsy, and was so far above the stream, that when we saw a woman and child pass over it, we drew our breath till they were safe on the other side. And yet we knew they were secure.

I have often passed over them myself; they are of the width of one bamboo, but the side railings give one confidence. Accidents do happen from carelessly allowing the rattan lashings to rot. Once when pressed for time I was passing rapidly across with many men following close behind me, when it began to sway most unpleasantly, and crack, crack was heard as several of the supports gave way. Most of my men fortunately were not near the centre, and relieved the bridge of their weight by clinging to the branches, otherwise those who were with me in the middle would have been precipitated on the rocks far below. After that we always passed singly over such neglected bridges.

Towards the afternoon we reached the first house, inhabited by the Orang Kaya's younger brother. This tribe is more scattered than is usually the case here,

four, six, eight families live together; and we nowhere
noticed those immense long village houses so common
in other tribes.

We found some Chinese trading for pigs and rice,
one of whom had been established in this place for
about six years. The house where we stopped for
the night was tolerably comfortable, with the walls
roughly planked. It is evident that these Dayaks
are very pleased to see us, and upon their pressing
invitations we have agreed to stay some days to give
time for the whole tribe to be collected.

In the evening we took a long walk over the steep
hills at the back of the village, and had a fair view
of Penrisen, one of the highest mountains in Sarawak.
It is estimated at above 5,000 feet. It is scarcely in
Sarawak, as a portion of its southern face belongs
to those countries beyond the border claimed by the
Dutch. We had a good view of the interior of the
Sadong country, a fine succession of hill and dale,
with blue mountains in the distance.

We stayed in the house nearly the whole day, as
the Dayaks wished to dance and feast in our presence.
The gongs were kept going, the drums beaten, and
all within five yards of us, until our heads were dizzy.
Occasionally, from sheer weariness, or from anxiety to
partake of the good things produced for the feast,
this din would cease, and then we could enter into
conversation with the elders.

The dress of the Dayaks is very simple; the men
wear the chawat, a strip of cloth round their loins;
a jacket and head-dress, the last sometimes of bark,
and fantastically put on; their ornaments are brass
rings, necklaces of beads and sometimes of tiger-cat's

teeth, and very neat plaited rings of rattan, stained black. The women have a short petticoat reaching from the hips to the knees, a jacket, and round their waists a band, often ten inches wide, of bark or bamboo, kept together by brass wire or rattans. It fits tight, and is only removed on the woman becoming pregnant.

Captain Brooke's principal object in making this tour was to inquire into the complaints which had been brought against the Datu Patinggi of forcing the Dayak tribes to deal with him, whether they wanted his goods or not, and insisting upon fixing his own price on the articles supplied. The complaints were more than substantiated; even the Chinese were unable to procure rice, and were forced to content themselves with the pig trade.

This was the Datu's system: he sent up a cha-nang, a kind of small gong much esteemed by the Dayaks, and ordered them to buy it at an exorbitant rate; before they had paid for that he sent another, keeping up a constant supply to prevent them trading with other people. When he heard that another Malay had sold a chanang in fair trade to these Dayaks, he would instantly send two more and force them to receive them. He had done the same with regard to salt, and to the clothes of both male and female, striving to his utmost to secure a monopoly. In this path he was followed by all his relations and connexions, their threats bullied and terrified the Dayaks, who loudly complained also of being used as beasts of burden without receiving hire.

The Senahs are altogether an interesting tribe; in manner the men are more polite; the women are fuller of life; some of the girls were pretty, their best age being six to sixteen, after that they begin to fall off. They appear to marry very young, and have for Asiatics rather large families—four, five, and six children were quite common. Some of the old gentlemen observed that, though they were only allowed to marry one wife, yet they were not strictly faithful to her if a favourable opportunity occurred, which observation seemed much to amuse the assembly.

Among the women was the widow of a Dayak, whose story is well worth relating as illustrative of their character and of their ways. He was a fine, handsome man, certainly the most handsome Dayak I have ever seen, tall and powerfully made, with a bold, open countenance; he was called Pa Bunang. The Orang Kaya of the Senahs took a liking to him, and having no children adopted and found him a wife among his own relations. She was a nice-looking girl, plump and well made. In former times the husband had been much noticed by Europeans, and in the pride of his heart determined to be the first man in the tribe: the only one he thought likely to oppose his pretensions was Pa Mua, the Orang Kaya's brother, who would not allow him to interfere in public affairs, and opposed his pretensions to superiority, in which he was supported by the sympathies of the whole community. Pa Bunang then determined on more violent methods than he had yet practised; he left the tribe for a few days and returned with the announcement that the Sarawak Government was so pleased with him, that they intended to make him a great man in the tribe. Resolving to get rid

of his rival, he lay in wait for him one day in a
by-path, concealing himself carefully behind some
bushes; the unsuspecting Pa Mua passed by, when
he sprang upon him, and with one blow of his sword
laid him dead at his feet, and then rushed into the
jungle, thinking he had done the deed unnoticed, but
at the moment of striking, the son of the murdered
man came round the turning of the path in time to
witness the act and to recognize the culprit.   The
alarm was given, and before the man could reach the
Orang Kaya's house, where his wife and child resided,
a menacing crowd had assembled.   He coolly assured
them that he was acting under the orders of the
Sarawak Government, and was now going to report
the accomplishment of the deed.   Though the people
did not believe him, they suffered him to depart with
his family, but followed closely in his track.   They
denounced him, he was instantly seized, thrown into
prison, and after ten days, to allow witnesses to
assemble, the affair came on before the Sarawak
Court.

It was so curious a case that I determined to be
present at the trial.   I found the court crowded, at
least a dozen Englishmen were assembled, who, with
the Malay chiefs, acted as a kind of jury.   Though
the case was clear in many respects, yet the greatest
pains were taken to obtain the best evidence: the son
of the murdered man was present, but it was at first
feared from the preliminary inquiries, that he would
be afraid to give his evidence before the prisoner.
When he was called into court the lad appeared
perfectly changed; he gave his evidence with a cool-
ness, a precision, and yet with an intensity that

nothing but the deepest feelings could excite; he never faltered once, but wound up his story by point-ing to the prisoner and saying, " My father was killed by that man." The prisoner could offer no defence; at first he denied the deed, then said that Pa Mua had seduced his wife, then confessed and implored for mercy. The verdict was unanimous, and he was con-demned to death. A fearful scene now took place; the constables had very improperly allowed the wife and child to sit close beside him, and he had, while the lad was giving his evidence, unnoticed by any, got his little child to crawl in between his manacled arms. When he heard the sentence he threw himself on his knees and begged in piteous terms for mercy, but finding it was useless he declared his wife and child should die with him; he first struck at the former and then tried to strangle the little thing between his arms, and failing in that, while struggling with the police, he fixed his teeth so tightly in the child's neck that they had to be forced open with the point of a drawn sword. His wife fled, and the child was saved, but he continued to struggle, and his roars could be heard until he was secured in his cell. I never witnessed a more painful scene. A marked contrast to that of the Malay who, calm and placid to the last moment, receives his condemnation with the observation, " It is your sentence," and walks quietly to prison and to execution.

The evening was spent in dancing, singing, and drinking, until the fun waxed fast and furious.

The next station up the river is San Piuh, which we did not visit, as business prevented our extending our tour. We were delighted with the position of the house in which we were staying; it was on the bank of the stream, here but a foot deep, occasionally not even six inches, so that the canoes had to be dragged over the pebbly bottom. The water coming from the neighbouring high mountains is both clear and cool, offering delightful places for bathing. In one large and deep pool, a little below the landing-place, the Dayaks say alligators congregate; but if so, they must be harmless, as I saw very little children bathing there; but yet I did not venture, as they might have been attracted by the unusual colour of my skin. The baths we obtain in the interior are of themselves worth the exertion of reaching those sequestered spots; the refreshing and invigorating feeling after a plunge into the cool stream is indeed delightful.

About midday we parted from our kind hosts, not before we had given solemn promises to return again as soon as possible, and now directed our faces homeward. The descent of the river was exciting, now leisurely suffering the canoe to float with the stream; then, as the distant roar announced a rapid, intelligent were the movements of the Dayaks, as they chose the least dangerous part, the waters increasing in speed as we approached the fall; then caught by the stream, we hurried along at the pace of a race-horse, and dashing through the foam were shot into the tranquil pool that generally forms below a rapid. At one we were compelled to take out all our baggage, and the non-swimmers walked past the obstruction to be re-shipped below. It was with feelings, half of envy, half of admiration, that I saw Captain Brooke tempt the danger.

About half-way down to Sibuñgoh we saw white flags overhanging the river at a landing-place, and there in a temporary hut was waiting the Orang Kaya of Brang; we stayed with him about an hour, and resisting his pressing invitation to his village, on account of our previous engagement, heard what he desired to communicate, and then continued our course to Sibuñgoh. We soon transhipped our goods to the large boat, and were not sorry, as many hours in a small canoe is fatiguing. We found that the Orang Kaya was no longer under taboo, so we stayed some little time with him, and then hurried on to the next landing-place, where we found a large party of Dayaks ready to escort us to the village of Grung.

The walk was pleasant, principally over the land that had formerly been farmed, and was now covered with brushwood and young trees, affording but little shelter from the burning sun. The country was un-dulating, with pretty pebbly streams in the hollows. Much rain having fallen in this neighbourhood during the last few days the paths were execrable, even for Dayak paths, which are, perhaps, the worst in the world. Over a marshy soil a line of single trees is laid, end to end, on which you balance yourself as you move along; there is no danger here, except of a slip into the oozy mud, sometimes up to the waist, affording to the non-sufferers great cause of merriment as you struggle and flounder to a drier spot; but these trunks of trees thrown over ravines are dangerous after rain, as when deprived of their bark they are slippery. But it is astonishing what use will do; we soon began to criticize and pronounce a wretched quagmire a tolerable path. The Dayak is so active, and so

accustomed to the work, that he seldom thinks of
doing more than felling a small tree, clearing it of its
branches, and throwing it across the smaller streams
as a bridge, except after harvest, when carrying home
the rice, a slight railing is added to give steadiness to
his movements.

The village of Grung is prettily situated near a
small and clear stream, and is surrounded by dense
groves of fruit-trees, particularly of durians, while
occasionally the graceful areca palm rises near the
houses. In one thing the Grungs excel every other
tribe of Dayaks I have ever seen, and that is in dirt;
their houses were dirty, their mats were dirty, and
their little children could only be described as positively filthy.

We found the village crowded with the representatives of all the neighbouring tribes; long strings of
men, women, and children were continually arriving
as we approached. Directly we ascended the notched
tree that served as a ladder to the Orang Kaya's
house, we found that we were no longer free agents.
A crowd of old women instantly seized us, and pulled
off our shoes and stockings, and commenced most
vigorously washing our feet; this water was preserved
to fertilize the fields. We were then conducted to a
platform but slightly raised above the floor, and
requested to sit down, but the mats were so dirty
that we could scarcely prevail upon ourselves to do so
—perhaps the only time it has occurred to us; generally the mats are charmingly neat and clean. The
arrival of our bedding freed us from this difficulty.

We were surrounded by a dense mass of men,
women, and children, who appeared all to be talking

at once; in fact, more excitement was shown than I have before observed. We had to do so many things, and almost all at once: to sprinkle rice about, to pour a little water on each child that was presented to us, until, from force of example, the women and even the men insisted upon the same ceremony being performed on them.

Silence being at last restored, Kasim explained in a long speech the object of Captain Brooke's visit; he spoke in Malay, interlarding it occasionally with Dayak phrases—I say Malay, but Malay that is only used when addressing the aborigines, clipping and altering words, changing the pronunciation, until I find that some have been deceived into believing this was the true Dayak language. It is to these people what the Lingua Franca is to Western Asia.

We got a little respite while eating our dinner, but as soon as we had finished we were again surrounded; the priestesses of the place were especially active, tying little bells round our wrists and ancles, and bringing rice for us to—how shall I explain it—in fact, for us to spit on, and this delectable morsel they swallowed. No sooner had these learned women been satisfied, than parents brought their children, and insisted upon their being physicked in the same way, taking care to have a full share themselves. One horrid old woman actually came six times.

The Orang Kaya now advanced, and there was strict attention to hear what he was about to say. He walked to the window, and threw some grains out, and then commenced a kind of prayer, asking for good harvests, for fertility for the women, and for health to them all. During the whole invocation he kept scattering rice about. The people were very attentive at first, but soon the murmur of many voices almost drowned the old man's tones. He did not appear very much in earnest, but repeated what he had to say as if he were going over a well-remembered but little understood lesson; in fact, it is said these invocations are in words not comprehended even by the Dayaks themselves—perhaps they are in some Indian language.

Then a space was cleared for dancing; the old Orang Kaya and the elders commenced, and were followed by the priestesses. They walked up to us in succession, passed their hands over our arms, pressed our palms, and then uttering a yell or a prolonged screech went off in a slow measured tread, moving their arms and hands in unison with their feet until they reached the end of the house, and came back to where we sat; then another pressure of the palm, a few more passes to draw virtue out of us, another yell, and off they went again; at one time there were at least a hundred dancing. Few of the young people joined in what appeared in this case a sacred dance.

For three nights we had had little sleep, on account of these ceremonies, but at length, notwithstanding clash of gong and beat of drum, we sank back in our beds, and were soon fast asleep. In perhaps a couple of hours I awoke; my companion was still sleeping uneasily; the din was deafening, and I sat up to look around. Unfortunate movement! I was instantly seized by the hands by two priests, and led up to the Orang Kaya, who was leisurely cutting a fowl's throat.

He wanted Captain Brooke to perform the following ceremony, but I objected to his being awakened, and offered to do it for him. I was taken to the very end of the house, and the bleeding fowl put in my hands; holding him by his legs, I had to strike the lintels of the doors, sprinkling a little blood over each; when this was over, I had to waive the fowl over the heads of the women, and wish them fertility; over the children, and wish them health; over all the people, and wish them prosperity; out of the window, and invoke good crops for them. At last I reached my mats, and sat down, preparatory to another sleep, when that horrid old woman led another detachment of her sex forward to re-commence the physicking; fortunately but few came, and after setting them off dancing again I fell asleep, and, in spite of all the noises, remained so till morning.

It is a fact unnoticed by us before, that among the Dayak tribes there are few girls between the age of ten and fifteen (1852). It is a striking proof of the effects that have attended the change of system from native lawlessness to English superintendence. Before Sir James Brooke held the reins of Government the little female children were seized for slaves and con-cubines by the Rajahs and Malay chiefs; since that practice has been put an end to, the houses are crowded with interesting girls of nine and younger.

The expression of all classes and of both sexes of these people is that of a subdued melancholy. A man fresh from Europe would doubtless notice many more peculiarities in these tribes, which being familiar to me pass without remark. Their houses I have before described, and what is suitable for the one is so for the other. Nearly all the representatives present are but those of the branches of a single tribe which has for many years been scattered. Their language is the same in words, though the accent is occasionally different—the effect of separation and other causes. It is difficult, without long and minute investigation, to familiarize oneself with their individual history and politics.

# CHAPTER V.

LAND DAYAKS OF SIRAMBAU—THEIR SOCIAL LIFE.

Madame Pfeiffer—Chinese Village—Chinese Maidens—Sirambau—
Ascent of the Mountain—Difficult Climbing—Forests of Fruit
Trees—Scenery—Sirambau Village—Houses—The "Look-
out"—Scenery—Head-houses—Orang Kaya Mita—His modest
Request—Sir James Brooke's Cottage—Natural Bath-house—
Chinese Gold Workings—Tapang Trees—Social Life of the
Land Dayaks—Ceremonies at a Birth—Courtship—Betrothe-
ment—Marriage—Burial—Graves—The Sexton—Funeral
Feast—Children—Female Chastity—Divorces—Cause of Sepa-
rations—Anecdote.

MADAME PFEIFFER, the traveller, suddenly made her
appearance among us in December, 1851 ; she was a
woman of middle height, active for her age, with an
open countenance and a very pleasant smile. She
lived with us for some days, and then we took her to
visit the Dayaks of Sirambau on the right hand
branch. We selected a very fast, long prahu, fitted
up with a little cabin for her, and another for ourselves, and having a numerous crew, pulled past our
usual resting-place at Ledah Tanah, and did not stop
till we reached the Chinese village of Siniawan, where
we took up our quarters for the night.

There are about three hundred Celestials settled
here, principally engaged in shop-keeping, though a
few cultivate gardens. They are evidently thriving,
as the Dayaks of the surrounding country resort to
this place, and there is a constant influx of Chinese

and Malay gold workers. Their women, half-breeds, are better-looking than any others in this part of the world; some of the girls were handsome, in one point they set a bright example to their neighbours, and that is in cleanliness. The Malay girls bathe at least three times a day, but are not careful of the condition of their clothes, while the Dayaks are too often neglectful of both their skins and their coverings.

It was quite a pleasure to look at the little Chinese maidens in their prim, neat dresses, and their parents evidently have a pride in their appearance. To them Madame Pfeiffer was a great attraction, and a crowd followed her everywhere, and wondered at the eagerness she displayed in the chase of a butterfly, or the capture of an insect.

Siniawan is situated on a plain near the foot of the Sirambau mountain, and affords an excellent market for the produce of the interminable fruit groves that cover the lower part of its slopes, and extend for miles beyond.

As Madame Pfeiffer had never seen a Dayak village, we thought she would like to visit these rather primitive people, who reside about eleven hundred feet up the sides of the mountain. Sirambau is separated from the surrounding ranges, and from the sea appears of great length, while from one view near Siniawan, it is a single peak seventeen hundred feet in height. At a few spots, we saw groves of cocoanuts varying the colour of the jungle, and these were at the villages of the Dayaks, all more than a thousand feet above us.

In the morning we collected a band of mountaineers to shoulder our baggage, and proceeded towards the

hill. The soil around had lately been cleared, and
afforded no shelter from the burning sun. I imagine
Madame Pfeiffer, in all her travels, had never met
worse paths, particularly when we commenced ascending the hill. It appeared exactly as if the Dayaks
had chosen the bed of a mountain torrent as the
proper approach to their houses. At first the stones
were arranged as a rough paving, then as rougher
steps, and at last it became so steep, rock piled on
rock, that notched trunks of trees leaning against
them were the only means of ascending.

But, if the climbing were difficult, we were partly
compensated by the shade of the lofty fruit-trees growing in glorious confusion on either side of our path.
Crowded as closely as in the jungle, durians, man-
gustins, and every variety of fruit-tree, jostled each
other for the light, and spoilt the symmetry of their
forms. I have not seen elsewhere durian-trees of
proportions so magnificent, some above ten feet in
circumference, and rising to the height of a hundred
and twenty feet. When the season is good, it is
dangerous to walk in a grove of these trees, as a
breeze gently shaking the ripe fruit from its hold, it
falls heavily to the ground. They are often a foot in
length, and eight inches in diameter, and many a
story was told us of Dayaks being brought home
insensible through a blow from a falling durian.

As we advanced up the side of the mountain, we
rested at spots where we could obtain partial views of
the surrounding country; large Dayak clearings now
completely brown, varied the otherwise continuous
jungle; gently swelling hills encircled the base of
Sirambau, and stretched onwards to the foot of the

steep and distant mountains. The Dayaks have led
rills of water to the edge of the path, at which they
refresh themselves, and occasionally there are rough
benches on which they rest their heavy loads, for
they carry up their whole rice crop to their mountain
villages.

After a toilsome ascent, which Madame Pfeiffer
feelingly describes, we passed the village of Bombok
on our left, and continued our course to that of
Sirambau, a little distance farther. Here the path
was more level, though it lay among huge rocks
detached from the summit of the mountain.

Sirambau is one of the most curious villages I have
seen; it is large, and the long houses are connected
together by platforms of bamboo or by rough bridges
—a very necessary precaution, as the numerous pigs
had routed up the land; and as every description of
dirt is thrown from their houses and never removed,
it is almost impossible to walk on the ground. Thick
groves of palms surrounded the village and buried it
from the world: indeed, it looked as isolated a spot
as any in wooded Borneo.

We found the chief Mita ready to receive us, and
to conduct us to his apartments; they were very
confined, but on the raised platform under the sloping
windows we found place for our beds. They very
politely gave Madame Pfeiffer an inner room, and
provided her with neat white mats.

In the evening the apartments were crowded, and
being small, not much space was left for dancing.
This village house was altogether uncomfortable; its
verandah was not five feet wide, and was totally
unfitted for their feasts; the rooms were not twelve

feet by sixteen, and the space was still further lessened
by a large fireplace that occupied an eighth of the
area. Some rough planks were laid on the floor and
then covered with earth; on it were arranged a few
stones, and that constituted the fireplace. At each
corner was a small post that supported a platform,
and on this was a heap of firewood kept here to dry
and to be ready at hand.

We have had much more intercourse with the
villagers on this hill, than with any other, as Sir
James Brooke had a country house near the upper-
most groves of palms that are seen from Siniawan.
Formerly it was a Dayak village, but the inhabitants
removing to join another section of their tribe who
were in a more sheltered spot, Sir James purchased
the fruit-trees around, and built a pretty cottage there.

Peninjau, or the "look-out," was the name of this
spot, and it well deserved its name, as from a rock
which terminated the level summit of a buttress can
be seen a view unsurpassed in extent. I have spent
many months at this cottage, and rarely an evening
passed without my witnessing the sunset from this
favourite rock.

The peak of Santubong is the centre of the picture,
and the undulating ground between and the winding
of the river may be seen clearly in all its varied detail.
The calm sea—from this distance it seems always calm
—bounds the horizon. Two effects of light I have
often witnessed here; just at sunset, the rays thrown on
the hills, the woods, the water, have a sickly tint;
and when rain threatens, the trees in the jungle on
the distant hills of Matang stand out distinctly
visible, and it is only at such times they do so.

There are three villages on this Sirambau hill—
the Peninjau, now visible below my favourite rock,
Bombok, and Sirambau, where we have left Madame
Pfeiffer.

Each of these villages contains a head-house; in
that at Sirambau there were thirty-three heads, at
Bombok thirty-two, and at Peninjau twenty-one, with
the skull of a bear killed during a head-hunting
expedition. They were all very ancient-looking, in
fact none had been added to their store since Sir
James Brooke assumed the government of the
country. That they still have a longing for a fresh
skull, I have little doubt, though previously to the
Chinese insurrection the apparent impossibility had
made them rather careless on the subject.

There is a custom in these tribes to assist the
Orang Kaya in making his farms; in fact, it is one of
the most lucrative of his perquisites. Mita of
Sirambau had pushed his prerogative too far, and had
forced his people to make him three farms, and as
from this and many other reasons, he had ruined his
popularity, he looked about him for a means to
recover it. At last it struck him that a fresh head
would make the whole tribe look up to him with
respect.

I was visiting the village one day, when he told me
he had a great favour to ask, which was, that I would
endeavour to obtain from Sir James Brooke permission for him to make a foray into the neighbouring
districts. All the elders of the tribe were present,
and it was evident that they were deeply interested in
the answer. The earnest way in which they assured
me that the crops had not been good for many years,

because the spirits were angry at the ancient rites
having fallen into disuse, showed that he had worked
upon them to believe in the necessity of a head being
procured, but my answer was so discouraging that
they never ventured to mention the subject to Sir
James Brooke. Mita was afterwards removed from
his office, to the great satisfaction of the tribe.

Our cottage was just twelve hundred and thirty
feet above the level of the sea, and had a pure and
cool atmosphere about it; but the most remarkable
spot near was a natural bath-house. In a ravine
close by rose a huge rock, seventy feet in length by
forty in breadth; somewhat of the shape of a mighty
but very blunt wedge. The thicker end was buried
in the ground, the centre, supported on either side
by two rocks, left a cave beneath, while the thinner
part, thrust up at an angle of thirty degrees, overshadowed a natural basin, improved by art, at which
we bathed. A rill that glided from under the rock
supplied us plentifully with cool, clear water. It was
a beautiful spot, a charming natural grotto, in which
to pass the burning midday hours; twenty or thirty
people could sit there with comfort, and admire the
vegetation that grew thickly around, but yet affording
glimpses of distant hills through the trees.

That spot for years was our boast; there was no
bathing-place like Peninjau, no water so cool, no air
so bracing. Once our grotto fell to a discount, and that
was when some one unromantically brought from our
basin a huge leech, fifteen inches long; but that was
the only intruder that ever invaded the sacred spot.
I may say that we never enter the basin when we
bathe in these places, or at our houses, but pour

small buckets of water on our heads, and let it run over our bodies ; it is the most refreshing plan. But up country, in the cool mountain streams, we always take a plunge into the water.

At night, looking south, the prospect appeared quite lively with fires and flashing lights ; these came from the villages of Chinese gold-workers occupying the valleys below. They extended irregularly for about ten miles until they reached their chief town of Bau, romantically situated among limestone hills, presenting perpendicular sides.

To the eastward was one of the noblest valleys in Sarawak, perfectly uninhabited. At the nearer end the Sirambau Dayaks occasionally had a farm, but thousands of acres, untrodden by man, lay there uncultivated.

To the left of Sirambau are some very fine Tapang trees, in which the bees generally build their nests ; they are considered private property, and a Dayak from a neighbouring tribe venturing to help himself of this apparently wild honey and wax, would be punished for theft. This tribe, also, is rich in edible birds'-nests, while the Peninjaus are becoming wealthy from the great extent of their fruit-groves. In former times, the Malays used to gather them without thinking of asking permission, but now the government has forbidden this practice, and the amount realized by the Dayaks is, for Borneo, something surprising. One good fruit season, a hundred and fifty families realized two pounds sterling each, enough to buy rice to last them six months.

I have said I am more familiar with the manners and customs of these Dayaks than with those of any others, and having had the advantage of receiving full and careful replies to a list of queries I addressed to all those I thought likely to be able to give me assistance, particularly from the Rev. Mr. Chalmers, the able missionary who formerly resided there, and whose departure from Borneo all sincerely regret, I will enter an account of the ways of the Land Dayaks, noticing in what manner they vary from those of the surrounding tribes. Though I am greatly indebted to Mr. Chalmers's notes, I by no means bind him to the opinions expressed, as we differ on some points, particularly regarding the belief in the Supreme Being.

*Births.*—After pregnancy is declared a ceremony takes place.* Two priestesses† attend, a fowl is killed, rice provided, and for two nights they howl and chant, during which time the apartment is "pamali," or interdicted. The husband of the pregnant woman, until the time of her delivery, may not do work with any sharp instrument, except what may be absolutely necessary for the cultivation of his farm; he may not tie things together with rattans, or strike animals, or fire guns, or do anything of a violent character—all such things being imagined to exercise a malign influence on the formation and development of the unborn child. The delivery is attended by an old woman, called a "Penyading," or midwife. A fowl is killed, the family tabooed for eight days, during which time the unfortunate husband is dieted on rice

* Dayak,—beruri.
† The Land Dayak word "borich," and the Sea Dayak "manang," are generally translated male and female doctors, but from their employment and duties, I think "priest" and "priestess" would better convey the idea.

and salt, and may not go out in the sun, or even
bathe for four days ; the rice and salt diet is to prevent the *baby's* stomach swelling to an unnatural
size.

*Courtship.*—Besides the ordinary attention which
a young man is able to pay to the girl he desires
to make his wife—as helping her in her farm work,
and in carrying home her load of vegetables or wood,
as well as in making her little presents, as a ring,
or some brass chain work with which the women
adorn their waists, or even a petticoat—there is
a very peculiar testimony of regard, which is worthy
of note. About nine or ten at night, when the
family is supposed to be fast asleep within the musquito curtains in the private apartment, the lover
quietly slips back the bolt by which the door is
fastened on the inside and enters the room on tip-toe.
He goes to the curtains of his beloved, gently awakes
her, and she on hearing who it is rises at once, and
they sit conversing together, and making arrangements for the future in the dark over a plentiful
supply of sirih-leaf and betel-nut, which it is the
gentleman's duty to provide. If when awoke the
young lady rises and accepts the prepared betel-nut,
happy is the lover, for his suit is in a fair way to
prosper, but if on the other hand she rises and says,
" Be good enough to blow up the fire," or to light the
lamp (a bamboo filled with resin), then his hopes
are at an end, as that is the usual form of dismissal.
Of course if this kind of nocturnal visit is frequently
repeated, the parents do not fail to discover it, although it is a point of honour among them to take no
notice of their visitor, and if they approve of him

matters take their course, but if not, they use their
influence with their daughter to ensure the utterance
of the fatal "please blow up the fire." It is said on
good authority that these nocturnal visits but seldom
result in immorality.

*Betrothment.*—There is no ceremony at a betrothment, the bridegroom expectant (if a young bachelor)
generally presents his betrothed with a set of three
small boxes* made of bamboo, in which are placed
the tobacco, gambir, and lime, with the sirih-leaf and
betel-nut, and sometimes also with a cheap ring or
two purchased from the Malays, or in the Sarawak
bazaar.

*Marriage.*—At a marriage, a fowl is killed, rice
boiled, and a feast made by the relations of the bride
and bridegroom. The bridegroom then generally
betakes himself to the apartment of his wife's parents
or relations, and becomes one of the family. Occasionally, as for example when the bride has many
brothers and sisters, or when the bridegroom is the
support of aged parents, or of younger brothers and
sisters, the bride enters and becomes one of the family
of her husband. It is a rare occurrence for a young
couple at once to commence housekeeping on their
own account; the reason is, that the labours of a
young man go to augment the store of the head of
the family in which he lives, be it that of his parents
or others, and not till their death can he claim any
share of the property in rice, jars, crockery, or gongs,
which by his industry he has helped to create; yet
most young men now have generally a small hoard
of copper coin, or even a few dollars, which they have

* Dekan.

acquired by trading, or by working for Europeans, Malays, or Chinese during the intervals of farm labour.

*Burial.*—When a Dayak dies the whole village is tabooed for a day ; within a few hours of death the body is rolled up in the sleeping mat of the deceased, and carried by the " Peninu," or sexton of the village, to the place of burial or burning.* The body is accompanied for a little distance from the village by the women, uttering a loud and melancholy lament. In the Peninjau tribe the women follow the corpse a short way down the path below the village to the spot where it divides, one branch leading to the burning ground, the other to the Chinese town of Siniawan. Here they mount upon a broad stone, and weep and utter doleful cries, till the sexton and his melancholy burden have disappeared from view. Curiously enough, the top of this stone is hollowed ; and the Dayaks declare that this has been occasioned by the tears of their women, which during many ages have fallen so abundantly, and so often, as to wear away the stone by their continual dropping.

In Western Sarawak the custom of burning the dead is universal, in the districts near the Samarahan, they are indifferently burnt or buried, and when the Sadong is reached the custom of cremation ceases, the Dayaks of the last river being in the habit of burying their dead. In the grave a cocoa-nut, and areca-nut are thrown, and a small basket of rice, and that one containing the chewing condiments of the deceased are hung up near the grave, and if he were a noted warrior, a spear is stuck in the ground close

* Tinungan.

by. The above articles of food are for the sustenance of the soul in his passage to the other world.

The graves are very shallow, and not unfrequently the corpse is rooted up and devoured by wild pigs. The burning also is not unfrequently very inefficiently performed, and portions of the bones and flesh of a deceased person have been brought back by the dogs and pigs of the village to the space below the very houses of the relatives. In times of epidemic disease, and when the deceased is very poor, or the relatives do not feel inclined to be at much expense for the sexton's services, corpses are not unfrequently thrown into some solitary piece of jungle not far from the village, and there left. The Dayaks have very little respect for the bodies of the departed, though they have an intense fear of their ghosts.

The office of sexton is hereditary, descending from father to son, and when the line fails, great indeed is the difficulty of inducing another family to undertake its unpleasant duties, involving, as it is supposed, too familiar an association with the dead and the other world to be at all beneficial. Though the prospect of fees is good, and perhaps every family in the village offers six gallons of unpounded rice to start the sexton elect in his new, and certainly useful career, among the Quop Dayaks it is difficult to find a candidate. The usual burial fee is one jar, valued at a rupee, though if great care be bestowed on the interment, a dollar is asked; at other places as much as two dollars are occasionally demanded, and obtained when the corpse is offensive.

On the day of a person's death, a feast* is given by

* Man buiya.

the family to their relations; if the deceased be rich,
a pig and a fowl are killed, but if poor, a fowl is considered sufficient. The apartment, and the family in
which the death occurs, are tabooed for seven days
and nights, and if the interdict be not rigidly kept,
the ghost of the departed will haunt the house.
Among the Silakau, the Lara, and the true Lundu
tribes, the bodies of the elders and rich are burned,
while the others are buried.

*Children.*—All children are very desirable in Dayak
eyes. Mr. Chalmers thinks that if a Dayak could
have but one child, he would prefer a female, as she
will always assist in getting wood and water (labours
held in little esteem by those males who have arrived
at the age of puberty); and, moreover, at marriage a
son may have to follow his wife, whereas a daughter
obtains for her parents the benefit of her husband's
labour and assistance; but my opinion is contrary,
I think male children are generally desired.

*Female Chastity.*—With regard to female chastity,
I imagine they are better, certainly not worse, than
the Malays. The " Orang Kayas " have many cases
of adultery to settle, which do not, however, cause
much excitement in the tribe.

*Divorces* are very common, one can scarcely meet
with a middle-aged Dayak who has not had two, and
often three or more wives. I have heard of a girl of
seventeen or eighteen years who had already had
three husbands. Repudiation, which is generally done
by the man or woman running away to the house of a
near relation, takes place for the slightest cause—
personal dislike or disappointments, a sudden quarrel,
bad dreams, discontent with their partners' powers of

labour or their industry, or in fact, any excuse which
will help to give force to the expression, " I do not
want to live with him or her any longer."

A woman has deserted her husband when laid up
with a bad foot, and consequently unable to work,
and returned to him when recovered, but this is
perhaps to obtain her food on easier terms. A lad
once forced his mother to divorce her husband, the
lad's stepfather, because the latter tried to get too
much work out of his stepson, and let his own
children by a former marriage remain idle. The
stepson did not understand why he should contri-
bute to the support of his half-brothers, so he
told his mother she must leave her husband, or he
would leave her, and live with his late father's
relatives. She preferred her son's society to her
husband's.

In fact, marriage among the Dayaks is a business
of partnership for the purpose of having children,
dividing labour, and by means of their offspring pro-
viding for their old age. It is, therefore, entered
into and dissolved almost at pleasure. If a husband
divorces his wife, except for the sake of adultery, he
has to pay her a fine of two small jars, or about two
rupees. If a woman puts away her husband, she pays
him a jar, or one rupee. If a wife commits adultery
the husband can put her away if he please; though
if she be a strong, useful woman, he sometimes does
not do so, and her lover pays him a fine of one
" tajau," a large jar equal to twelve small jars, valued
at twelve rupees. If a separation take place, the
guilty wife also gives her husband about two rupees.
If a husband commit adultery, the wife can divorce

him, and fine his paramour eight rupees, but she gets
nothing from her unfaithful spouse. There is one
cause of divorce, where the blame rests on neither
party, but on their superstitions. When a couple are
newly married, if a deer, or gazelle, or a mouse deer
utter a cry at night near the house in which the pair
are living, it is an omen of ill—they must separate, or
the death of one would ensue. This might be a
great trial to a European lover ; the Dayaks, however,
take the matter very philosophically.

Mr. Chalmers mentions to me the case of a young
Peninjau man who was divorced from his wife on
the third day after marriage. The previous night
a deer had uttered its warning cry, and separate they
must. The morning of the divorce he chanced to
go into the " head-house," and there sat the bridegroom contentedly at work.

" Why are you here? " he was asked, as the
" head-house " is frequented by bachelors and boys
only ; " what news of your new wife ? "

" I have no wife, we were separated this morning,
because the deer cried last night."

" Are you sorry ? "

" Very sorry."

" What are you doing with that brass wire ? "

" Making perik "—the brass chain-work which the
women wear round their waists—" for a young woman
whom I want to get for my new wife."

# CHAPTER VI.

SOCIAL LIFE OF THE LAND DAYAKS—*Continued.*

Religion—Belief in Supreme Being—Traces of Hinduism—Sacrifices
—Pamali or Interdict—Mr. Chalmers's Account of the Dayak
Religion—A Future State—Spirits by Nature—Ghosts of
Departed Men—Transformations—Catching the Soul—Con-
version of the Priest to Christianity—Story—Other Ghosts—
Custom of Pamali, or Taboo—Sacrifices—Things and Actions
Interdicted—Not to Eat Horned Animals—Reasons for not
Eating Venison—Of Snakes—The Living Principle—Causes of
Sickness—Spirits Blinding the Eyes of Men—Incantations to
Propitiate or Foil the Spirits of Evil—Catching the Soul—
Feasts and Incantations connected with Farming Operations—
The Blessing of the Seed—The Feast of First Fruits—Securing
the Soul of the Rice—Exciting Night Scene—The Harvest
Home — Singular Ceremony — Head Feasts — Offering the
Drinking Cup—Minor Ceremonies—Images—Dreams—Love—
Journeys of the Soul—Warnings in Sleep—Magic Stones—
Anecdote—Ordeals—Omens—Birds of Omen—Method of Con-
sulting them—Beneficial Effects of the Head Feasts—Languages
of the Land Dayaks—Deer—The Sibuyaus free from Prejudice—
Story of the Cobra De Capella—Names—Change of Name—Pro-
hibited Degrees of Affinity—Heights—Medical Knowledge—
Priests and Priestesses—Origin of the latter—Their Practices
—Manufactures—Agriculture—Story of the Origin of Rice—
The Pleiades.

*Religion.*—This principally consists of a number
of superstitious observances. They are given up to
the fear of ghosts ; and in the propitiation of these by
small offerings and certain ceremonies consists the
principal part of their worship. But though this is
the case, I am quite convinced that they have a firm,
though not clear belief in the existence of one

Supreme Being, who is above all, and over all; and in this lies the best hope of the missionary. If we could trace back the origin of their superstitions, we should probably find that many of their inferior spirits are simply heroes of old who have assumed the form of demi-gods; in fact, all my inquiries among the wild tribes confirm me in the opinion that they believe in a Supreme Being. I have mentioned in my *Limbang Journal* old Japer saying, — " When I speak of the God of the Pakatan tribe, I mean Him who made the heavens, the earth, and man." I have always thought that the three inferior spirits mentioned by Mr. Chalmers in the extract I will give, Tenabi, Iang, and Jirong are merely agents of Tapa, and occasionally their subordinate position is overlooked by the Dayak narrators. It reminds one of the three powers in the Hindoo religion, " Brahma," " Vishnu," and " Siva," issuing from the Godhead Bram—and, in the Dayak religion, "Tenabi," the maker of the material world; Iang, the Instructor, and Jirong, the Renovator and Destroyer, emanating from the Godhead Tapa, the great Creator and Preserver. Before proceeding, I will give the substance of Mr. Chalmers's account of the religion of the Land Dayaks; I may also premise by saying, that the Sarawak Land Dayaks call their God " Tapa," the Silakaus and Laras " Jewata," and the Sibuyaus, " Batara."

In common with many other barbarous tribes, their religious system relates principally to this life. They are like the rest of mankind, continually liable to physical evils, poverty, misfortune, sickness, and these they try to avert from themselves by the practice of ancient customs which are supposed to be effectual for the purpose. This system may be classed as follows :—

The killing of pigs and fowls, the flesh of which is eaten, small portions being set aside with rice for the spiritual powers; and from the blood mixed with spittle, turmeric, and cocoa-nut water, a filthy mess is concocted, and called physic, with which the people attending the feast are anointed on the head and face. Dancing by the elders and the priestesses about a kind of bamboo altar, erected on these occasions either in the long room or on the exterior platform of one of the houses, round which the offerings are placed, always accompanied by the beating of all the gongs and drums of the tribe by the young lads, and singing, or rather chanting, by the priestesses. The "pamali," or taboo of an apartment, house, or village for one, two, four, eight, and even sixteen days, during which in the case of a village, no stranger can enter it, in the case of a house, no one beside the families residing therein, and in the case of an apartment no one out of the family.

It cannot be denied that they have some belief in the Supreme God who is called " Tapa," the Creator or Maker, though their idea of Him as a moral governor is very hazy and confused. They possess also some glimmerings of a future existence, though scarcely any idea of a future state of rewards and punishments. The following are a few particulars of the Dayak theology.

There are four chief spirits : " Tapa," who created men and women, and preserves them in life; "Tenabi," who made the earth, and, except the human race, all things therein, and still causes it to

flourish; " Iang," or " Iing," who first instructed
the Dayaks in the mysteries of their religion, and
who superintends its performance; " Jirong," who
looks after the propagation of the human species, and
also causes them to die of sickness or accident.
" Iang " is frequently associated with " Tapa," and
" Tapa Iang " often stands for the Supreme Being.

An intelligent man of the tribe Setang, gave another account. He says that " Tapa " and " Tenabi "
are but different names for the same Great Being,
and that with Him is associated " Jirong," the Lord
of birth and death. That when Tapa made the
world, he first created " Iang," then the spirits
" Triu " and " Komang," and then man. That man
and the spirits were at first equal, and fought on fair
terms, but that on one woful occasion, the spirits got
the better of man, and rubbed charcoal in his eyes,
which made him no longer able to see his spirit foes,
except in the case of certain gifted persons, as the
priest, and so placed him at their mercy.

With respect to a future state, the common Dayak
story is that when a man dies, he becomes a spirit,
and lives in the jungle, or (this Mr. Chalmers heard
in one of the dead body burning tribes) that as the
smoke of the funeral pile of a good man rises, the soul
ascends with it to the sky, and that the smoke from
the pile of a wicked man descends, and his soul with
it is borne down to the earth, and through it to the
regions below. Another version is, that when a man
dies a natural death, his soul on leaving the body
becomes a spirit, and haunts the place of burial or
burning. When a spirit dies, for spirits too, it would
seem, are subject unto death, it enters the hole of

Hades, and coming out thence again becomes a Bejawi. In course of time the "Bejawi" dies, and lives once more as a "Begutur;" but when a "Begutur" dies, the spiritual essence of which it consists, enters the trunks of trees, and may be seen there damp and blood-like in appearance, and has a personal and sentient existence no longer.

I have introduced this account, and it is curious to trace in it a similarity to the Budhist religion professed in Siam. There, they believe that after passing through many and various transmigrations, they will, as the last and best existence, sink into "neiban" and be lost to all sense, and fade away without retaining personality any longer.

With regard to a future state, the Dayaks point to the highest mountain in sight as the abode of their departed friends.

The spirits are divided into two classes, "Umot," spirits by nature, and "Mino," as I understood it to be, ghosts of departed men.

Umot.—The "Trui" and "Komang" live amid the noble old forest on the tops of lofty hills. They delight in war and bloodshed, and always come down to be present at the Dayak "head feasts." They are described as of a fierce and wild appearance, being covered with coarse red hair like an orang-utan. By some the "Komang" are said to be the spirits of departed heroes, associated after death for their valour with the war-loving "Trui." "Umot Sisi" is a harmless kind of spirit which follows the Dayak, to look for the fragments of food which have fallen through the open flooring of their houses, and who is heard at night munching

away below. " Umot Perubak" cause scarcity among
the Dayaks, by coming invisibly and eating the rice
from the pot at mealtime; their appetite is insa-
tiable. " Umot Perusong" and " Tibong" come slily
and devour the rice which is stored within a recep-
tacle made of the bark of some gigantic tree, and is
in the form of a vat. It is kept in the garrets of the
houses, and a large one will contain a hundred and
fifty bushels, and the family live in constant fear
that these voracious spirits will visit their store and
entirely consume it.

" Mino Buau" are the ghosts of those who have
been killed in war. These are very vicious and
inimical to the living ;—they dwell in the jungle, and
have the power of assuming the form of beasts or
headless men. A Quop Dayak declared he met with
one. He was walking through the jungle, and saw
what he thought was a squirrel sitting on the large
roots of a tree which overhung a small stream. He
had a spear in his hand, this he threw at the squirrel,
and thought he had struck it; he ran towards the
spot at which it had apparently fallen, when to his
horror it faced him, rose up, and was transformed
into a dog. The dog walked on a few paces, and
then turning into a human shape, sat slowly down
on the trunk of a fallen tree—head there was none.
The spectre body was parti-coloured, and at the top
drawn up to a point. The Dayak was smitten with
a great fear, and away he rushed home and fell into
a violent fever; the priest was called, and he pronounced that the patient's soul had been summoned
away from its corporeal abiding place by the spirit;
so he went to seek it, armed with his magic charms.

Midway between the village and place where the "Buau" had appeared, the fugitive soul was overtaken and induced to pause, and having been captured by the priest, was brought back to its body, and poked into its place through an invisible hole in the head: the next day the fever was gone.

This shows how the priests practise on the ignorance and superstition of the people. Mr. Gomez, aware of it, used his utmost efforts to convert the principal " Manang " or priest of the Lundu branch of the " Sibuyaus," and succeeded; since then there have been many baptized. This, however, is not the principal effect; he has enlisted the learned man on his side instead of against him, and I have little doubt of his ultimately winning over the whole tribe of that section of Sea Dayaks.

Some accuse the Buau of being occasionally guilty of running off with women. In former times, a wife named Temunyan was, in her husband's absence, carried off. On his return he searched for, and found the spirit, slew him by a trick and recovered his wife; not, however, until she had suffered violation. She was pregnant by the Buau, and in due time she brought forth a son—a horrible monster, which her enraged husband chopped up into small pieces; and these immediately turned into leeches, with which the jungles are to this day unpleasantly infested.

" Mino Pajabun."—These are the ghosts of those who meet with an accidental death. Their name seems to be derived from a Dayak word meaning " To long for," because it is said they pass their time in useless wailings over their hard fate.

"Mino Kok Anak."—The spirits of women who
have died in childbed. They delight to mount high
trees, and to startle belated Dayaks by horrible noises
as they are hurrying home in the twilight. There is
also a ghost or spirit—whether "Mino" or "Umot,"
I have not ascertained—known to the "Peninjaus,"
which lives amid the holes of the rocks on the hills;
it is called "Sedying," and on a rainy day may
be heard in its cave shivering and bemoaning as if
suffering from the ague.

I have already mentioned that the custom "pamali,"
called by the Land Dayak "porikh," obtains among all
the tribes, and is constantly practised. To propitiate
the superior spirits, they shut themselves up in their
houses a certain number of days, and by that, among
other means, hope to avert sickness, to cure a favourite
child, or to restore their own health. They also have
recourse to it when the cry of the gazelle is heard
behind them, or when their omen birds utter unfavourable warnings. They likewise place themselves under
this interdict at the planting of rice, at harvest home,
and upon many other occasions. During this time,
they appear to remain in their houses, in order to eat,
drink, and sleep; but their eating must be moderate,
and often consists of nothing but rice and salt.
These interdicts are of very different durations and
importance. Sometimes, as at the harvest home, the
whole tribe is compelled to observe it, and then no
one must leave the village; at other times it only
extends to a family, or to a single individual. It is
also considered important that no stranger should
break the taboo by entering the village, the house, or
the apartment, placed under interdict. If any one

should do so intentionally, he would subject himself to a fine.

The taboo lasts from one to sixteen days, according to the importance attached to the event. The animals used in the sacrifice are fowls and pigs, and I hear also that even dogs in certain tribes are occasionally employed. The fowls and pigs are eaten, but the dogs not, the blood only being required in their incantations. When a fowl is killed a taboo may last one, two, or four days; when a pig—and then it is usually a very important occasion—the ceremony may last four, eight, or sixteen days.

People under interdict may not bathe, touch fire, or employ themselves about their ordinary occupations. In conversation you continually hear even the Malays say, "It is pamali," or interdicted by their superstitions, but if contrary to their religion they say "haram."

I will notice a few things which the Dayaks consider must not be done by them; for instance, most are not allowed to eat the flesh of horned animals, as cattle and goats, and many tribes extend the prohibition to the wild deer. In their refusal to touch the flesh of cows and bulls they add another illustration of the theory that their religion is indirectly derived from the Hindu, or if not actually derived, greatly influenced by their intercourse with its disciples. They say that some of their ancestors, in the transmigration of souls, were formerly metamorphosed into these animals; and they slily, or innocently add, that the reason why the Mahomedan Malays will not touch pork is, that they are afraid to eat their forefathers, who were changed into the unclean animal.

It has often struck me that the origin of many of
their superstitions arose from the greediness of the
elders; as in some of the tribes they, together with
the women and children, but not the sturdy young
men, may eat eggs.    In other instances the very old
men and the women may eat of the flesh of the deer,
while the young men and warriors of the tribe are
debarred from venison for fear it should render them
as timid as the graceful hind.

The taboo which prevents certain families from
consuming the flesh of snakes and other kinds of
reptiles, most probably arose from some incident in
the life of one of their ancestors, in which the
rejected beast played a prominent part.    It is reli-
giously forbidden to all those intending to engage
in a pig-hunt from meddling with oil before the
chase, for fear the game should thus slip through
their fingers.    I may add, if a certain kind of
bird flies through a house the inhabitants desert
it; as they likewise do if a drop of blood be seen
sprinkled on the floor, unless they can prove whence
it came.

In addition to the incantations (Beruri) which
accompany every feast (Gawei), there are special
ones on occasions of sickness both in men and rice.
The Dayak idea of life is this, that in mankind,
animals, and rice there is a living principle called
"semungat" or "semungi;" that sickness is caused
by the temporary absence, and death by the total
departure of this principle from the body.    Hence
the object of their ceremonies is to bring back the
departed souls; and some of the feasts are held to
secure the soul of the rice, which, if not so detained,

the produce of their farms would speedily rot and decay. At sowing time, a little of the principle of life of the rice, which at every harvest is secured by their priests, is planted with their other seeds, and is thus propagated and communicated.

Sickness among mankind is occasionally caused by spirits inflicting on people invisible wounds with invisible spears; indeed, they themselves sometimes enter men's bodies and drive out the soul. As a rule, to be ill is to have been smitten by a spirit,* for it is these implacable foes of mankind who under all circumstances entice forth and endeavour to carry away the souls of men. If any one in his wanderings through the jungle is wounded or killed by the spring traps † set near the farms to destroy pigs who may attempt to break through into the fields, it is because the spirit of the trap has caused darkness to pass over his eyes, so that he should not see the regular warning mark, consisting of two bamboos crossed, which tells of the neighbourhood of danger.

To return, however, to the incantations by which the inimical spirits are propitiated or foiled in their machinations. They are three: "Nyibaiyan," or the ceremony for restoring health. At this only one fowl is killed; two priestesses are the actors, and they spend their time chanting monotonously; the taboo lasts two nights. The invalid and the person who prepares the magic ointment (a near relative of the patient) are the only persons subject to its restraints.

* " Kena antu."
† " Peti," made by bending back a sharp bamboo spear. An animal touching a stick, placed across an opening, lets fly the spring, and the spear is driven through the unheeding stranger, whether human or animal.

"Berobat Pinya" is also for sickness. At this one priest and four or five priestesses attend, the interdict lasts four days, and one pig and one fowl are killed. Outside the door of the family apartment in which the incantation is held are gathered together, in a winnowing basket, an offering of fowls, yams, and pork, fowl and pig's blood in a cup, boiled rice and sirih-leaf, and areca-nut: these are for the various spirits. On the first day of the incantation two priestesses pretend to fight with each other with drawn swords, which they wave and slash about in so furious a manner, as at once to put to flight the trembling ghost. After this display of valour, chanting begins, accompanied by the music of a small gong and a drum, the latter beaten by the priest; this continues for a day and night. Towards midnight he proceeds to get the soul of the patient. Carefully wrapping up a small cup in a white cloth, he places it amidst the offerings before mentioned, then, with a torch in one hand and a circlet of beads and tinkling hawk bells in the other, he stalks about shaking his charms. After a little time he orders one of the admiring spectators to look in the cup previously wrapped up in white cloth, and sure enough there the soul always is, in the form of a bunch of hair to vulgar eyes, but to the initiated in shape and appearance like a miniature human being. This is supposed to be thrust into a hole in the top of the patient's head, invisible to all but the learned man. He has thus recovered the man's soul, or, as it may be called, the principle of life that was departing from him.

The Land Dayaks of Sarawak say they have only

one soul; the "Sibuyaus" talk of several; but their souls, as shown by the priest to the friends of the patient, bear a suspicious resemblance to the seeds of the cotton plant.

"Berobat Sisab" has a similar aim to the above. At this, one priest, but no priestess, is present. The priest first makes a bamboo altar * in the commom verandah outside the door of the patient's room, round which are placed offerings, and a pig and a fowl are killed. The interdict lasts for eight days. For two there is beating of gongs and drums, and dancing by the man who makes the charm, usually some relation of the sick person. On the first night the soul is recovered, and the patient washed in the milk of the cocoa-nut. I have often been present when these ceremonies were going on; it is astonishing that any patient should recover, stunned as he must be by the beating and clanging of these ear-splitting instruments close to him. It has effectually prevented my closing my eyes; and the melancholy wail of the priestesses is sufficient, one would imagine, to drive hope itself from the bedside of the sufferer.

The feasts and incantations connected with farming operations are as follows:—First, in the midst of cutting down the jungle; second, when it is set on fire. These are small affairs, the interdict lasting but one day, and only a fowl being killed. They are called " Mekapau," only one gong and one drum are beaten; and also " nyirangan," because a bamboo altar is built by the road-side, and upon it a small offering of rice and blood is placed for the spirit. The second feast

* " Sikurung," a bamboo altar,

is to drive away all evil influences from the earth, when ready for the seed.

The third feast* is the blessing of the seed before planting. It is brought out, and the priestesses wave over it their flat brush-like wands, which consist of the undeveloped fruit of the areca palm, stripped of its sheath, and is in itself one of the prettiest objects in the world, and in its natural bursting spreads around the parent stem a delicious perfume that scents a whole grove. They thus expel all malign influences; the interdict lasts two nights, one fowl is killed, and there is music and dancing.

During the growth of the rice, if the rats be making havoc among it, or the pale green leaf appear blighted, there are similar ceremonies to awe the vermin, and charm back the colour to the plant. But the harvest feasts are the great days; there are three:—The feast of first fruits,† when the priestesses, accompanied by a gong and a drum, go in procession to the farms and gather several bunches of the ripe padi. These are brought back to the village, washed in cocoa-nut water, and laid round a bamboo altar, which at the harvest feasts is erected in the common room of the largest house, and decorated with white cloth and red streamers, so as to present a very gay appearance, and is hung around with the sweet-smelling blossom of the areca palm. This feast and interdict last two days; only fowls are killed; dancing and gong-beating go on night and day; and when it is over, the Dayaks may set themselves to repair their bamboo platforms outside the houses, on which the rice is trodden out from the

* " Mamuk Benih."          † " Nyipa 'an."

car, and then dried in the sun. They may now also gather in their crops.

The second feast* is a more important affair : it is held about the middle of harvest, and lasts four days; fowls and a pig are killed, and dancing and beating of gongs go on almost continually. The first part of this feast is celebrated, not in the village, but in a shed at some distance from it, frequently built by the roadside, and sometimes on the very summits of the hills on which the villages are situated. Although strangers are forbidden to approach the place during these ceremonies, yet at Sirambau I have often been invited to be present during this and the other feasts. They choose a lovely spot for the erection of their shed, which is tastefully decorated with green boughs and climbing plants, and situated under the loftiest fruit-trees I have ever seen; and here as in other villages, around the spot where the shed was erected were planted yellow bamboos, and their golden tapering stems and graceful feathery tufts are a charming and pleasing contrast to the rude leaf walls and roof of the neighbouring building.

At this, and at the third and last harvest feast, the soul of the rice is secured. The way of obtaining it varies in different tribes. In the Quop district it is done by the chief-priest alone; first, in the long and broad verandah where the altar is erected, and afterwards in each separate family apartment. Sometimes it is performed by day, sometimes by night; and the process is this: the priest, fixing his eyes on some object visible only to him, takes in one hand his bundle of charms and in the other a second composed of pigs'

* " Man Sawa," or " Nyitungid."

and bears' and dogs' tusks and teeth, and large opaque-coloured beads; a little gold dust is also necessary in this ceremony, during which he calls aloud for white cloth; when it is brought and spread before him, he waves his charms towards the invisible object in the air, and then shakes it over the white cloth, into which there fall a few grains of rice, which Tapa, in reward for their offerings and invocations, sends down to them. This is the soul, and it is immediately wrapped up with great care and laid among the offerings around the altar.

The gold dust and white cloth are generally furnished at their earnest request by the government, as the Dayaks think it exercises a beneficial effect to receive it from white men. It used to be supplied by the Malay rulers.

In some tribes it is a far more exciting spectacle, especially when done at night. A large shed is erected outside the village, and lighted by huge fires inside and out, which cast a ruddy glow over the dense mass of palms surrounding the houses; while gongs and drums are crashing around a high and spacious altar near the shed, where a number of gaily-dressed men and women are dancing with slow and stately step and solemn countenances, some bearing in their hands lighted tapers, some brass salvers on which are offerings of rice, and others closely covered baskets, the contents of which are hidden from all but the initiated. The corner-posts of the altar are lofty bamboos, whose leafy summits are yet green and rustle in the wind; and from one of these hangs down a long, narrow streamer of white cloth. Suddenly elders and priests rush to it, seize hold of its extremity, and amid

the crashing sound of drums and gongs and the yells
of spectators, begin dancing and swaying themselves
backwards and forwards, and to and fro.  An elder
springs on the altar, and begins violently to shake the
tall bamboos, uttering as he does so shouts of triumph,
which are responded to by the swaying bodies of those
below; and amid all this excitement, small stones,
bunches of hair and grains of rice, fall at the feet of
the dancers, and are carefully picked up by watchful
attendants.  The rice is the soul sought for, and the
ceremony ends by several of the oldest priestesses falling, or pretending to fall, to the earth senseless; where,
till they recover, their heads are supported and their
faces fanned by their younger sisters.

The third feast* is held after the end of the harvest,
when the year's crop has been carefully stowed away.
A pig and fowls are killed, for four days gong-beating
and dancing are kept up, and the taboo lasts for eight
days.  Sometimes no stranger may approach the village for sixteen days.  At this period also the soul of
the rice is likewise secured, which is to ensure the
non-rotting of the crop.  At this feast there is a
general physicking of the children.  They are washed
with cocoa-nut water, and then laid down in a row in
the common room where the feast is held, and scarcely
suffered to move about for four days.  At this time
also the elder priestesses physic their younger sisters,
and children of a tender age are entered among the
number of this learned and accomplished body; partly
because admission into it is supposed to secure them
against violent sickness.  For each one who is now to
be initiated, a young cocoa-nut is obtained, and their

* Nyishupen, or "nyipidang menyupong."

elder sisters cause those on whom they are to exercise
their power to lie down in a line along the room, and
to cover themselves with long sleeping sheets. The
cocoa-nuts belonging to the patients are then taken
into the hands of the priestesses, and with them they
run violently about the long room, tossing them up
and down and to and fro. In some villages they
are rolled in soot and oil, and then kicked furiously
about from one priestess to the other. During this
part of the process the room presents a curious scene.
Here some six or seven gaily-dressed women are rushing frantically up and down, tossing in their hands
the heavy young cocoa-nuts; there a dozen old women
are moving to and fro on a rude swing suspended from
the rafters, and howling dolefully round the altar. A
number of others are shrieking and dancing; while
from the farther end of the room beyond the line of
prostrate patients resounds a clatter of gongs and
drums, beaten as vigorously as twenty pair of young
hands can apply themselves to the work.

One by one the old priestesses cease their wild
running backwards and forwards, and each in succession presents herself before an elder of the tribe,
who stands, chopper in hand, over a mortar, into
the hollow of which each in turn places her cocoa-
nut. With one blow the old man splits the nut,
and out gushes the water. If it simply fall into the
mortar, the prospect is good, but if it shoot up towards
the roof, then evil is the lot of the patient whose
cocoa-nut it may be, for there is sickness before her
in the coming year. When a cocoa-nut is split, she to
whom it belongs is raised from her recumbent position
and the water is poured over her; she is then laid

down again and carefully wrapped up in her sheet. When all have been so treated a lighted taper is waved over the prostrate, motionless patients, and a form of words chanted, and then the ceremony is concluded by the head priestess going round and blowing into the face of each of the patients; after which they are allowed to chatter and amuse themselves, but are confined to the long room, in company with the elders and such of the children as had been previously subjected to the ceremony, until the close of the interdict.

*Head Feasts.*—These are held only after some new heads have been added to the ghastly trophies of the bachelor's house; consequently among the Dayaks of Sarawak there has not been a feast for many years, except those celebrated over the heads of the rebellious Chinese killed in 1857, who, confident in their firearms, attempted to capture the villages on the mountain, their chief object being to burn down Sir James Brooke's cottage. They offered to cease their attack if the Dayaks would put fire to it themselves; but they refused, and defended their steep paths by the aid of barricades. The Chinese were foiled and driven back to the plain, and were pursued by the mountaineers, who inflicted heavy loss upon them. Chinese heads, however, are esteemed of little value in comparison with those of their ancient enemies. The head feast is the great day of the young bachelors. The head-house and village are decorated with green boughs, and the heads to be feasted are brought out from their very airy position, being hung from one of the beams, where they rattle together at every breath of wind, and are put into a rice measure in some very prominent place. The whole population are robed in their best, the young men in red jackets, yellow and red head-dresses, and gay waist-cloths or trousers.

For four days and four nights an almost incessant beating of gongs and drums is kept up, and dances are performed by the young men only.   The priestesses are decked out in their usual style, but upon this occasion their occupation is gone.   Strong drinks, made from rice or the fruit of the tampui-tree, and also from the gomuti palm, flow freely; shrieks, yells, laughter, and shoutings, are heard in all directions, and the whole village seems given up to riot and dissipation.   The interdict lasts eight days, two pigs are killed, and as many fowls as they can afford. An offering of food is made to the heads, and their spirits, being thus appeased, cease to entertain malice against, or to seek to inflict injury upon, those who have got possession of the skull which formerly adorned the now forsaken body.

A curious custom prevails among the young men at this feast.   They cut a cocoa-nut shell into the form of a cup, and adorn it with red and black dye. Into one side of it they fasten a rudely carved likeness of a bird's head, and into the other the representation of its tail.   The cup is filled with arrack, and the possessor performs a short wild dance with it in his hands, and then with a yell leaps before some chosen companion, and presents it to him to drink.   Thus the "loving cup" is passed around among them, and it need not be said that the result is in many cases partial, though seldom excessive, intoxication.

Before leaving the subject of feasts and incantations, I will mention some of their occasional ceremonies.

They perform some on account of a bad dream, any threatening evil, or because of actual sickness; sometimes also by way of precaution, but this is only after harvest when they have nothing better to do. The theory of their ceremonies appears to be this: that the offering of food made to the spirits assuages their malice and secures their departure, these spirits being considered the proximate cause of nearly all the evils to which they are subjected.

The minor ceremonies are called "nyirañgan," because a bamboo altar* is erected by the roadside, and a fowl killed near it, part of which, with rice and betel-nut, is offered upon it: the taboo is only for a day. If any one meets with an accidental death in the jungle, a ceremony is gone through near the spot; at this a pig is occasionally killed, but in all such cases the taboo lasts only one day. If during farming time a tree fall across the path, a ceremony is held, and all whose farms are in that direction are tabooed. If during harvest the basket into which the ears of rice are cut be upset, a fowl is killed, and the family to whom the basket belongs is tabooed. Again, when the Government rice-tax is paid, there is a ceremony. On this occasion a shed is erected just at the entrance to the village, and in addition to the offerings of food, it is hung with a number of split cocoa-nut shells, which the spirits are supposed to appropriate as gongs.

*Images.*—Although the Dayaks adhere with great strictness to the command not to make any graven image for purposes of worship, yet in some tribes they are in the habit of forming a rude figure of a naked

---

* Sirangan, also a bamboo altar.

man and woman, which they place opposite to each
other on the path to the farms. On their heads are
head-dresses of bark, by their sides is the betel-nut
basket, and in their hands a short wooden spear
These figures are said to be inhabited each by a
spirit who prevents inimical influences from passing
on to the farms, and likewise from the farms to the
village, and evil betide the profane wretch who lifts
his hand against them,—violent fever and sickness
are sure to follow.

Among the tribes of Western Sarawak the priestesses
have made for them rude figures of birds. At the
great harvest feasts they are hung up in bunches of
ten or twenty in the long common room, carefully
veiled with coloured handkerchiefs. They are supposed
to become inhabited by spirits, and it is forbidden for
any one to touch them, except the priestesses.

*Dreams.*—The Dayaks regard dreams as actual
occurrences. They think that in sleep the soul sometimes remains in the body, and sometimes leaves it
and travels far away, and that both when in and out
of the body it sees, and hears, and talks, and altogether
has a prescience given it, which, when the body is in
its natural state, it does not enjoy. Fainting fits, or
a state of coma, are thought to be caused by the
departure or absence of the soul on some distant
expedition of its own. When any one dreams of a·
distant land, as we exiles often do, the Dayaks think
that our souls have annihilated space, and paid a
flying visit to Europe during the night. Elders and
priestesses often assert that in their dreams they have
visited the mansion of Tapa, and seen the Creator
dwelling in a house like that of a Malay, the interior

of which was adorned with guns and gongs and jars innumerable, Himself being clothed liked a Dayak.

A dream of sickness to any member of a family always ensures a ceremony; and no one presumes to enter the priesthood, or to learn the art of a black-smith, without being, or pretending to be, warned in a dream that he should undertake to learn it.    I have known a man with only two children give his younger child to another who was no relation, because he dreamed that he must give it to him or the child would die.

In dreams also "Tapa" and the spirits bestow gifts on men in the shape of magic stones, which, being washed in cocoa-nut milk, the water forms one of the ingredients in the mass of blood and turmeric which is considered sacred, and is used to anoint the people at the harvest feasts.    They are ordinary black pebbles, and there is nothing in their appearance to give an idea of their magic power and value.    The ones in the Quop village were procured in a dream by the late "Orang Kaya Bai Malam," in order to replace those lost in the civil wars which desolated the country before Sir James Brooke's arrival.    He dreamt that a spirit came unto him and gave him a number of these sacred stones; and lo! when he awoke, they were in his hand.    In some villages they are kept in a rude kind of wooden bowl covered and fastened down, then fixed to the top of an iron-wood post in the middle of the outside platform.    In others they are deposited in a small house built in the jungle, at some distance from the village, and all around it is sacred.    I will relate an anecdote Mr. Chalmers told me :—

A Quop woman who had turned Malay was staying at her village when the clergyman was there; he had a number of coloured-glass marbles, and one of these this woman got hold of, and no doubt thought it very strange and wonderful. Next morning, when she awoke, she called loudly for white cloth, declaring at the same time that the late Orang Kaya had appeared to her in the night and given her a sacred stone, at the same time producing the marble, and expected, no doubt, a good price for it from the Dayaks. But they are wiser now than of yore, and would have nothing to do with it; and the young fellows, hearing how she had procured the marble, teased her on the subject until her departure.

*Ordeals.*—One of the ordeals practised among them is the following: When a quarrel takes place which the elders find it impossible to settle, from conflicting evidence, the disputants are taken to a deep pool in a neighbouring stream, and both standing up to their necks in the water, at given signals plunge their heads below the surface: the first that rises to take breath, loses the case. Among the Land Dayaks, these ceremonies are not often practised. Another is by listening to the night-birds: if their cry be such as to be considered a favourable omen, the accused is declared not guilty; if a bad omen, he is pronounced guilty and must pay the fine demanded of him. The most common ordeal, however, is this: two wax tapers of equal size and length are prepared, they are lighted, and the owner of the one that is first extinguished, or burnt out, loses his case.

*Omens.*—If a man be going on a war expedition, and has a slip during his first day's journey, he must return to his village, especially if by the accident blood be drawn, for then, should he proceed, he has no prospect but wounds or death. If the accident occur during a long expedition, he must return to his last night's resting-place. In some tribes, if a deer cry near a party who are setting out on a journey they will return. When going at night to the jungle, if the scream of a hawk, or an owl, or of a small kind of frog be heard, it is a sign that sickness will follow if the design be pursued; and, again, if the screech of the two former be heard in front of a party on the war-path, it is an evil sign, and they must return. Omens derived from the cry of birds are always sought previously to setting out on a journey, and before fixing on a spot to build new houses, or to prepare their farms.

The birds which give the omen for a journey are three, the "Kushah," "Kariak," and "Katupung." The traveller goes to a spot near the village where the feast sheds are usually erected, and sometimes a stage of bambu is also made ready for the purpose. There he waits till he hears the ofttimes long-awaited cries. When the "Kushah" or "Katupung" are heard on the right or the left only, or in front, no success will attend the journey; but if their cry be heard on the left and then answered on the right, the traveller may start in peace. The "Kariak's" omen, however, is more important still. If heard on the right hand, the omen is good; if on the left, some slight inconvenience may follow; if behind, sickness or death awaits him in the place to which he is bound. How common is the saying used, "I had a bad bird," to excuse every breach of engagement!

In house-building and farm-making all the birds of night are consulted. During the day, a place in the forest, which appears suitable, is fixed upon, and a small shed erected near. Some boiled rice, stained yellow with turmeric, and other offerings, are prepared, and at night a party takes them to the hut already built. This they enter, and an elder having invoked the spiritual powers, and cast the yellow rice in all directions, they await the omen. If a bird cry and twitter in front, and if it then fly past the hut towards the village, it is a good omen; but if the birds fly and alight near the hut, and there cry and twitter, evil and sickness await those who build or farm there, for many spirits have made that their dwelling-place.

The reason assigned for using these bird omens is that they are half Dayaks. Long ago, a spirit married a Dayak woman, and the result of the intercourse was the production of birds. These were tenderly cared for and cherished by the Dayaks, and, in return, from that time to this, they have ever warned their former protectors of impending evil, if duly consulted according to the customs which have descended to the tribes from their ancestors.

Having thus given a brief account of Dayak ceremonies, and feastings, and omens, I may conclude with a remark, that, of all the feasts and ceremonies, the most beneficial in its influence is the " Head Feast." The object of them all is to make their rice grow well, to cause the forest to abound with wild animals, to enable their dogs and snares to be successful in securing game, to have the streams swarm with fish, to give health and activity to the people themselves, and to ensure fertility to their women. All these blessings, the possessing and feasting of a fresh head are supposed to be the most efficient means of securing. The very ground itself is believed to be benefited and rendered fertile, more fertile even than when the water in which fragments of gold, presented by the Rajah, have been washed, has been sprinkled over it; this latter charm, especially when mixed with the water which has been poured over the sacred stones, being, next to the possession of a newly acquired head, the greatest and the most powerful which the wisdom of the "men of old time" has devised for the benefit of their descendants. It may, therefore, be understood what importance Orang Kaya Mita attached to his request that permission should be given to him to seek another victim, and what influence he would have gained with the tribe had they secured these blessings by his means.

*Language.*—The vocabularies printed in the Appendix will, as Mr. Chalmers observes, show that there is a great affinity betwixt the Dayaks of Sarawak, Sadong, and some Sambas tribes. This connection is not so visible in the dialects of others, as, for instance, the Silakau tribe, who formerly lived on a stream of the same name between the Sambas and Pontianak. In the dialects of the Sea Dayaks, there are perhaps a few words radically the same as their correspondents in Land Dayak, but only a few which are not derived in common from Malay. In the dialect of the Dayaks of Banjermasin, I have also noticed words the same in form and meaning, but they are not very frequent.

My own experience has led me to the conviction that it is very difficult to draw any safe conclusion from the vocabularies generally collected, because the best are usually made through the medium of the Malay, and the worst by merely showing articles and guessing that the response is the name of the thing shown. I made a list of Bisaya words on the Limbang, another among the Idaán at the foot of "Kina Balu." I was certain of a great affinity between the languages, as men from one tribe could freely converse with those of the other, though their dwellings were a hundred and fifty miles apart; but on comparing the written vocabularies, I found a surprising difference. Just before I left Borneo, I spoke to a Bisaya on the subject: he said, "Repeat me a few words of the Idaán that are different." I did so. He answered, "I understand those words, but we don't often use them," and he instantly gave their meaning in Malay, to show that he did understand them.

My sudden and unexpected return to this country prevented my pursuing the investigation. I mention this circumstance to show that differences are often more apparent than real. Mr. Chalmers's vocabularies are trustworthy, as he can speak the Land Dayak freely.

*Deer.*—The Dayaks of the Quop district do not refuse to eat deer. The custom of doing so, however, obtains in Western Sarawak, but chiefly in the Singgi tribe, and then only among the young men.

As will be found mentioned in my account of Samarahan, they do so because deer's flesh produces in those who eat it faint hearts; and as I have elsewhere observed, the interdict on certain

13—2

kinds of food to the young people is merely selfish-
ness on the part of the elders to secure to themselves a greater share of articles that are not
plentiful.    The Silakau and Lara Dayaks who
have emigrated from Sambas into Lundu, do not
eat the flesh of the deer, from an opinion that they
descended from Dayak ancestors, but Mr. Chalmers,
in his experience of the Sarawak Land Dayak, never
heard of any prejudice existing against killing or
even eating any animals except the faint-heartedness
supposed to be produced by venison; nor did he
notice that the serpent had any sacred character.
Many people eat it; some, however, refuse, considering it foul-feeding.

The Sibuyau Dayaks of Lundu, from their greater
intercourse with Malays and Chinese, and from
the advantages they have derived from local self-
government, and freely trading with the surrounding districts, have lost most of their old superstitions, as I have noticed in my account of the Sea
Dayaks : nor must I omit to mention that their intercourse with a succession of able European officers,
and the constant presence among them of Mr. Gomez,
a missionary of singular tact, have had a remarkable
effect upon their characters, and rendered them a very
superior tribe.  They kill the cobra and other reptiles,
but the Land Dayaks of Lundu, as well as the Silakaus,
consider it wrong to destroy it.   They say that in
former times one of their female ancestors was pregnant
for seven years, and ultimately brought forth twins,
one a human being and the other a cobra de capella.
They lived together for some time, the snake always
keeping his head well out of the way for fear of

hurting his brother with his venomous teeth, but allowing him to amuse himself with his tail. When they grew up the cobra left the house to dwell in the forest, but before leaving he told his mother to warn her children, that should, unfortunately, one of them be bitten by the hooded snake, not to run away, but remain a whole day at the spot where the injury was received, and the venom would have no poisonous effect. Not long after he was met in the forest by his brother, who, under the effect of surprise, drew his sword and smote off his tail, which accounts for that blunted appearance observable in all his brethren. The superstition of the snake curing the bite is believed; the wounded person being still allowed to remain twenty-four hours in the jungle. During my fourteen years' residence in Borneo, I have only heard of two persons dying from the effects of snake bites.

*Names :—*

| Names of Men. | | Names of Women. | |
|---|---|---|---|
| Mobon. | Si Ngaruk. | Si Kudon. | Tika. |
| Doden. | Si Gindai. | Si Risi. | Si Nyat. |
| Magè. | Si Raru. | Si Tuk. | Monog. |
| Nyait. | Si Rugi. | Si Ngada. | Sakot. |
| Rinyang. | Si Kangon. | Si Risok. | Si Rawang. |
| Si Ngais. | Sonyam. | Si Kûdi. | Sopop. |
| Marik. | Si Mara. | Si Bior. | Si Nuag. |
| Si Neg. | Sanyung. | Sanut. | |

The above are personal names; when young the parents often change them, especially if the child be sickly, there being an idea that they will deceive the inimical spirits by following this practice. As the children grow up they are dignified further by a change of name: thus, " Si Mara" becomes " Ma Kari," *i.e.* the father of Kari, being the name of a

child of his father's or mother's younger brother or
sister. If this younger brother or sister have no
children, whose names are to spare, "Si Mara" must
wait until he gets a child of his own, and then he
takes his child's name with "Ma" prefixed.   The
same custom holds good with women ;—" Si Risi," a
personal name, being changed into " Nu Sangut," *i.e.*
the mother of Sangut.   So, again, if the younger
brother or sister (and this is a most comprehensive
relationship) of a person's father or mother have
grandchildren, then the " Ma" and " Nu" are abandoned for "Bai" and " Muk," the grandfather or
grandmother: thus, " Ma Kari" might become " Bai
Kinyum," and " Nu Sangut " be metamorphosed into
" Muk Weit."

*Marriage.*—The prohibited degrees seem to be the
same as adopted among ourselves: marriage with a
deceased wife's sister, it is said, is prohibited, as well
as that between first cousins; and second cousins are
only permitted aftèr the exchange of a fine of a jar,
the woman paying it to the relation of her lover, and
he to her relations.   Among the Sibuyaus, however,
I have known an uncle marry his niece.

*Heights.*—MALE ADULTS: 4 ft. 10 in. (short);
5 ft. 1 in.;  5 ft. 3 in.;  5 ft. 4 in.;  5 ft. 5½ in.;
5 ft. 7 in.  FEMALE ADULTS: 4 ft. 6 in. (short);
4 ft. 8 in.;  4ft. 9 in.;  4ft. 10½ in.;  5 ft.;  5 ft. 2 in.
(tall).

They have little or no knowledge of medicine,
though they sometimes collect pepper and onions with
which to make physic, a kind of stomachic.   The
grated flesh of old cocoa-nut is occasionally applied to
wounds and bruises, but there is no general knowledge

even of the powers of rice poultices. Blue-stone they
eagerly inquire for, and they have learnt its properties.
Their most common physic is to get a friend to chew
up a mass of sirih-leaves, areca and lime, until it is
reduced to a thick red juice, which is then squirted
from the mouth over the part affected. If this physic
be thus administered by a regular doctor it will be
more efficacious, but any one may do it. This mess is
used indiscriminately for all diseases: stomach ache,
sore eyes, ulcers, wounds, boils, rheumatism, as well as
fever. When it is squirted on to the forehead it is
supposed to be efficacious in relieving the accompanying headache. This is very much practised by the
Malays, who thus render their sick, objects of disgust.
I have often thought it necessary to insist upon the
patient being washed carefully before administering
European medicines.

I have already spoken of a mixture of blood
and turmeric being plastered on the head at the
regular ceremonies. On these occasions also the
cheek and forehead of those who take part in
them are marked with blood. I have also spoken
of bathing the patient in cocoa-nut water, and these
comprise all the medical applications of which I am
aware.

In most tribes, there are five or six priests, and in
some districts half the female population are included
under the denomination of priestesses.

In Western Sarawak they are not so numerous.
The power of these women consists chiefly in their
chanting, which is supposed to be most effectual in
driving away spirits. Strange to say, some of the
sentences they chant are not in their own language,

but in Malay. These women are not necessarily impostors; they but practise the ways and recite the
songs which they received from their predecessors, and
the dignity and importance of the office enable them
to enjoy some intervals of pleasurable excitement
during their laborious lives. Their dress is very gay;
over their heads they throw a red cloth, on the top of
which they place a cylindrical cap, worked in red,
white, and black beads, and their short petticoats are
fringed with hundreds of small, tinkling hawk-bells.
Around their neck is hung a heavy bead necklace,
consisting of five or six rows of black, red, and white
opaque beads strongly bound together. In addition,
they hang over their shoulders, belt-fashion, a string
of teeth, large hawk-bells and opaque beads. There
are several stories concerning the origin of the
priestesses. That which is current in the Quop district
is as follows:—

Long ago, when the Dayaks were quite ignorant of
religion, a certain man and his wife had two daughters.
Both of them fell ill; the parents knew of no remedy,
so they took a pig's trough, placed the children within
it, and sent them floating down the river towards the
sea. The great "Iang," from his lofty seat, saw
them in this pitiful situation and crying helplessly, he
had compassion on them and took them to his dwelling
on the mountain of Santubong.

There he cured them himself, and then taught them
the mysteries of religion, the formulas they were to
chant, the taboo they were to observe, and the rites
and ceremonies they were to perform. This done, he
transported them back to their own village, where
they were welcomed and reverenced, and it was they

who founded the sacred order of priestesses, as it now exists throughout these countries.

The priests must in many respects be regarded as impostors, though, of course, even with their deceitful practices is mixed much superstitious credulity. They pretend to meet and to converse with spirits, to receive warnings, and sometimes presents from them, to have the power of seeing and capturing the departed soul of a sick man, and to be able to find and secure for the Dayaks that vital principle of the rice which " Tapa " sends down from above at their two chief harvest feasts. To increase their authority, they do not hesitate to declare that they have predicted every event. No accident happens to man or goods of which they do not say that they had previous warning; and a sick man scarcely ever calls upon them for their aid when they do not tell him that for some time previously they had known he was going to have an attack. One of their commonest practices is to pretend to extract from a sick man's body, stones and splinters, which they declare are spirits; they wave charms over the part affected, and jingle them upon it for a moment, then bring them to the floor with a crash, and out of them falls a stone, or piece of wood, or small roll of rag. At least half a dozen of these evil spirits are occasionally brought out of a man's stomach, one after the other, and great is the influence, and not small the profit, of a successful priest. For getting back a man's soul he receives six gallons of uncleaned rice; for extracting a spirit from a man's body, the same fee, and for getting the soul of the rice at harvest feasts he receives three cups from every family in whose apartment he obtains it. The

value of six gallons of uncleaned rice is not very great,
but it is the sixtieth part of the amount obtained by
an able-bodied man for his annual farm labour.

The priestesses have their fees, but they do not
make so much from the superstition of their countrymen as the male professors.

*Manufactures.*—Among these are baskets of fine
rattan and coarse rattan mats.  In each village there
is generally a blacksmith who can make, as well
as repair, their spears and choppers; each man,
moreover, is his own carpenter, gardener, and farmer;
in fact, does almost everything necessary for the wel-
fare of his family.

*Agriculture.*—They plant rice, Indian corn, cucum-
bers, bananas, sweet potatoes, sugar-cane, kiladis,
yams, beans in their farms and gardens, and all kinds
of fruit-trees around their villages and on neighbouring hills.

I will add a story which was kindly communicated
to me by Mr. Chalmers as to the introduction of rice
among the Dayak tribes.

Once upon a time, when mankind had nothing to
eat but a species of edible fungus that grows upon
rotting trees, and there were no cereals to gladden and
strengthen man's heart, a party of Dayaks, among
whom was a man named Si Jura, whose descendants
live to this day in the Dayak village of Simpok, went
forth to sea.  They sailed on for some time, until they
came to a place at which they heard the distant roar
of a large whirlpool, and, to their amazement, saw
before them a huge fruit-tree rooted in the sky, and
thence hanging down with its branches touching the
waves.  At the request of his companions, Si Jura

climbed among its boughs to collect the fruit which
was in abundance, and when he was there he found
himself tempted to ascend the trunk and find out
how the tree grew in that position.  He did so, and
at length got so high that his companions in the boat
lost sight of him, and after waiting a certain time
coolly sailed away loaded with fruit.  Looking down
from his lofty position, Si Jura saw his friends
making off, so he had no other resource but to go on
climbing in hopes of reaching some resting-place.  He
therefore persevered climbing higher and higher, till
he reached the roots of the tree, and there he found
himself in a new country—that of the Pleiades.
There he met a being in form of a man, named Si
Kira, who took him to his house and hospitably
entertained him.  The food offered was a mess of soft
white grains—boiled rice.  "Eat," said Si Kira.
"What! those little maggots?" replied Si Jura.
"They are not maggots, but boiled rice;" and Si
Kira forthwith explained the process of planting,
weeding, and reaping, and of pounding and boiling
rice.  Before eating, Si Kira's wife went to get
some water, and during her absence Si Jura looked
into a large jar near where he was sitting, and there,
as in a telescope, he saw his father's house, and
his parents and brothers and sisters all assembled
and talking.  His spirits were much depressed at the
remembrance of a home he perhaps might not see
again, and instead of eating he began to weep.  Si
Kira, who perceived at once what was the matter,
bade him cheer up and eat away, for he would arrange
everything for him satisfactorily.  So Si Jura made
a hearty meal, and after eating, Si Kira gave him

seed of three kinds of rice, instructed him how to cut down the forest, burn, plant, weed, and reap, take omens from birds, and celebrate harvest feasts; and then, by a long rope, let him down to earth again near his father's house.

Si Jura it was who taught the Dayaks to farm, and to this day they follow the instruction he received from Si Kira—nay, more, the Pleiades themselves tell them when to farm; and according to their position in the heavens morning and evening, do they cut down the forest, burn, plant, and reap.   The Malays are obliged to follow their example, or their lunar year would soon render their farming operations unprofitable.

# CHAPTER VII.

STARTED in the evening from our house at Kuching amid a storm of rain, thunder, and lightning. Our well-covered boat protected us, though the rain fell in torrents and dashed impetuously against the matted roof, creating so great a noise as to prevent our voices being heard even when shouting. At last the gusts of wind sweeping up the reaches became so violent, that we were forced to draw under the shelter of the banks, and await the abating of the storm. I never saw lightning more vivid, or heard the crash and rattle of the thunder more deafening. The storm was evidently increasing: one bright, blinding flash, and one ear-splitting peal, that made my heart stand still, marked the crisis; gradually the lightning became less bright and the thunder less loud, as the high wind carried the tempest before it. In about an hour we were enabled to proceed.

As the night was very dark, and the ebb tide nearly run out, we avoided passing into the Samarahan by the Rhium, as the rocks there are dangerous at low water, but chose another passage, very narrow, and, if possible, to be avoided, as the name alone is a warning —" the musquito passage." It is famous for the size and venom of that insect,—in fact, there is but one other spot worse, and that is Paknam at the entrance of the Siam river. The men, however, repented their choice, as it took us the whole night to get through, and no one was able to close his eyes. The nipa palm nearly met over our heads, and every time a leaf was disturbed a swarm of musquitoes settled on us. I endeavoured to shelter myself under a blanket, but the heat was so great as to compel me unwillingly to face the enemy. I have heard of men, exposed to this annoyance for several days, being thrown into a fever by constant irritation, and I can well believe it.

It was daylight when we reached the Samarahan, at a spot about twelve miles from the sea. The banks of this river are low, and consist entirely of rich alluvial deposit. When cleared, they form the best ground for rice; when drained the sugar-cane flourishes with extraordinary luxuriance. It is, therefore, a very favourite farming ground for all those strangers who have sought refuge in Sarawak. There are several thousands scattered along its banks, besides the native population of the river.

The Samarahan Malays are a quiet, inoffensive people, and live almost entirely by farming and gardening; there is also a large Dayak population in the interior. On the left-hand branch are the Bukar tribe, divided into four villages—Munggu Babi, or the hill of pigs, Jenang, Lanchang, and Kumpang—which contain about three hundred families that pay revenue. On the right-hand branch are the two tribes of Sring and San Pok, each containing about eighty families. I say "pay revenue," as it is seldom that seventy-five per cent. do so. The custom is to pay by the "door," that is, each division in their village houses pays the Government rice to the value of from three to four shillings. To avoid this, two or three families will crowd into a space barely sufficient for one; however, measures have been taken to ensure a proper enumeration.

Pulled on towards the village where Orang Kaya Stia Bakti, the principal Malay officer, lived, and passed on our way the houses of a branch of the Sibuyau tribe of Dayaks. At the landing-place we were met by a crowd of Malays, looking especially miserable, thus showing, that like good Mahomedans, they were strictly keeping the fast; while a crowd in the neighbouring mosque where chanting in a loud voice verses from the Koran.

The old Orang Kaya, a pleasant, fine-looking man, came down to our boat, and our follower, Kasim, explained to him the object of Captain Brooke's tour of inspection, which was to inquire into the charges

brought against certain Malays of oppressing the
Dayaks.   He said he was extremely pleased, as
it would then prove how well he and his people had
conducted themselves.   He offered to accompany us,
but this was politely declined on account of the fast,
but the real reason was that the Dayaks would not
have entered into their complaints before their local
ruler.   As the flood-tide had just ended, and there
was a six hours' ebb before us, we fell down the river
to the Sibuyau village to while away the time, and
give the men an opportunity to cook and sleep.   We
were received with much hospitality by the Orang
Kaya Tumanggong.   The hamlet consists of two long
houses, surrounded by a rough palisade, called by
them a fort.

The Samarahan was a favourite attacking ground
of the pirates, and owed much of its safety to the
courage of these Dayaks, who were formerly more
united than they are now.   The Sibuyau are, in
fact, strangers.   They were harassed out of their
own country by the Seribas pirates and retired to
Samarahan; they are now scattered, a section here,
a larger one on the Lundu river, another at Meradang
on the Quop, besides smaller villages on the Sarawak,
the Sadong, and in other districts.

Their houses are like the others belonging to the
Sea Dayaks; the Orang Kaya's own division is large,
with musquito curtains, and has an air of comfort and
tidiness very unusual.   These Sibuyaus are more independent than the Land Dayaks, and keener traders.
One of the chief's married daughters was quite
pretty, extremely fair, with soft expressive features,
and a very gentle voice; she was making an elegant

mat of the finest rushes; other women were employed
in forming coarser ones from the rougher leaves,
while those that were not so engaged were turning
the padi into rice by beating it in their mortars,
and winnowing it. They show a skill in the latter
process truly marvellous: they put the beaten padi
into a flat basket with slightly rounded raised edges,
and standing on the platform to catch the slight
breeze, quietly throw the contents in the air, and
catch the grains while the wind carries away the
chaff; it is quickly cleaned. There was an appearance of activity and bustle about this village that was
really pleasing.

On the beams above our heads were some roughly
carved dragons' heads ornamented with China paper,
which some wise Dayak had informed them must be
guarded and preserved with care. They were quite
modern, and most probably a knave had worked on
these simple people to purchase them of him, as they
could not tell their use except to stick up during
their feasts, in the same way as the other Sea Dayaks
do with their rudely-carved figures of birds. In
front of their village was erected one of their
climbing-poles, at the raising of which the Orang
Kaya proudly declared one hundred and fifty jars
of tuak were consumed; and he added, with an appearance of the greatest satisfaction, that his tribe
and all their visitors were intoxicated for six days.
At their convivial meetings some strong-headed fellow
will sit down before a jar holding, perhaps, a dozen
gallons, and help those around; for every one he
serves out he should drink one himself, and it is his
pride if he can manage to keep his seat until all

have lost their senses around him.   To take glass for
glass with each man until the jar was emptied being
a manifest impossibility, there must be some sleight
of hand practised to deceive the others.   On inquiring
whether they never felt headaches the next day, they
said no; but their Lingga visitors at the last great
feast had cried from the pains they suffered; it was
ludicrous to notice the boastful look with which they
said, "The Sibuyaus get no headaches."

The Orang Kaya furnished us with fresh tuak,
which has rather a sickly, unpleasant taste, excellent
omelettes, and slices of fried kiladi, a species of arum;
in return we presented him with Batavian arrack,
tobacco, and sugar.   I have said that these Sibuyaus
are not so easily oppressed as the other Dayaks; in
fact, when the Orang Kaya was a young man, the
most powerful Malay chief on the coast, Abdulraman,
the governor of Siriki, entered their village, and tried
to force them to purchase his goods at exorbitant
prices.   They refused, upon which he directed his
followers to seize some baskets of rice, but to his
astonishment the Dayaks resisted, drove him and his
party to their prahus, and in the struggle killed
several of his followers.   The remembrance of this
and other similar deeds has given them confidence
and preserved them from oppression.

On the flood tide's making, we took leave of our
hospitable friends and pulled up the river. Both banks
are covered with gardens filled with fruit and vegetables, as well as with remarkably fine sugar-cane,
which is grown, not to be manufactured into sugar,
but to be eaten in its natural state.

Before daylight, we were again on the move.   The

appearance of the country continues the same, but
the houses, as we proceed farther up, are not quite
so numerous ; the gardens do not extend above a few
hundred yards from the river, and we could observe
the line of the forest even from our boat. We nowhere found the water shallow till we turned up the
left-hand branch that leads to the Bukar tribe; here
it becomes very narrow and is obstructed by trees
and branches, and occasionally little pebbly rapids.
It was often almost impassable from the old trunks
of fallen trees that stretched from bank to bank;
but by the greatest patience and perseverance, and
by removing the covering of our boat, we passed over
some and under others of these obstructions: at last
all these difficulties were surmounted, and we reached
the landing-place of the Munggu Babi Bukars about
half-past two, after upwards of eight hours' hard
work.

It was pleasant to leave the perpetual mud flat of
the Samarahan and get into this branch, where
occasionally rocks, and banks overshadowed by the
enormous trees of the old forest, with glimpses of
hills and distant mountains, varied the scene. The
Samarahan, though not a very picturesque river,
would afford great satisfaction to any one who con-
templated sugar plantations. The soil is of the richest
description, and, from the existing cultivation, we
may infer what it would become in the hands of
able Chinese agriculturists. These Malays neither
use the spade, the hoe, nor the plough, but simply stir
the soil with a pointed stick, or with their iron
choppers.

At the landing-place we met a party of Sadong and

Bukar Dayaks, who shouldered our baggage; we then started on our way to Munggu Babi. The path at first was detestable—the worst of paths, over slippery trunks and branches of huge trees lying scattered over the sites of their old rice farms, very perilous, as the slightest slip endangered the safety of a limb. To the bare-footed Dayak it is nothing, but shoes render it unpleasant; however, it soon changed into the ordinary style; and getting rapidly over about four miles, we arrived at the foot of the hill on which the houses are built. They were entirely hidden by fruit-trees. Beyond rose the mountains of Sadong, which can be seen from the decks of the ships that pass along the coast. At the foot of Munggu Babi flowed a delightful stream into which we plunged to dispel some little fatigue arising from the heat. Our Dayak attendants had pushed on with our baggage, and being now refreshed we began climbing the steep that separated us from the houses; no sooner was this observed, than every available brass wall-piece was fired in our honour, and it was under this salute that we entered the village.

It is an illustration of the state of insecurity in which these people formerly lived, and which is still vivid in their imagination, that when those who were returning from their farms heard the guns fired, they hid themselves in the forest, thinking their homes were surrounded by enemies; and it was not until the gongs beat out joyful sounds that they were reassured and returned to their abodes.

The village is, as I have said, situated on the summit of a little hill covered with every kind of fruit-tree; and was, the Bukars say, named Munggu Babi, from the innumerable wild pigs that used to swarm upon it, very well represented at the present day by their civilized brethren. The first house is the Pangga or head-house, lately erected, very comfortable, in which we took up our lodgings ; a rough sort of street beyond it, lined with very old-looking houses, rising one above the other with the slope of the hill until the village was completed by two more head-houses.

We appeared to be very welcome guests, and were soon surrounded by the elders of the tribe and by crowds of young men. We were the second party of white visitors who had slept at this place, but the first probably who travelled in European style, and as usual our proceedings excited much curiosity. Just as dinner was over, we heard the pleasing announcement that a Sambas Malay, who lived among the Dayaks, had shot a fine buck which he very obligingly presented to us. No one who has not lived principally on ducks and fowls for many years can appreciate the importance of such an event. We agreed to visit the famous caves of Sirih the next day, and in the evening to have a search for deer. They are represented as very numerous, as the Bukars do not eat their flesh,—a fortunate event for their visitors, but not for themselves, as they are thus deprived of good and easily-acquired food.

Up early, and after a hearty breakfast of deer-steaks, started for the caves of Sirih. We passed up the street that runs through the centre of the village, the houses looking very dilapidated in comparison with those of the Sibuyau Dayaks, but all were swarming with children. An abrupt descent brought us to a lower part of the stream that runs at the foot of Munggu Babi, affording beautifully clear water for

the villagers. Continuing our course over the low
buttress of the Sadong mountains, where the Dayaks
have enclosed several spots for gardens, we had a beautiful prospect of the surrounding country, better seen
however from the heights above, which we intended
passing over the next day. Two miles' walk through
old farms and fresh felled jungle brought us to the foot
of a very steep hill in which the cave was situated.
Clambering up the rocks for a couple of hundred feet,
we suddenly found ourselves at the mouth of the cave.
The entrance is peculiar: divided formerly into three,
the fall of a pillar has united two of the openings into
one, which is above thirty feet in breadth; at first
there appeared no far interior, but to the left a
descending passage led into the great cave. To the
right was a separate apartment with a fine opening,
forming the first division of the mouth, but inacces-
sible from the outside. The Dayak boys beckoned
us to come in. We went, thinking they wished us to
look out from thence on the beautiful valley below and
the lofty mountain beyond it; but our surprise was
great when they pointed into a deep hole where lay the
skeleton of a human being.

Among the guides who were with us was a resolute
but very good-tempered looking Sarawak man, and as
he was standing near we asked him to explain the cause
of those bones being there. He answered very quietly,
"It is only a Dayak that I shot many years ago." We
asked him to explain, which he did without any hesitation. Some years before these districts came under
Sir James Brooke's influence, a chief named Bandhar
Kasim ruled over the Sadong province; he was a
very harsh man and oppressed the Dayak more than

was usually the case among the neighbouring chiefs.
One tribe on the right-hand branch of the Sadong had
suffered very severely from his exactions.  They only
murmured when he took their goods: when he
demanded their children they refused to give them
up, and flying to the Sirih caves threw up a barricade across the entrance.  This example he thought
might prove contagious among the neighbouring
tribes, so he determined to attack them; besides he
was delighted with the opportunity of acquiring slaves,
as every one he captured would be reduced to that
state.  By promising to divide the booty and the captives
he soon collected a force of three hundred men, many
with firearms.  These marched boldly to the attack,
but being received with a shower of heavy stones
and rolling rocks quickly withdrew to an open space,
a little grass spot which the narrator pointed out to
us.  There being none present who appeared willing
to expose his life for the sake of Bandhar Kasim, the
whole affair seemed likely to terminate in a distant
but harmless fire being kept up at the entrance of the
cave.  At last Bandhar Kasim cried out, "I will
give a slave to any man who will drive those devils
from their position." The Sarawak man instantly
volunteered, if the others would support him.  Plung-
ing into the jungle he reached the foot of the hill, and
by dint of strength and activity, contrived to climb
the almost perpendicular side of the mountain, and
reach a spot above the cave, from whence he came
down until he could look well over the barricade.  The
descent was now very dangerous, but he prepared for it.
The first Dayak who showed himself he shot through
the body; then throwing away his gun and taking

advantage of the confusion caused by the fall of their companion, he boldly swung himself down the rocks, and sprang in among the astonished Dayaks crying, " Who is brave enough to fight me ? " The unfortunate wretches, thinking he must be well backed, fled into the cave and were soon pursued by Bandhar Kasim's followers: two were killed and seven taken prisoners; the rest escaped, as the cave extends quite through the mountain.

While we were listening to this story, the Dayaks had prepared dried sticks of a resinous wood by splitting one end until it had the appearance of a brush ; they were tolerable substitutes for torches. We followed our guides down the narrow passage that leads into the interior cave. They walked with the greatest care, examining the ground before they placed a foot ahead, knowing that the men who now collect the edible birds' nests here often place sharp pointed pieces of bamboo sticking up in the path to punish unwary interlopers. The cave gradually became broader and more lofty, and our slight torches could scarcely pierce the gloom that hung thickly around us.

As we advanced the form of the cave varied but slightly, until we reached a spot where we had to pass through a sort of opening, like some of those diminutive doors occasionally seen in odd nooks of old cathedrals. Here we found ourselves in a small chamber that appeared for a moment the termination of our walk, but in the right corner was a narrow descending interstice in the rock, through which we could just squeeze our bodies to find ourselves again in the lofty cave. The gentle fall of water told of the neighbourhood of a stream, which now and then became our path. The Dayaks say that there are fish that see not, in the dark pool, which may at times be observed, particularly under the rocks.

We soon arrived at a sloping surface over which the water spread, rendering it difficult to prevent our feet from gliding from under us. This I gladly climbed, as we had been informed that during a heavy shower of rain the water would suddenly rise to such a height in the depressed portion of the cave we had just passed, that all non-swimmers would be drowned. The walking now became often unpleasant; slippery mud and no less slippery rock; the ascents and descents were very abrupt, and occasionally we passed a deep chasm where a slip might be fatal.

The stream that runs through the cave now and then disappears under some rock to reappear fifty yards ahead.

After continuing our course about a quarter of a mile, we came on a spot where the height of the cave from seventy feet decreased to three, and through this aperture the wind blew sharply and felt very cold. The Dayaks now proposed we should stop, as our torches would not last longer than the time required to return to the entrance; but we said we wished to advance as far as the chamber in which the edible birds' nests were collected; so putting out some of the torches we pushed on in a stooping position. One fresher blast blew out some of the lights, and I thought for a moment that we were about to be left in the dark. A hundred yards brought us to the spot where the Dayaks take up their abode during the gathering season: it was a more lofty chamber than any we had as yet passed through. The birds build

as near as possible to the top of the cave, and the
dangerous operation of collecting the nests is performed by Dayaks who climb long poles fastened
together to the height of eighty or ninety feet, which
looked very poor scaffolding to sustain men at that
dizzy height. The gathering is slow work, taking them
five days. The nests found in these caves are very
inferior to those of Baram; the former being like
dirty glue, the latter like the finest isinglass.

We should like to have penetrated farther and seen
the country on the opposite side, but the cave was
reputed dangerous and but seldom frequented, as the
Dayaks never go beyond the profitable chamber.
This would have rendered our progress slow, and the
blasts of cold wind might have blown out our torches,
now nearly consumed; and if the chasms were as bad
even as those we had passed over, we could scarcely have
finished our journey in safety. Reluctantly, we gave
the order to return, when the whole body of little
Dayak boys who had accompanied us, half frightened
of ghosts and half in fun, started away yelling and
whooping, their torches occasionally throwing light on
the rocky sides and now fading away to mere specks
of light. The loftiness of this cave, its great extent,
the cry of the disturbed swallows, the peculiarly grave
look of our almost naked guides, the knowledge that
we were the first Europeans who had ever penetrated
to this spot, the distant shouts of the boys as they
were re-echoed back—all combined to render the scene
interesting and impressive.

From every calculation we could make, we were
convinced that we penetrated the cave above a third
of a mile. It is the finest I have ever seen, but I

afterwards heard that there is another called Gua Mawap, or the cloudy cave, which is infinitely larger. It is said that some Malays who had entered it to look for birds' nests lost their way and were no more heard of. The Dayaks from this, or some superstitious reason, did not mention its existence to us, as they are very well aware that Englishmen have a propensity to search every spot, whether dangerous or not.

We returned under a very hot sun to find that all the villagers were in active preparation to have a dance and a feast. We agreed after dinner to go to the Orang Kaya's house, and submit ourselves to their will. They sent us a large decanter—where they got it from I forgot to inquire—full of a very sweet and pleasant liquor, of the colour of dark sherry, made from the tampui fruit : it was stronger than it tasted. While we were waiting for our dinner, we observed two very pleasant-looking girls of sixteen come cautiously up the ladder of the head-house. As it was very unusual for women to enter this bachelor's hall, we quietly watched, while pretending to be en- gaged in our toilette. Glancing at us, and thinking themselves unobserved, they made their way over to two Dayak youths who had accompanied us from the Sibuyau village. The fair Hebes bore in their hands two large bowls of fresh tuak, which they pressed their visitors to drink, but they laughed and declined. The young girls opened a regular battery of blandish- ments, put their arms round them and besought them to drink, not to give them the shame of having to take the liquor back to their houses to be laughed at by all the other girls; they wound up by saying, " What ! are the Sibuyaus so weak-headed as to fear to drink

Bukar tuak?" This was the *coup de grace;* the youths, already half overcome, raised the bowls to their lips, and were not allowed to set them down till they had drained the last drop. The girls then ran away laughing, knowing the effect that must soon follow the draught.

The Dayak women seldom, if ever, drink, but some of them appear delighted to see their husbands and brothers in a wretched state of intoxication. Mr. Crookshank told me that he arrived at a Sadong village during one of their drinking feasts: the men were already staggering in their walk, and towards evening were sitting and lying about too drunk to be able to raise the bowls to their lips, when the women took that office upon them and poured the liquor down the drunkards' throats. It must not be supposed, however, that the Dayaks are habitual drinkers; on the contrary, except at their feasts, they are a very sober people.

In the evening, we went to the Orang Kaya's house, and had to go through most of the ceremonies I have already described in the account of our visit up the left-hand branch of the Sarawak river. During the dancing of the old people, we inquired whether the young women never danced, and on our promising a gift of a brass chain that the girls wear round the waist to all who would join the elders: there was no lack of competitors. It was mischievously suggested to the Orang Kaya's daughter that I was a famous dancer, and it was amusing to notice the eagerness with which the girls besought me to join them; as four drew me gently into the vortex it was impossible to resist, though I quickly disengaged myself by assuring them that on their split bamboo floors no European could dance.

The most remarkable peculiarity of many of these men is their being so hairy in comparison to those of other tribes, some having regular whiskers, and others beards. The women have their limbs spoilt from carrying heavy weights, even from their tenderest age, over exceedingly steep ground; their legs appeared bent. I saw one mother bearing on her back two children, and a basket containing twenty or more bamboos full of water, the latter a sufficient load for one person. In the harvest, they act as beasts of burden, and bring the bulk of the rice home. The children, in general, were very clean and pleasing.

We started early in the morning for Lanchang, the second division of the Bukar tribe that we intended to visit. The path was over the Sadong mountains, where a depression in the range renders its elevation not perhaps over a thousand feet. As we moved along the open ground among the fenced-in gardens, we were enabled to obtain a very extensive view of the surrounding country, and I have rarely seen one of greater beauty; the variety of form assumed by the hills from the mountain range to the isolated peak rising from the fertile plain of the Samarahan and Quop, the extent of ground over which the eye could travel from the Santubong and the sea to the interior hills of Sadong, rendered it almost as lovely and as interesting as the famous scene from the summit of the Penang Hill. It wanted but the civilized appearance which is found there—the houses, villas, churches, ships, and roads. The way over the hill was very difficult, consisting entirely of small felled trees, notched, and in a very rotten state, and sometimes both steep and slippery. However, we got over it without a fall, and managed to work our way to the opposite side, whence the valley of the Bukar stream and the interior of the Sadong are visible—pretty enough, but all scenery here has similar characteristics.

The sun was very warm, and the perspiration ran from me in streams; but meeting with a cool rivulet, shaded by overhanging rocks, not by trees, we sat still till perfectly cooled, and then refreshed ourselves by a bathe under a tiny but foaming cascade. The two Sibuyau youths who had been so fascinated by the fair maidens the previous night looked very woful this morning, and could hardly get along at all or carry their own baggage, but sat moodily looking at the water, with their heads pressed lightly between their hands.

From this spot our path continued among the valleys, over rice plantations, without any remarkable feature. At length we reached the village of Lanchang, on the borders of a pebbly stream. It is built on the low land, and has a greater appearance of comfort than Munggu Babi. As we were their first European visitors, we excited a great deal of curiosity; but forcing our way through the crowd, we took up our quarters in the head-house, making our beds, as usual, beneath a ghastly row of skulls.

We were welcomed by the old Orang Kaya Sunan in the absence of the rival chiefs. In this village five men claim the supremacy, having been appointed at different times by various people. Sunan had been promoted some thirty or forty years before by the Sultan of Brunei, but was now too old to do his work effectually: the other four Orang Kayas were irregularly named by certain native officers without any authority. As I have elsewhere observed, under the former system, the Malay chiefs received half the revenues of the Dayak tribes instead of salary, which opened the door to many abuses. The great evil-doer was the Datu Patinggi of Sarawak, who had charge of Lanchang. When he found that an Orang Kaya would not sufficiently second him in his endeavour to monopolize the trade, he would appoint another. All this was quite illegal; it was to do away with these abuses, and to inaugurate a new system, that Sir James Brooke had directed Captain Brooke to make these tours of inspection through all the principal districts of Sarawak and its dependencies.

The consequence of having five Orang Kayas in this village was of necessity a series of disputes, and the day before our arrival two of them had quarrelled violently, and one proposed that, to settle the matter, they should sally out into the neighbouring countries, and the first who should bring home a head should be declared victor, and have the case decided in his favour. It was their ancient custom, not that they dared to carry it into practice.

Captain Brooke summoned the five Orang Kayas before him, and ordered them to appear at the capital, when it would be settled who should be appointed by the Government; in the meantime he set our followers to make inquiries among the principal families, who was considered fittest for the office and was most popular among the tribe.

Presently a small crowd assembled, and asked to have their cases settled; but finding that none of them were of less than twenty years standing, they were told that it would be impossible to finish them so quickly, and they were put off. None of them really expected to have their disputes arranged, but they appeared delighted to have a grievance to relate. I have never seen any Land Dayaks with an air of greater comfort; they appear to be well fed, and, consequently, are more free from skin diseases than their neighbours.

In the evening, we went out to look for deer. After making a circuit of a few miles, I reached a stream near which the animals are usually found, when, to my disgust, I heard a shot fired, followed immediately by another. I ran forward only in time to see a fine buck spring into the forest and another stretched lifeless at Captain Brooke's feet. He came to the spot, saw two grazing together, and with an old-fashioned cavalry carbine knocked over one; the other stood astonished, which gave him time to reload and hit him heavily. We tracked him for a little distance, but the night closing in prevented our finding him. Our follower, Kasim, saw eight, wounded one, but did not succeed in securing him. My indignation at the mistake of my guide in bringing me to a spot already engaged was much mitigated by the prospect of deer-steaks for dinner.

That night there were the usual ceremonies and dances without an incident to vary them: they kept us up rather late.

Walked over to Jenang: it was but three miles off, through gardens, groves of fruit-trees, old rice-

grounds, and underwood. We noticed with much
indignation that hundreds of fine fruit-trees were
destroyed, and on inquiry found it had been done
by the old Orang Kaya Sunan, who wanted to have
a farm near his own house. The trees belonged to
the tribe, who vainly tried to persuade him not to
do it; but being backed by the Datu Patinggi, he
would not listen to them. The village of Jenang
is small and of little consequence, numbering but
twenty-five families, and had not arrived at the
dignity of an Orang Kaya. Their head-house was
very old and small, the worst we had seen.

All the elders were called together in the morning
to choose an Orang Kaya; and instead of fixing on
one of themselves, their choice fell on a young man
of rather heavy appearance, who seemed, however, to
be an universal favourite. After this ceremony we
started off to Munggu Babi, through the valleys and
lowlands between the hills. The walk was long and
very much exposed to the sun, but we reached that
village by one, and after a short rest pushed on to our
boat.

As we had heavy rain the previous night, the
stream was much swollen, but it helped us over many
obstructions, though it rendered some few more
difficult. We brought up for the night a short
distance from the junction.

Started up the right branch of the Samarahan to
meet the San Poks, who were a primitive tribe, never
yet visited by Europeans. We were detained several
hours by the numerous obstructions in the river. At
one place, a huge tree had fallen across, and rendered
a passage impossible, except by dragging the boat

over. We tried; but an ominous crack made us quickly push her back into the stream. We then with axes removed a portion of the trunk, and at last got safely over. We met a party of San Poks coming down the river, who returned with us. We did not reach their landing-place till three P.M. A very dirty walk of two miles brought us to their village-house, which was new : the tribe having but lately removed hither. The country we passed over was undulating, occasionally descending in abrupt ravines. The San Poks had chosen a low, cleared hill for their domicile. We were welcomed by a perfect storm of good wishes, seized on by a dozen women, who insisted on washing our feet, tying little bells round our wrists, and dancing before us enthusiastically. Very few could understand Malay. We inquired about the deer-grounds; but as these Dayaks are partial to deer's-flesh, there was no game to be found in the neighbourhood.

The San Poks appeared mad with excitement; they danced, and drank, and beat their gongs and drums till daylight, affording us but snatches of slumber. Their ceremonies were exactly similar to those I have formerly described.

Turned our faces towards home. When we came to the Bukar branch, we entered a small Dayak canoe and paddled a short distance up to land near a spot where a hot spring was said to exist. We went ashore, and wandered on for about a mile, our guides evidently not quite certain of the path. At length we reached a small stream flowing through a flat tract of jungle—the soil a dark mud; tried it, and certainly it was very warm. Following its course, we came to the place where the water bubbled up from the ground through the black soil. The spring was about six feet by three where it issued from the earth, and supplied a shallow rill about a yard in breadth. The water we could see bubbling up through liquid mud. I tried to keep my feet in it, but it was far too hot, and left a burning sensation. A vapour rose above it, but the water had no perceptible taste or smell.

A few planks of an old boat that we found at this spot have given rise to a story among the Dayaks of an ancient ship being lost here when this lowland was covered by the sea. The planks evidently were part of a Sea Dayak boat, from the way they were cut, and were of a fine wood called marbau. They have been here for many years—perhaps this water has a preservative effect. The aborigines say that this spring is the work of evil spirits, and therefore will not approach it alone. We brought away a few bottles of it. It appeared a curious place to find a warm-water spring: no high land near; indeed, no rocks, but all an alluvial flat.

Fell down the river till night. We sent our men ashore in one place to examine a stone that was, as usual, in some way connected with spirits. We had it removed to Sarawak. It proved to be the representation of the female principle so common near Hindu temples: its necessary companion was not found, or, being more portable, had been removed, though formerly it was observed there.

There is but one more known material remnant of Hindu worship in these countries: it is a stone bull—an exact facsimile of those found in India. It is cut

from a species of stone said not to be found in
Sarawak : the legs and a part of the head have been
knocked off.  Its history is this : Many years ago, on
being discovered in the jungle, the Malays and Dayaks
removed it to the bank of the river, preparatory to
its being conveyed to the town ; but before it could
be put into a prahu, they say, a tremendous storm
of thunder and lightning, wind and rain, arose, which
lasted thirty days.· Fearing that the bull was angry
at being disturbed in his forest home, they left him
in the mud.  When Sir James Brooke heard that
this sacred bull was half-buried in the soil, he had it
removed to his house.  Several of the Dayak tribes
sent deputations to him to express their fears of the
evil consequences that would be sure to ensue—everything would go wrong, storms would arise, their crops
be blighted, and famine would desolate the land.
Humouring their prejudices, he answered, that they
were mistaken, that the bull, on the contrary, would
be pleased to be removed from the dirty place in
which the Malays had left him, and that now he was
kept dry and comfortable, they would find he would
show no anger.  They were satisfied with this reply
and departed.  Occasionally, some of the Dayaks
will come and wash both of these Hindu relics, and
bear away the water to fertilize their fields.

Among some of the aborigines there is a superstition that they must not laugh at a dog or at a
snake crossing their path.  Should they do so, they
would become stones.  These Dayaks always refer
with respect and awe to some rocks scattered over the
summit of a hill in Sadong, saying that they were
originally men.  The place was a very likely one to

be haunted—noble old forest, but seldom visited. They tell the following story:—Many years ago, a great chief gave a feast there, in the midst of which his lovely daughter came in: she was a spoilt child, who did nothing but annoy the guests. They at first tried to get rid of her by mixing dirt with her food: finding she still teazed them for more, they gave her poison. Her father, in his anger, went back to his house, shaved his dog, and painted him with alternate streaks of black and white. Then giving him some intoxicating drink, he carried him in his arms into the midst of the assembly, and placed him on the ground. The dog began to caper about in the most ludicrous manner, which set all off laughing, the host as well the guests, and they were immediately turned into stone.

230

# CHAPTER VIII.

## THE MOUNTAIN OF KINA BALU.

### FIRST EXPEDITION.

First Ascent by Mr. Low—Want of Shoes—Set Sail for the Tampasuk
—Beautiful Scenery—The Abai—Manufacture of Nipa Salt—
Uses of the Nipa Palm—A Lanun Chief—Baju Saddle—Baju
a Non-walker—Our ride to the Tampasuk—Gigantic Mango
Trees—The Datu's House—Its Arrangements—The Datu and
his People—Piratical Expedition—A Bride put up to Auction
—The Bajus—Mixed Breeds—Quarrels with the Lanuns—
Effect of Stealing Ida'an Children—Fable of the Horse and his
Rider—Amount of Fighting Men—Freedom of the Women—
Killing the Fatted Calf—Beautiful Prospect—A new Gardinia
—Pony Travelling—Difficulty of procuring Useful Men—
Start—An Extensive Prospect—Cocoa-nuts and their Milk—
A View of Kina Balu—Granite Debris—Our Guides—Natives
Ploughing—Our Hut—Division of Land—Ginambur—Neatest
Village-house in the Country—Its Inhabitants—Tatooing—
Curiosity—Blistered Feet—Batong—Granite Boulders—Ford-
ing—Fish-traps—Tambatuan—Robbing a Hive—Search for
the Youth-restoring Tree—Our Motives—Appearance of the
Summit of Kina Balu—A long Story—Swimming the River—
Koung—Palms not plentiful—Lanun Cloth—Cotton—Nominal
Wars—The Kiladi—Attempt to Levy Black-mail at the Village
of Labang Labang—Resistance—Reasons for demanding it—
Bamboo flat-roofed Huts—Ingenious Contrivance—Kiau—
Dirty Tribe—Recognition of Voice—A Quarrel—Breaking the
Barometer—Opposition to the Ascent of Kina Balu—Harmless
Demonstration—Thieves—Mr. Low unable to Walk—Continue
the Expedition alone—Cascade—Prayers to the Spirit of the
Mountain—Flowers and Plants—Beautiful Rhododendrons—
Cave—Unskilful Use of the Blow-pipe—Cold—Ascent to the
Summit — Granite Face — Low's Gully — Noble Terrace —
Southern Peak—Effect of the Air—The Craggy Summit—
Distant Mountain—Dangerous Slopes—Ghostly Inhabitants—
Mist — Superstitions — Collecting Plants — Descent — Noble

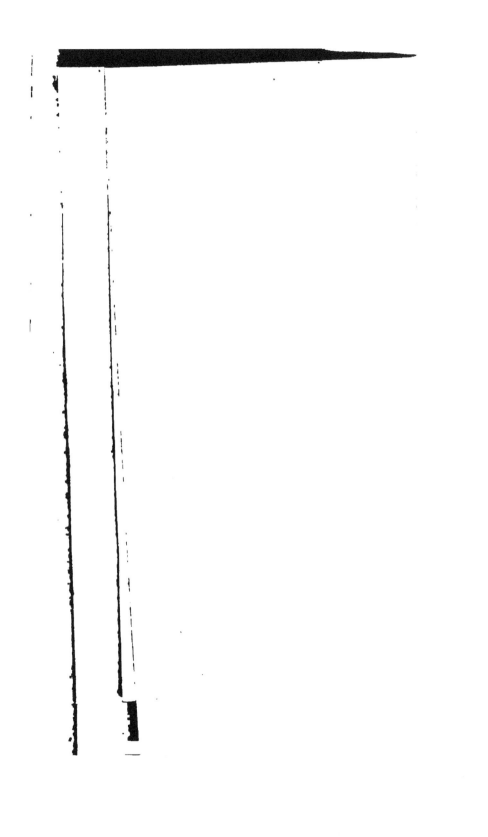

To ascend Kina Balu had been an ambition of mine,
even before I ever saw Borneo. To have been the first
to do it would have increased the excitement and the
pleasure.     However, this satisfaction was not for me.
Mr. Low, colonial treasurer of Labuan, had long
meditated the same scheme, and in 1851 made the
attempt.     It was thought at the time but little likely
to succeed, as the people and the country were entirely
unknown; but by determined perseverance Mr. Low
reached what may fairly be entitled the summit,
though he did not attempt to climb any of the rugged
peaks, rising a few hundred feet higher than the
spot where he left a bottle with an inscription in it.

In 1856, Mr. Lobb, a naturalist, reached the foot
of the mountain, but was not allowed by the natives
to ascend it.

In 1858, Mr. Low and I determined to make
another attempt; and early in April I went over from
Brunei to Labuan to join him. We waited till the
15th for a vessel, which we expected would bring us a
supply of shoes, but as it did not arrive we started.
This was the cause of most of our mishaps,—as a
traveller can make no greater mistake than being
careless of his feet, particularly in Borneo, where all
long journeys must be performed on foot.

In 1851, Mr. Low had gone by the Tawaran, but
the Datu of Tampasuk, who was on a trading voyage
to Labuan, having assured us that it was easier to
get to the mountain from his river, we determined

to try that route.  He started before us, and on
April 15th we followed, in a pinnace, obligingly
lent us by Dr. Coulthard, of the Eastern Archipelago
Company, our party being very large for the con-
veyance—Mr. Low and myself, two servants, six
crew, and seventeen followers.  During the night
we passed Pulo Tiga, and were off Papar in the
morning.  We sailed along as beautiful a coast as
can be conceived: ranges of hills rising one beyond
the other, some grass-covered, others still clothed in
forest, with soft valleys and lovely bays, and here and
there patches of bright sandy beach, with Kina Balu
towering in majestic grandeur as a background.   In
fact, the prospect increased in beauty until, on the
evening of the 17th, we reached Abai, where we found
the Datu of Tampasuk in his prahu.  The little bay
at the entrance of the Abai affords shelter from all
winds except the N.W.; the bar, however, having
only a fathom at low water prevents any but small
craft from entering the river.  On the sandy point
of the grassy plain, at the west side of the entrance,
is a small well where boats may water.  The Datu
came off and agreed to go up the Abai with us, and
send his own boat round by sea to Tampasuk.

Started at four A.M., but made very slow progress, the wind blowing down the river, and the
flood-tide not being strong.  However, by towing
and warping, we managed to reach our anchorage
about ten P.M.  The banks near the entrance appear
to be high, but it was almost dark as we passed
them; then narrow mangrove swamps fringed the
shores with occasionally grassy hills in the background.  On the left bank there are two small

branches, Gading and Paka Paka, inhabited, the
Datu said, by some villages of Ida'an. There appear
to be but few people living on this river, or rather
salt-water creek. Three very small hamlets, containing altogether about thirty houses, were all I saw.
There are numerous sheds for making salt, which
appears to be the principal industry of the Bajus.
The manufacture is conducted as follows :—Great
heaps of the roots of the nipa palm, that always grows
in salt or brackish water, are collected and burnt ;
the residue is swept up and thrown into half-filled
pans, where the ashes and small particles of wood are
separated, and the water boiled ;—a coarse, bitter
salt is the result. It is not disagreeable after a little
use, and I much prefer it to the common article
brought from Siam, and generally sold in these
countries. The natives of the north seldom use the
imported salt, except for preserving fish ; whereas,
towards Sarawak, the Siamese is rapidly taking the
place of that procured from the nipa palms.

The nipa palm is indeed a blessing to the natives ;
as we have seen, they make a salt from the ashes of the
root ; they extract a coarse sugar from the stem ; they
cover in their houses with the leaf ; from the last also
they manufacture the mat called kejang, with which
they form the walls of their houses, and the best
awning in the world for boats, perfectly water-tight,
and well adapted to keep out the rays of the sun.
Their cigars are rolled up in the fine inner leaf; and
a native could doubtless tell of a dozen other uses to
which it is put. In ascending rivers there is nearly
always deep water near the nipa, but shallow near
the mangrove.

The Abai creek has generally more than two fathoms from the mouth to the hamlets, but never less.   We anchored opposite a Lanun chief's house, which, though on the left bank, is still towards Tampasuk, as the river, after proceeding in a southerly direction, suddenly turns to the north-east.

The Rajah Muda, the Lanun chief, came on board, and was very civil.   He is a handsome-looking, manly fellow, and extremely polite.   From what I have heard and seen, he is a type of his countrymen—a different race from the Baju : a slight figure, more regular features than the Malays, a quiet, observant eye ; he wore a delicate moustache.   He is the son of the late Pangeran Mahomed, of Pandasan, whose grave, ornamented with seven-fold umbrellas, we passed on the river's bank.

Knowing that we could ride from Abai to Tampasuk, we had brought our English saddles, and were soon mounted on indifferent ponies, making our way towards the Datu's house in an easterly direction. The Baju saddle, made of wood, covered with thin cloth, is very small.   Instead of stirrups they have a rope with a loop in the end, into which they insert their big toe, and ride with the soles of their feet turned up behind ; and when they set off on a gallop they cling with their toes under the pony's belly.

The Baju is essentially a non-walker.   He never makes use of his own legs if he can possibly get an animal to carry him.   He rides all the horses and the mares, even when the latter have but just foaled. Cows are equally in requisition, and it was laughable to observe one of these animals with a couple of lads on her back trotting along the pathways, a calf, not a week old, frisking behind her. The water buffalo, however, appeared to be the favourite—the strong beast constantly carrying double. Every man we met had a spear, which was extremely useful in fording rivers, as well as for defence.

We rode at first over a small plain, about two miles in extent, half of which we had to traverse: it was bounded on either side by a low sandstone range, and before us was a connecting ridge, which we had to cross before entering the Tampasuk district. From its top, we had a view of the country: beneath us was a plain, extending some miles beyond the river; not very pleasant riding, as every here and there a slushy, muddy stream crossed the path, into which our ponies sunk up to their girths, and found some difficulty in floundering through. There were signs that cultivation is occasionally carried on here, and I should imagine it well adapted for rice fields. As it happened to be a very warm day, we were not sorry, after a ride of two miles and a half, to reach the river's bank, where we found a most agreeable shade under gigantic mango trees. I call them gigantic—they were for this country, being above two feet in diameter, and probably sixty feet high. Unfortunately, it was not the fruit season. Very few mangoes in Borneo are worth eating. Occasionally we find them with delicate flavour; but nothing to equal the magnificent fruit of Bombay. I was anxious to taste the produce of these trees, as from former intercourse with the Spaniards the natives might have obtained seeds from Manilla, where the fruit arrives at great perfection. A half mile of shady ride brought us to the ford opposite to the Datu's house, where we found the Tampasuk, a hundred yards wide, but not more than three feet deep—clear, cool, and rapid.

After enjoying a pleasant bathe, we strolled on for a hundred yards to the Datu's house, which is really a good and comfortable one, and we were agreeably surprised at the excellent accommodation. It is double-storied, with plank walls. The lower part of the house consisted of one great room, surrounded by broad verandahs; the end ones being partially partitioned off. In one of these we were lodged, and found all the ladies of the family engaged in preparing our apartment and covering the floor with nice clean mats of brilliant colours, which, with our own bedding, soon made us comfortable. The great room, or hall, was the chief's, in the centre of which was an immense resting-place or bed, and behind were heaps of boxes, containing the wealth of the family, piled as I had seen done in Sùlu. The upper story appears to be reserved for the daughters and other unmarried girls, who, as their floor was only of split bamboo, could look through and watch all our movements; and the occasional light laughter showed that we afforded them some amusement.

The Datu of Tampasuk is considered the head of the Bajus in these districts, but his power is more nominal than real. The race is, individually, very independent, and no one appears ready to obey authority; and the same character may be given to their neighbours, the Lanuns and Ida'an. Mengkabong and Tampasuk are their chief ports, though they are scattered in many other districts, both on this and the north-eastern coast. They were formerly very piratical, and even now are unwilling to let a favour-

able opportunity pass. Their lawlessness is proverbial :
one instance will suffice. A large party went on an
expedition to the island of Banguey, where they
anchored opposite a village, and commenced trading,
being, they said, particularly anxious for tripang,
or edible sea-slug. The fishermen dispersed in quest
of this article, but had no sooner gone than the
crews of the prahus landed, surprised the village,
killed or drove away the few men that remained,
and captured about twenty-eight women and children.
This little incident was much talked of at the time,
as they managed to seize a young bride, just decked
out for a wedding, loaded with all the gold ornaments of the village. This young girl, contrary to
their usual custom, was, it is said, put up to auction
by her captors, as she was too valuable to be one
man's share. Yet both the people of Banguey and
Mengkabong are claimed by the Brunei Government
as their subjects. I have little doubt that, on hearing of this affair, the only reflection of the ministers
was — " We wish those Mengkabong people were
nearer, that we might have a share of the plunder."

When not engaged in sea expeditions, the Bajus
employ themselves in a peddling trade with the aborigines, exchanging nipa salt, with a little iron and
cloth, for tobacco and rice ; the former they sell to
the Malays. I must not omit to notice that the
Bajus are very expert fishermen, and catch and salt a
great quantity every year, which they sell to the
inhabitants of the hills. Some few have gardens,
and plant rice, and, in a lazy, careless way, rear
cattle, ponies, and buffaloes. They profess Islamism,
but do not probably understand much beyond the

outward observances, though they keep the fast with greater strictness than most of the Malays. No one can accuse the Bajus of being a handsome race ; they have generally pinched-up, small faces, low fore-heads, but bright eyes; the men are short, slight, but very active, particularly in the water ; the women have similar features, and are slighter and perhaps taller than the Malay ; they wear their hair tied in a knot on the fore part of the head, which has a very unbecoming appearance. I never saw a good-looking face among them, judging even by a Malay standard. The Datu had five daughters, as well as five sons—a large family, but a thing by no means rare in Borneo.

We saw many men that differed totally from the above description, but, on inquiry, found they were of mixed breed. I asked one of what race he was. He answered four—Baju, Lanun, Malay, and Chinese. He was a broad-faced, ugly-looking fellow, one of our guides. Another, rather good-looking, claimed to be descended of four races also—Baju, Sulu, Lanun, and Malay. Almost all those we asked were of mixed parentage, which renders it difficult to describe a particular tribe ; yet the Baju is a distinct animal from the Malay, and does credit to his name of Sea Gipsy, as he has quite the appearance of that wandering tribe.

We heard much of their differences with the Lanuns, who occupy the mouth of the Tampasuk, and were formerly very powerful on this coast; their own oppressive conduct turned the people of the interior against them, and at Tawaran they were driven out. They were accused of stealing the children of the Ida'an. I say driven out—I should rather have

said, teazed out. No people in this country can cope
with them in battle; so the Ida'an kept hovering
around the Lanun villages to cut off stragglers. At
last, no one could leave the houses even to fetch firewood, unless accompanied by a strong armed party,
which interfered so much with their piratical pursuits
that they at last abandoned the country, and retired
to Tampasuk and Pandasan. Here they were in 1845
attacked by Sir Thomas Cochrane, and their villages
burnt. This again broke up their communities, and
most of those who were addicted to piracy retired to
the north-east coast, to Tungku and the neighbouring
rivers. Since then they have gradually so dwindled
away in these countries, that now, it is said, they
scarcely muster two hundred fighting men. Even
these are under various chiefs, who delight in giving
themselves high-sounding names, as Sultan, Rajah,
Rajah-Muda; though, perhaps, scarcely able to man
a war prahu with their followers.

The present cause of quarrel between the Lanuns
and Bajus is theft, mutual reprisals ending in the
death of one of the latter. The Datu talked of
nothing but war; he said he had been advised by the
Spanish missionary, Signor Cuateron, to apply to the
Spaniards at Balabak to assist him in expelling the
Lanuns, and that he was determined to do so. I
related to him the fable of the horse and his rider,
and left him to find out its application. His ready
laugh told he had caught the meaning. The Datu
said he could muster 600 fighting men in Abai and
Tampasuk, and that the Lanuns have but 150. At
Pandasan the Lanuns have but forty men to oppose
to 400 Bajus. Still, the latter have no stomach for

the fight. I doubt if they give very correct information about the numbers at Pandasan, as in 1851
they were very much more numerous; in fact, several
hundreds were then seen around the houses of the
chiefs. They themselves said that comparatively few
lived on the Tampasuk. Mr. Low ascended the Pandasan and found a village under Panquan Mahomed,
whose grave we saw on the Abai; and, farther up
this shoal and narrow river, he came to the village
of Asam, the residence of Pañgeran Merta and other
chiefs. Beyond that, on the tongue of land caused
by the river dividing, was the village of Sultan Si
Tabuk. About twenty-five miles to the north of
Pandasan are the small rivers of Kanio Kanio and
Layer Layer, also inhabited by Lanuns. They are
very fond of boasting of their courage, and say, if
the Europeans would but meet them sword in hand,
they would fight them man to man.

I may notice that the Lanuns, Bajus, and Sulus do
not shut up their women in the same manner as is
practised by the Malays of the capital and most other
Mahomedans; on the contrary, they often sit with the
men, and enter freely into the subject under discussion. I should like to be able to ascertain whether
this comparative freedom renders them more chaste
than the Malay women; they could not well be less
so. In Sulu, the wives of the chiefs are entrusted
with the principal management of the accounts, and
carry on much of the trade; it is said that they have
acquired considerable knowledge from the Manilla
captives, who are often of a superior class.

We stayed a day at the Datu's house, waiting the
arrival of our baggage, for which we had despatched

buffaloes. The chief, to show his hospitality, determined to kill a fatted calf to feast us and our followers. The endeavours, first to catch a cow, then a
calf, were very amusing. The beasts were particularly active, half-wild things; and the Bajus gave
chase on horseback, galloping boldly over the rough
ground, and through the long grass. We expected
every moment to see man and horse roll over, but by
dint of hard chasing, at last a half-grown heifer was
driven into the enclosure; man, horse, and game
being equally blown.

In the afternoon we rode over towards Pandasan,
in search of plants; from the summit of the first low
hill we had a beautiful view of the lovely plain of
Tampasuk, extending from the sea far into the interior. Groves of cocoa-nuts were interspersed among
the rice grounds, which extended, intermixed with
grassy fields, to the sea-shore, bounded by a long
line of casuarinas. Little hamlets lay scattered in
all directions, some distinctly visible, others nearly
hidden by the rich green foliage of the fruit-trees.
The prospect was bounded on the west by low sandstone hills, whose red colour occasionally showed
through the lately-burnt grass, affording a varied
tint in the otherwise verdant prospect; to the south,
Kina Balu and its attendant ranges were hidden by
clouds.

Riding on over the undulating ground, we entered
a plain that lies between the districts of Tampasuk
and Pandasan; it looked parched, and was in no way
to be compared to the one we had left: clouds of
smoke from the burning grass occasionally obscured
the prospect. Here Mr. Low found a beautiful gar-

dinia, growing on slight elevations, on barren, decomposing rock, and plentiful wherever the land was undulating. It seemed to flourish in positions exposed to the hottest rays of the sun, and in situations where the reflected heat was also very great. It was a bush, varying from a few inches to two feet in height, and bore flowers of a pure white. We observed some of the shrubs not six inches in height, which were covered with blossoms, yielding a powerful aromatic odour. In fact, as we rode among them, the whole air appeared filled with their fragrance. I imagine the dwarfing of the plants resulted from the inferior nature of the soil, and the great heat which kept the moisture from their roots. The high range that separates these districts from Maludu Bay does not appear to be very far off; in fact, it is but two days' journey on horseback, which, in the mountains, would not be much faster than walking, since the paths are very bad. We galloped home, the natives evidently amused by our novel style of sitting a horse. Our ride had been in a north-easterly direction.

On our arrival at the Datu's house, we found all our followers assembled, and the baggage in heaps near our beds. We therefore made preparations for starting in the morning. On dividing our luggage, however, it appeared that we should require at least a dozen Bajus to assist; these had been promised, but were not forthcoming. Guides to carry nothing were easily procurable; but it being the month of the Ramadhan was an excuse for any amount of laziness.

When we started next morning, the Datu came with us a few miles and helped us with some of his men ; so that, having packed up, we were enabled to leave about nine A.M.  Our route lay through low land for about a mile and a half, crossing the river once.  We stopped at a village situated on and about a low hill.  By the way, we saw a herd of fine cattle, both white and piebald—an unusual colour in Borneo; they were in a very flourishing condition, and I endeavoured in vain to make arrangements to transport the whole lot to my grounds near the Consulate.  We stayed at a house occupied by Rajah Ali, a Baju, for about an hour, trying to get men to take the place of the Datu's, who had helped us so far, but could not tempt really useful men.  We had already four guides, and might have had as many more as we pleased, but porters were not to be procured.

The house where we rested was on top of a little hill, commanding a very extensive prospect: at the foot the river divided into two, one branch stretching away towards the E.S.E., whose course we could trace for eight or ten miles; it then appears to take a southerly direction, towards Kina Balu, from which the natives say it issues : the right-hand branch bore S. by E., and this is visible for several miles—perhaps eight; it then appears to turn more easterly.  Near the banks the ground is generally flat, while towards the west the hills are numerous.

Finding it impossible to get men enough to carry all our things, we resolved to push on with those we had, and then send back for the remainder.  Our impedimenta were numerous, as we had boxes for specimens, planks with quires of brown paper, besides the cloths and brass wire required to purchase provisions.  Every man also was provided with a musket.

16—2

Our course lay at first over hills with soil of a red-dish colour, but a couple of miles brought us to the low land bordering the river.  Here we brought up under a clump of cocoanut palms, to allow our strag-gling party to collect, and having obtained permission, our men soon secured a supply of the fruit.  I have no doubt that many travellers in tropical countries will agree with me, that nothing is more refreshing after a walk in a broiling sun (and it was indeed broiling to-day) than a draught of cocoanut-milk, duly tempered with a dash of wine or brandy.  For some time I preferred a glass of sherry or madeira, now I incline to a tablespoonful of brandy, as forming the most agreeable and healthy compound.  I have seen to day a great many clumps of cocoanut-trees very unhealthy.  I think they must be injured by the constant drain to which they are subjected by the aborigines in extracting toddy from them.  These trees belonged to the Piasau Ida'an, whose villages were scattered in every direction.  Piasau is the word used by the Borneans of the capital for cocoanut.

While reclining under the shade of these palm-trees, we had a beautiful view of the country beyond. The Tampasuk flowed past us, bubbling and break-ing over its uneven bed ; here shallower, and there-fore broader, than usual.  To the left the country was open, almost to the base of the great mountain ; to the right the land was more hilly, and Saduk Saduk showed itself as a high peak, but dwarfed by its neighbourhood to Kina Balu, whose rocky precipices looked now of a purple colour.  The summit was beautiful and clear, and I remained in earnest study of its features till aroused by an exclamation of my companion, who, pointing to a remarkable indentation surmounting an apparently huge fissure in gloomy shade, said, " I am sure that is the spot where I left a bottle in 1851." With the aid of a telescope we could distinctly note the position of every crag, and I determined, if possible, we would visit that fissure, and see if the bottle still remained. Kina Balu looked more grand to-day than ever as there were no hills between us to mar its noble proportions. I made a sketch of the crags on the summit in order to recognize them again, if we should be sufficiently fortunate to reach them.

Having collected our party, now amounting to about thirty, we moved on. Our path lay near the river, which we had to ford eight times, and where the stream was rapid, the operation proved very fatiguing. Between the reaches our path ran over granite *débris* of the size of coarse sand ; it was so hot that it felt painful through our shoes, and those who were barefoot danced along over it as if they were on burning stones :—it was trying walking. We fully intended to have reached Ginambur, but having had so many detentions, we found that at 4 P.M. it was still several miles off; it was useless, therefore, to expect to reach it, particularly as our men, unaccustomed to walking, were greatly fatigued. We determined, therefore, to put up at the farm-houses of the Buñgol Ida'an, which were built conveniently on the banks of the river. It had been threatening rain, which came on before the evening closed in. Our general direction all day had been a little to the east of south.

The Datu of Tampasuk had promised to accompany us himself, but the fast gave him an excellent excuse ; he, however, sent some men as guides, whom

he called his relations.  These men of course came
with us, fancying that by trading for us with the
Ida'an they would be enabled to make a great profit
beyond the regular pay.  They did not fail to let us
know their intentions, by telling us that the Ida'an
were asking half a dollar's worth of goods for a fowl;
so we declined taking it, telling the Bajus that we were
well aware that they themselves could get a dozen for
the same amount.  We expected and intended to let
them fleece us moderately, but this was too barefaced.
We had tin meats,—so managed to make an excellent dinner without the fowl.  Such provisions are
certainly of great assistance to the traveller, but the
addition of a fowl, or of any fresh vegetable, takes
away that unpleasant taste always observable in preserved meats.

It was here I first saw natives ploughing.  Their
plough is of a very simple construction, and serves
rather to scratch the ground than really to turn it
over : it is made entirely of wood, and is drawn by a
buffalo, and its action was the same as if a pointed
stick had been dragged through the land to the depth
of about four inches.  After ploughing, they use a
rough kind of harrow.  Simple as this agriculture
is, it is superior to anything that exists south of
Brunei, and it would be interesting to investigate the
causes that have rendered this small part of Borneo,
between the capital and Maludu Bay, so superior in
agriculture to the rest.  I think it is obviously a
remnant of Chinese civilization.  I must elsewhere
dwell upon the Chinese intercourse, as it is too extensive a subject to be introduced into a journal while
waiting for the cook to get the dinner ready.  The

farm hut in which we spent the night was about twelve feet by six, and of exceedingly neat construction: the bamboo was employed for posts, and split afforded both good flooring and walls; the roofing leaves were also excellent, and made from the sago palm. The musquitoes were very numerous, and soon drove us to bed: the natives assert that these insects are not to be found near running fresh water—a statement which experience completely disproves.

The farmhouse we occupied was one of many scattered over a narrow plain, perhaps four or five hundred yards in breadth, which skirted the banks of the river for several miles. It was evident that these Ida'an kept this land under continued cultivation, and that each portion was strictly private property. We found every house had about four acres of ground belonging to its owner, which were divided from one another by slight embankments. The soil appeared of admirable quality—in fact, a rich black mould. Heaps of panicles were lying near the houses, and the amount seemed to show that they must have had a very good crop last year.

Having induced three Buñgol Ida'an to start with buffaloes to fetch the baggage that was left at Rajah Ali's house, we moved on a little before ten for Ginambur, intending to await their arrival there. Our path lay along the left bank, over low ground covered with long grass and brushwood, which prevented our obtaining other than glimpses of the mountain, but at a rapid we had a good view. The Baju guides gave these Ida'an the character of great thieves, and requested us to have everything carefully put away at night, affirming that these inhabitants

of the plain were of a different character from those
on the hills.  It may be so, but we have never found
the aborigines inclined to pilfer ; on the contrary,
they are remarkably honest ; and should these prove
to be of a different disposition, it will be an unique
instance.   Here as at Buñgol we could not purchase
fowls except at absurd rates, which we declined.  It
is curious that these people show no hospitality—
never offering us a single thing ; but, instead, trying
to overreach us in every transaction.

The house in which we lodged was the best I have
ever seen among the aborigines : it was boarded with
finely-worked planks ; the doors were strong and excellently made, with a small opening for the dogs to
go in and out ; everything looked clean—quite an
unusual peculiarity.   The flooring of beaten-out
bamboos was very neat, and free from all dirt, which
I have never before noticed in a Dayak house, where
the dogs generally render everything filthy.  As this
was the cleanest, so I think my friend the Bisayan
chief's house on the Limbang was the dirtiest—to
describe its abominations would turn the reader's
stomach.

These Ida'an are very good specimens of the interior people—clear-skinned, free from disease, with
pleasant, good-humoured countenances.  None of the
women are good-looking ; still, they would not be
called ugly.  We noticed two peculiarities : that all
the girls and young women wore a piece of black
cloth to conceal their bosoms, which was held in its
place by strips of coloured rattans ; their petticoats
were larger than usual, a practice that might have
been followed with advantage by their elders.   The

second was that the young girls had the front of the
head shaved, after the manner of the Chinese.

I have not noticed that any of the men are
tattooed, but during our walk to-day we met many
large parties of Ida'an loaded with tobacco, who
were on their way to Tampasuk to trade, among
whom there were some ornamented in this fashion:—
A tattooed band two inches broad, stretched in an
arc from each shoulder, meeting on the stomach,
then turning off to the hips; others had likewise
a band extending from the shoulders to the hands.
They were all small, slight men, and armed with
spears and swords.

As we were the first Europeans who had ever
penetrated so far into the country, we excited great
curiosity, particularly among the female portion of
the tribe: every action was watched and commented
upon, though I am bound to state that my little
China boy, Ahtan, with his long tail, excited equal
surprise; and when the black Madras cook commenced operations, we were totally abandoned, and
a most attentive crowd collected round him, watching
his every motion. As he proceeded to prepare the
curry and the stew, the pressure became too great for
his patience, so that he ran out declaring he could
not cook the dinner. The crowd then drew back
a little, but his actions did not escape the most attentive inspection. We were told that there was another
extensive village of their people on the slope of the
hills, embowered in groves of fruit-trees. It is a
great advantage to live on the banks of a running
stream, as all the population can keep themselves
clean by frequent bathing. Another great preven-

tive to disease is their having sufficient food : they
appear well off, with plenty of buffaloes and cattle—
a contrast, indeed, to their miserable brethren on the
Limbang.

We soon began to find the effect of starting without proper shoes : yesterday my boots had blistered
one heel so much that I determined to walk bare-
footed. Mr. Low's feet became likewise so painful
that he made up his mind to follow my example.

Our baggage did not arrive till the morning; we
were then detained to procure men to carry it. At
last Suñgat, the chief, agreed to follow us with six
of the villagers. We started about eleven. Our
course lay along the banks of the river, cutting off
the points, and occasionally in the bed of the old
stream. It having rained on the night previous, the
river was somewhat swollen, which prevented either
ourselves or our men fording it without Baju assistance; this rendered our progress slow. Mr. Low
having never before walked without shoes, suffered
much in passing over the pebbles, which were heated
by the bright mid-day sun, and I also, though more
used to it, felt it very much occasionally : in four
hours we did not make more than three miles.

Having passed a very deep ford at 2.45 P.M., we
agreed to stop for the night, and pitched our tents
on the banks of the river on some dry sand, to have
the benefit of the cool water that flowed by. We
might have gone to the Ida'an houses, but preferred
the independence of our own tents, both as more
cool and less crowded; besides, we were there free
from the suspicion of insects. The fords we passed
during the day were composed of black sand, with

small blocks of granite and serpentine mixed with sandstone.

The name of this place was Batong: from it Kina Balu bore S.E., and Saduk Saduk 15° east of south; the latter appears from this view to be a peaked mountain between 5,000 and 6,000 feet high. Kina Balu of course absorbed our attention: at night, as the sun shone brightly on its peaks, it wore a very smiling appearance. The summit seemed free from all vegetation, and streams of water were dashing over the precipices.

Started next morning at a quarter to eight, and soon arrived at a place where the river divided, the Penantaran coming from an E.N.E. direction. Its bed was full of large blocks of serpentine (though after passing the mouth of this branch we met with very few specimens of that kind of rock). There is a village of the same name as the branch close to the junction. We followed the right-hand branch— direction about south—keeping close to the banks, crossing and recrossing continually, seeing occasionally a few houses. We were now passing through sand-stone ranges, but the country had no remarkable features. At 9.40, stopped to breakfast, having made about four miles; our followers gradually closed up. At eleven we pushed on again. Huge granite boulders are now common, and under the shelter of one mighty stone we rested for half an hour, waiting the arrival of our straggling followers.

One of the greatest advantages of travelling with an intelligent companion is the interchange of ideas, and consequently the more accurate noting of obser-vations. As we sat beneath the shade of the huge granite boulder, surrounded on all sides by sandstone hills, we could not but speculate how it came there. Without having recourse to the glacier theory, the reason appeared to me simple.    It is evident that the level of the country was very much greater in former times than at present, and that water is the great agent by which these changes have been effected.

The streams continually cut their way deeper in the soil, as we may daily observe : the increasing steepness causes innumerable landslips, and the process going on for ages, the whole level of the country is changed, and plains are formed from the detritus at the mouths of the rivers.    Huge granite masses, falling originally from the lofty summit of Kina Balu, would gradually slip or roll down the ever-forming slopes which nature is never weary of creating.

In ascending some of the steeps that rise on either side of the streams near Kina Balu, we continually came across boulders of granite, which, in comparatively few years, will, through landslips, roll many hundred feet into the stream below, to commence their gradual movement from the mountain.    I have continually come across evidences of the Bornean rivers having flowed at a much higher level than at present, finding layers of water-worn pebbles, a hundred feet above the present surface of the stream.    In Borneo, where the rain falls so heavily, the power of water is immense.    After a heavy storm, the torrents rise in confined spaces often fifty feet within a few hours, and the rush of the stream would move any but the largest rocks, and wash away most of the effects of the landslips.

Standing on a height overlooking a large extent of country, it is instructive to be able to survey at a glance the great effect caused by the rivers and all their tributaries, deep gullies marking every spot where an accession joins the parent stream. After heavy rains, the rivers present the colour of *café au lait*, from the large amount of matter held in temporary suspension, and on taking out a glassful, I have been surprised by the amount of sediment which has immediately fallen to the bottom.

The walk was becoming rather tiring ; drizzling rain rendering the stones very slippery, and having continually to make the mountain torrent our path, it was severe work for our bare feet. The rain continuing, and the stream rapidly rising, we halted at some farmhouses in the midst of a long rice-field. Fording the river is difficult work ; the water rushing down at headlong speed, renders it necessary to exert one's utmost strength to avoid being carried away : the pole in both hands, placed well to seaward, one foot advanced cautiously before the other, to avoid the slippery rocks and loose stones. I found that this fatigued me more than the walking. The water became much cooler as we approached the mountain, while the land is rapidly increasing in elevation. The river was full of Ida'an fish-traps, made by damming up half the stream, and forcing the water and fish to pass into a huge bamboo basket. They appeared to require much labour in the construction, particularly in the loose stone walls or dams. As we advanced, we found the whole stream turned into one of these traps, in which they captured very fine fish, particularly after heavy rain. I bought one with large scales, about eighteen inches long, which was of a delicious flavour.

To see the young Ida'an ford the stream, raised both my envy and my admiration; with the surging waters reaching to their armpits, with a half-dancing motion, they crossed as if it were no exertion at all. So much for practice. During the last three hours we did not make more than four miles, though out of the stream the paths were good. The rain continuing to pour heavily, we determined to stop, as I have said, at these Ida'an huts, which were situated opposite the landing-place of the village of Tambatuan, concealed by the brow of a steep hill rising on the other bank. We sent a party there to buy rice, which became cheaper as we advanced: these villages also possessed abundance of cattle and buffaloes. We were much pleased to find the great confidence shown by the people; we often met parties of women and girls, and on no occasion did they run away screaming at the unusual sight of a white face. Several of them came this afternoon to look at us, and remained quite near for some time, interested in watching our proceedings. Kina Balu was cloud-hidden this evening.

During the night our rest was much disturbed by bees, who stung us several times, and Mr. Low, with that acuteness which never deserts him in all questions of natural history, pronounced them to be the "tame" bees, the same as he had last seen thirteen years ago among the Senah Dayaks in Sarawak. About midnight we were visited by a big fellow, who, our guides assured us, wanted to pilfer; but we found next morning that he had come to complain of his hives having been plundered. On inquiry, we discovered the man who had done the deed. He was fined three times the value of the damage, and the amount handed over to the owner.

A great many questions were asked as to what could be our object in visiting Kina Balu: to tell them that it was for curiosity would have been useless: to say that we were seeking new kinds of ferns, pitcher-plants, or flowers, would not have been much more satisfactory to them. Some thought we were searching for copper or for gold, while others were equally convinced we were looking for precious stones. One man sagaciously observed that we were seeking the *Lagundi* tree, whose fruit, if eaten, would restore our youth and enable us to live for countless years, and that tree was to be found on the very summit of Kina Balu. To-day an Ida'an came, I suppose to try us, and said he knew of copper not more than half a day's journey from our path, and offered to take us to it; seeing we were not to be tempted, another told us of a tree of copper that was to be found a few miles off; but even that did not alter our determination to make the best of our way to the mountain. We left the questioners sadly puzzled as to what possibly could be our object in ascending Kina Balu.

All the Bajus and Borneans are convinced that there is a lake on the very summit of this mountain, and ask, if it be not so, how is it that continual streams of water flow down its sides. They forget that very few nights pass without there being rain among the lofty crags, even when it is dry on the plains. Sometimes the sun, shining on particular portions of the granite, gives it an appearance of

great brilliancy; and those who formerly ascended
the summit with Mr. Low, reported that whenever
they approached the spot where these diamonds
showed themselves at a distance, they invariably disappeared: as these men have a perfect faith in
every wild imagination of the *Arabian Nights*.
they easily convinced themselves and their auditors
that the jinn would not permit them to take them.
The old story of the great diamond, guarded on
the summit of Kina Balu by a ferocious dragon,
arose probably from some such cause. The Malays
are great storytellers, and these wonders interest
them. I may notice that most of the men that were
with us accompanied us to the mountain of Molu the
preceding February, and then one of the Borneans
commenced a story which lasted the seventeen days
we were away, and he occasionally went on with it
during our present journey. It was the history of an
unfortunate princess, who for " seven days and seven
nights neither eat nor drank, but only wept."

Opposite our resting-place we observed some remarkably elegant tree ferns, whose stems rose occasionally to the height of ten feet, and with their long
leaves bending gracefully on every side, they were
an ornament to the river's bank. We noticed as yet
but little old forest. The only fine trees we saw
were near the villages, and these were preserved for
their fruits. Where the land is not cultivated, it is
either covered with brushwood, or trees of a young
growth.

Drizzling rain prevented our departure till near
eight, when we continued our course along the rice-
fields: we had been told we should find the path

very bad, but were agreeably surprised by it proving
dry and principally among plantations of kiladi.
We crossed the river only five times, and passed
over a sandstone range about five hundred feet
above the plain: it was nearly three miles from
our resting-place.   The stream had now become a
perfect mountain torrent, breaking continually over
rocks.

Occasionally the fords were difficult, as the continued rains rendered the river very full.   At one
place where an island divides the Tampasuk, it was
so deep that it was found necessary to swim over,
and only a very expert man could have done it, as
the water rushed down with great force.   The Bajus,
however, were quite prepared; they did not attempt
to cross the stream in a direct course, but allowed
themselves to be carried away a little, and reached
the other side about fifty yards farther down.   They
did it very cleverly, carrying all our luggage over,
little by little, swimming with one hand and holding
the baskets in the air with the other.   As we could
not swim, two men placed themselves, one on either
side of us, told us to throw ourselves flat on the water
and remain passive; in a few minutes we were comfortably landed on the opposite bank, drenched to the
skin, it is true, but we had scarcely had any dry
clothes on us during the whole journey ; however, no
sooner did we arrive at our resting-places, than we
stripped, bathed, rubbed ourselves into a glow, and
put on dry clothes.   Nothing is so essential as this
precaution, and I have twice had severe attacks of
fever from neglecting it.   The hills as we advanced
began closing in on the river's banks, leaving

occasionally but a narrow strip of flat ground near the stream.

At 11.20 A.M. we reached Koung, a large, scattered village on a grassy plain: it is a very pretty spot, the greensward extending to the river's banks, where the cattle and buffaloes graze: about a hundred feet up the side of a neighbouring hill is another portion of the village. The roaring torrent foams around, affording delicious spots for bathing, the water being delightfully cool. In the bed of the stream there were masses of angular granite, mixed with the water-worn boulders. It was the first time we had ever seen it of that sharp form, but similar blocks were afterwards noticed on the summit. The wild raspberry is very plentiful here. One cannot help having one's attention continually drawn to the air of comfort, or, rather, to the appearance of native wealth observed among the Ida'an: food in abundance, with cattle, pigs, fowls, rice, and vegetables; and no one near them to plunder or exact. Accustomed as I had been to the aborigines around the capital, the contrast struck me forcibly.

Next day we hoped to reach Kiau, the village from which Mr. Low started for the mountain in the spring of 1851. There was an apparent hitch about getting from that place; but we thought perhaps the reports arose from tribal jealousy. At four P.M., Koung: barometer, 28·678°; thermometer, 77·5°; unattached, 78·3°. So that this village must be about 1,500 feet above the level of the sea: a very rapid rise for the stream in so short a distance. The sandstone hill we crossed to-day had the same characteristics as those I had observed up the Sakarang, Batang Lupar, and near the capital

—all being very steep, with narrow ridges, and buttresses occasionally springing from their sides : on the one we crossed to-day was a quantity of red shale.

Near our last night's resting-place, I noticed, for the first time on this river, some sago palms; they have again shown themselves to-day, and there are a few round the village, but neither these trees nor cocoanut nor areca palms are plentiful. At every village I made inquiries about cotton, and, like the men with tails, it was always grown a little farther off; only we know cotton must be grown somewhere in this neighbourhood, as at the very moment I was writing my journal I saw an old woman engaged spinning yarn from native material. The Lanuns also furnish a cloth which is highly prized among every class of inhabitants in Borneo ; it is a sort of checked black cloth, with narrow lines of white running through it, and glazed on one size. This was formerly made entirely of native yarn ; but I am afraid this industry will soon decline, as connoisseurs are already beginning to discover that the Lanun women, finding English yarn so cheap, are using it in preference, though it renders the article much less durable. It is also worthy of notice that this cloth is dyed from indigo grown on the spot. These Ida'an purchase their supplies of cotton of the Inserban and Tuhan Ida'an who live on the road to the lake, while the Bajus obtain theirs from the Lobas near Maludu Bay. I saw one plant growing near the hut where we rested last night ; it was about ten feet high, and covered with flowers.

They told us at Koung that the Ida'an were at war; but though they may have quarrels, they must

17—2

be trifling, as we met every day women and children
by themselves at considerable distances from their
houses. Besides, parties of a dozen men and boys
of the supposed enemies passed us on their way to
Tampasuk to trade, and in none of their villages
did we notice heads.

All these Ida'an appear to pay particular attention
to the cultivation of the Kiladi (arum), planting it in
their fields immediately after gathering in the rice
crop, and keeping it well weeded: they grow it everywhere, and it must afford them abundance of food.
It is in shape something like a beetroot, and has the
flavour of a yam. Roasted in the ashes, and brought
smoking hot to table, torn open, and adding a little
butter, pepper, and salt, it is very palatable, particularly among those hills.

Saduk bore N.E. and Kina Balu due E. from the
southern portion of the village.

Started about seven in a S.E. by E. direction,
ascending a hill on which the village of Labang
Labang is situated: here occurred a scene. Mr. Low
and I, with a few men, were walking ahead of the party ;
as we passed the first house, an old woman came to
the door, and uttered some sentences which struck us
as sounding like a curse: however, we took no notice ;
but as we approached the end of the village, we were
hailed by an ugly-looking fellow, with an awful squint,
who told us to stop, as we should not pass through
his village: this was evidently a prepared scene, the
whole of the population turning out, armed: so we
did stop to discuss the point. We asked what he
meant: he answered that they had never had good
crops since Mr. Low ascended the mountain in 1851,

and gave many other sapient reasons why we should not ascend it now; but he wound up by saying that if we would pay a slave as black mail, they would give us permission to pass and do as we pleased: this showed us that nothing but extortion was intended; yet, to avoid any disagreeable discussion, we offered to make him a present of forty yards of grey shirting; but this proposition was not listened to, and he and his people became very insolent in their manner.

We sent back one of the men to hurry up the stragglers, and in the meantime continued the discussion. They then said they would take us up the mountain if we would start from their village; but being unwilling to risk a disappointment, we declined. They remembered how the Kiaus had turned back Mr. Lobb, because he would not submit to their extortions, and thought they might do the same with us. As the Ida'an were shaking their spears and giving other hostile signs, we thought it time to bring this affair to a climax; so I ordered the men to load their muskets, and Mr. Low, stepping up to the chief with his five-barrelled pistol, told the interpreter to explain that we were peaceable travellers, most unwilling to enter into any contest; that we had obtained the permission of the Government of the country, and that we were determined to proceed; that if they carried out their threats of violence, he would shoot five with his revolver, and that I was prepared to do the same with mine; that they might, by superior numbers, overcome us at last, but in the meantime we would make a desperate fight of it.

This closed the scene: as long as we had only

half a dozen with us, they were bullies; but as our
forces began to arrive, and at last amounted to fifty
men, with twenty musket-barrels shining among them,
they became as gentle as lambs, and said they would
take two pieces of grey shirting; but we refused to
give way, keeping to our original offer, and then only
if the chief would follow us on our return, and receive
it at Tampasuk.  We ordered the men to advance,
and we would close up the rear: no opposition was
offered; on the contrary, the chief accompanied us
on our road, and we had no more trouble with the
Labang Labang people.  We were detained forty
minutes by this affair.  Our guides explained the
matter to us: when Mr. Low was here last time, many
reports were spread of the riches which the Kiaus
had obtained from the white man, and they were
jealous that the other branch of their tribe should
obtain the wealth that was passing from them through
their village.  The Koung people tried to persuade
us last night to start from their place, and as they
were very civil we should have liked to oblige them,
but they were uncertain whether they could take us
to the summit.  Mr. Lobb, when he reached Kiau,
had but a small party, and was unarmed, so they
would not allow him to pass, except on terms that
were totally inadmissible.

Immediately after passing the village, we descended
a steep and slippery path to one of the torrents into
which the Tampasuk now divided.  After crossing it,
we were at the base of the spur on which the village
of Kiau is situated.  We passed several purling
streams which descended, in a winding course, the
face of the hill.  From one spot in our walk, we had

a beautiful view of two valleys, cultivated on both banks, with the foaming streams dashing among the rocks below. Over the landscape were scattered huts, which had the peculiarity of being flat-roofed: the Kiaus using the bamboo as the Chinese use their tiles, split in two; the canes are arranged side by side across the whole roof, with their concave sides upwards to catch the rain; then a row placed convex to cover the edges of the others, and prevent the water dropping through. They are quite water-tight, and afforded an excellent hint for travellers where bamboos abound.

The latter portion of the road was difficult climbing, the clay being slippery from last night's rain; but as we approached our resting-place, the walking became easier. Kiau is a large village on the southern side of the spur. The houses scattered on its face are prettily concealed from each other by clumps of cocoanuts and bamboos. It covers a great extent of ground, but is badly placed, being more than 800 feet above the torrent—that is, the portion of the village at which we stayed. The eastern end was nearer the stream. The inhabitants supplied themselves with drinking-water from small rills which were led in bamboos to most of their doors. We brought up about eleven, our course being generally E.S.E. Thermometer 73° at twelve in the house. We felt it chilly, and took to warm clothing.

The Kiaus are much dirtier than any tribes I have seen in the neighbourhood: the children and women are unwashed, and most of them are troubled with colds, rendering them in every sense unpleasant neighbours. In fact, to use the words of an experienced traveller, "they cannot afford to be clean," their climate is chilly, and they have no suitable clothing. We observed that the features of many of these people were very like Chinese—perhaps a trace of that ancient kingdom of Celestials that tradition fixes to this neighbourhood. They all showed the greatest and most childlike curiosity at everything either we or our servants did.

In the afternoon, Lemaing, Mr. Low's old guide, came in. Mr. Low recognized his voice immediately, though seven years had passed since he had heard it. Sir James Brooke has a most extraordinary faculty of remembering voices, as well as names, even of natives whom he has only seen once. It is very useful out here, and I have often found the awkwardness which arises from my quickly forgetting both voices and names.

Shortly after Lemaing's arrival, a dispute arose between him and Lemoung, the chief of the house in which we were resting : both voices grew excited ; at last, they jumped up, and each spat upon the floor in a paroxysm of mutual defiance : here we interposed to preserve the peace, and calm being restored, it was found that seven years ago they had disputed about the division of Mr. Low's goods, and the quarrel had continued ever since—the whole amount being five dollars. Lemoung said that his house had been burnt down in consequence of the white man ascending Kina Balu, and that no good crops of rice had grown since ; but it was all envy ; he thought in the distribution he had not secured a fair share. We asked if he had ascended the mountain ; he said no, but his son had brought some rice, for which, on inquiry, we found he had been paid. Drizzling rain the whole afternoon.

The thermometer registered 66° last night, and we enjoyed our sleep under blankets. At mid-day, we took out the barometer from its case, and found, to our inexpressible vexation, that it was utterly smashed. This will destroy half the pleasure of the ascent; in fact, our spirits are somewhat depressed by the accident, and by Mr. Low's feet getting worse. At twelve, thermometer 77°. (The lamentable accident so disgusted me that I find no further entry in that day's journal, but a pencilled note remarks that the Ida'an preserve their rice in old bamboos two fathoms long, which are placed on one side of the doorway. It is said that these bamboos are preserved for generations, and, in fact, they looked exceedingly ancient.)

Last night, thermometer 69°. At early dawn, we heard the war-drums beating in several houses, and shouts and yells from the boys. They said it was a fête day, but we rightly guessed it had something to do with our expedition. For some time, our guide did not make his appearance, and a few young fellows on the hill over the village threw stones as we appeared at the door—a very harmless demonstration, as they were several hundred yards off—but discharging and cleaning a revolver lessened the amount of hostile shouting. About nine, the guide made his appearance; the women seemed to enjoy the scene, and followed us to witness the skirmish; but the enemy, if there were an enemy, did not show, and the promised ambush came to nothing—it was but a trick of Lemoung to try and disgust Lemaing, and frighten us by the beating of drums and shouting. At the place where we were assured an attack would be made, we found but a few harmless women carrying tobacco.

Our path lay along the side of the hill in which the village stands, we followed it about four miles in an easterly direction, and then descended to a torrent, one of the feeders of the Tampasuk, where we determined to spend the night, as Mr. Low's feet were becoming very swollen and painful, and it was as well to collect the party. We had passed through considerable fields of sweet potatoes, kiladi, and tobacco, where the path was crossed occasionally by cool rills from the mountains. We enjoyed the cold water very much, and had a delightful bath. The torrent comes tumbling down, and forms many fine cascades. Mr. Low botanized a little, notwithstanding his feet were suppurating. The hut in which we spent the night was very pretty-looking, flat-roofed, built entirely of bamboos.

To-day, we had a specimen of the thieving of our Ida'an followers. One man was caught burying a tin of sardines; another stole a Bologna sausage, for which, when hungry, I remembered him, and another a fowl.

Next morning, Mr. Low found it impossible to walk, and I was therefore obliged to start without him. We showed our perfect confidence in the villagers of Kiau by dividing our party, leaving only four men with Mr. Low to take care of the arms; we carried with us up the mountain nothing but our swords and one revolver. They must have thought us a most extraordinary people; but we

knew that their demonstrations of hostility were
really harmless, and more aimed against each other
than against us. Probably, had we appeared afraid,
it might have been a different matter.

Our course was at first nearly east up the sub-spur
of a great buttress. The walking was severe, from
the constant and abrupt ascents and descents, and
the narrowness of the path when it ran along the
sides of the hill, where it was but the breadth of the
foot. At one place we had a view of a magnificent
cascade. The stream that runs by the cave, which is
to be one of our resting-places, falls over the rocks
forming minor cascades ; then coming to the edge of
the precipice, throws itself over, and in its descent of
above fifteen hundred feet appears to diffuse itself
in foam, ere it is lost in the depths of the dark-
wooded ravines below.

I soon found I had made a great mistake in permit-
ting these active mountaineers to lead the way at their
own pace, as before twelve o'clock I was left alone with
them, all my men being far behind, as they were
totally unaccustomed to the work. Arriving at a little
foaming rivulet, I sat down and waited for the rest of
the party, and when they came up, they appeared so
exhausted that I had compassion on them, and agreed
to spend the night here. The Ida'an were very dissatisfied, and declared they would not accompany us,
if we intended to make such short journeys ; but we
assured them that we would go on alone if they left us,
and not pay them the stipulated price for leading us
to the summit. I soon set the men to work to build a
hut of long poles, over which we could stretch our
oiled cloths, and to make a raised floor to secure us

from being wet through by the damp moss and heavy rain that would surely fall during the night. At three P.M. the thermometer fell to 65°, which to the children of the plain rendered the air unpleasantly cold; but we worked hard to collect boughs and leaves to make our beds soft; and wood was eagerly sought for to make fires in the holes beneath our raised floor. This filled the place with smoke, but gave some warmth to the men.

The Ida'an again tried to get back, but I would not receive their excuse that they would be up early in the morning: they then set hard at work going through incantations to drive away sickness. The guide Lemaing carried an enormous bundle of charms, and on him fell the duty of praying or repeating some forms: he was at it two hours by my watch. To discover what he said, or the real object to whom he addressed himself, was almost impossible through the medium of our bad interpreters. I could hear him repeating my name, and they said he was soliciting the spirits of the mountain to favour us.

The thermometer registered 57° last night in tent. Started at seven; I observed a fine yellow sweet-scented rhododendron on a decayed tree, and requested my men on their return to take it to Mr. Low; continuing the ascent, after an hour's tough walking, reached the top of the ridge. There it was better for a short time; but the forest, heavily hung with moss, is exposed to the full force of the south-west monsoon, and the trees are bent across the path, leaving occasionally only sufficient space to crawl through. We soon came upon the magnificent pitcher-plant, the *Nepenthes Lowii*, that Mr. Low was anxious to get. We could find no young plants, but took cuttings, which the natives said would grow.

We stopped to breakfast at a little swampy spot, where the trees are becoming very stunted, though in positions protected from the winds they grow to a great height. Continuing our course, we came upon a jungle that appeared to be composed almost entirely of rhododendrons, some with beautiful pink, crimson, and yellow flowers. I sat near one for about half an hour apparently in intense admiration, but, in fact, very tired, and breathless, and anxious about my followers, only one of whom had kept up with me.

Finding it useless to wait longer, as the mist was beginning to roll down from the summit, and the white plain of clouds below appeared rising, I pushed on to the cave, which we intended to occupy. It was a huge granite boulder, resting on the hill side, that sheltered us but imperfectly from the cold wind. The Ida'an, during the day, amused themselves in trying to secure some small twittering birds, which looked like canaries, with a green tint on the edges of their wings, but were unsuccessful. They shot innumerable pellets from their blowpipes, but did not secure one. In fact, they did not appear to use this instrument with any skill.

At four o'clock the temperature of the air was 52°, and of the water 48°.

Some of my men did not reach us till after dark, and it was with great difficulty that I could induce the Malays to exert themselves to erect the oiled cloths, to close the mouth of the cave, and procure sufficient firewood. They appeared paralyzed by the cold, and were unwilling to move.

During the night, the thermometer at the entrance of the cave fell to 36° 5'; and on my going out to have a look at the night-scene, all the bushes and trees appeared fringed with hoar frost.

After breakfasting at the cave, we started for the summit. Our course lay at first through a thick low jungle, full of rhododendrons; it then changed into a stunted brushwood, that almost hid the rarely-used path; gradually the shrubs gave way to rocks, and then we commenced our ascent over the naked granite. A glance upwards from the spot where we first left the jungle, reveals a striking scene—a face of granite sweeping steeply up for above 3,000 feet to a rugged edge of pointed rocks; while on the farthest left the southern peak looked from this view a rounded mass. Here and there small runnels of water passed over the granite surface, and patches of brushwood occupied the sheltered nooks. The rocks were often at an angle of nearly forty degrees, so that I was forced to ascend them, at first, with woollen socks, and when they were worn through, with bare feet. It was a sad alternative, as the rough stone wore away the skin and left a bleeding and tender surface.

After hard work, we reached the spot where Mr. Low had left a bottle, and found it intact—the writing in it was not read, as I returned it unopened to its resting-place.

Low's Gully is one of the most singular spots in the summit. We ascend an abrupt ravine, with towering perpendicular rocks on either side, till a rough natural wall bars the way. Climbing on this, you look over a deep chasm, surrounded on three sides by precipices, so deep that the eye could not reach the bottom ; but the twitter of innumerable swallows could be distinctly heard, as they flew in flocks below. There was no descending here : it was a sheer precipice of several thousand feet, and this was the deep fissure pointed out to me by Mr. Low from the cocoanut grove on the banks of the Tampasuk when we were reclining there, and proved that he had remembered the very spot where he had left the bottle.

I was now anxious to reach one of those peaks which are visible from the sea; so we descended Low's Gully, through a thicket of rhododendrons, bearing a beautiful blood-coloured flower, and made our way to the westward. It was rough walking at first, while we continued to skirt the rocky ridge that rose to our right; but gradually leaving this, we advanced up an incline composed entirely of immense slabs of granite, and reaching the top, found a noble terrace, half a mile in length, whose sides sloped at an angle of thirty degrees on either side. The ends were the Southern Peak and a huge cyclopean wall.

I followed the guides to the former, and after a slippery ascent, reached the summit. I have mentioned that this peak has a rounded aspect when viewed from the eastward ; but from the northward it appears to rise sharply to a point ; and when with great circumspection I crawled up, I found myself on a granite point, not three feet in width, with but a water-worn way a few inches broad to rest on, and prevent my slipping over the sloping edges.

During the climbing to-day, I suffered slightly from shortness of breath, and felt some disinclination to bodily exertion ; but as soon as I sat down on this lofty point, it left me, and a feeling came on as if the air rendered me buoyant and made me long to float away.

Calmly seated here, I first turned my attention to the other peaks, which stretched in a curved line from east to west, and was rather mortified to find that the most westerly and another to the east appeared higher than where I sat, but certainly not more than a hundred feet. The guides called this the mother of the mountain, but her children may have outgrown her. Turning to the south-west, I could but obtain glimpses of the country, as many thousand feet below masses of clouds passed continually over the scene, giving us but a partial view of sea, and rivers, and hills. One thing immediately drew my attention, and that was a very lofty peak towering above the clouds, bearing S. $\frac{1}{4}$ E. It appeared to be an immense distance off, and I thought it might be the great mountain of Lawi, of which I went in search some months later; but it must be one much farther to the eastward, and may be the summit of Tilong, which, as I have before mentioned, some declare to be much more lofty than Balu itself.

Immediately below me, the granite for a thousand feet sloped sharply down to the edge of that lofty precipice that faces the valley of Pinokok to the south-west.    I felt a little nervous while we were passing along this to reach the southern peak, as on Mr. Low's former expedition a Malay had slipped at a less formidable spot, and been hurried down the steep incline at a pace that prevented any hope of his arresting his own progress, when leaning on his side his kris fortunately entered a slight cleft, and arrested him on the verge of a precipice.

Among the detached rocks and in the crevices grew a kind of moss, on which the Ida'an guides declared the spirits of their ancestors fed. A grass also was pointed out that served for the support of the ghostly buffaloes which always followed their masters to the other world. As a proof, the print of a foot was shown me as that of a young buffalo; it was not very distinct, but appeared more like the impression left by a goat or deer.

Our guides became very nervous as the clouds rose and now occasionally topped the precipice, and broke, and swept up the slopes, enveloping us. They urged me to return; I saw it was necessary, and complied, as the wind was rising, and the path we were to follow was hidden in mist.

We found the air pleasantly warm and very invigorating; the thermometer marked 62° in the shade; and as we perceived little rills of water oozing from among the granite rocks, the summit would prove a much better encamping ground than our cold cave, where the sun never penetrates. The Ida'an, however, feared to spend one night in this abode of spirits, and declined carrying my luggage.

Our return was rather difficult, as the misty rain rendered the rocks slippery, but we all reached the cave in safety. Here I received a note from Mr. Low, but he was still unable to walk. The bathing water was 49°.

During the night the temperature fell, and the registering thermometer marked 41°. My feet were so injured by yesterday's walking that I was unable to

reascend the mountain to collect plants and flowers, so
sent my head man Musa with a large party.  I, however, strolled about a little to look for seeds and a
sunny spot, as the ravine in which our temporary
home was, chilled me through.  I was continually
enveloped in mist, and heard afterwards to my regret
that the summit was clear, and that all the surrounding country lay exposed to view.  The low, tangled
jungle was too thick to admit of our seeing much.
I climbed the strongest and highest trees there, but
could only get glimpses of distant hills.

Thermometer during the night, 43°, while in the
cave yesterday it marked 56° at two o'clock.

Started early to commence our descent, collecting
a few plants on our way ; the first part of the
walking is tolerably good—in fact, as far as the
spot where we rested for breakfast on our ascent.
It is in appearance a series of mighty steps.  Passed
on the wayside innumerable specimens of that curious
pitcher-plant the *Nepenthes villosa*, with serrated
lips.

After leaving the great steps, our course was along
the edge of a ridge, where the path is extremely narrow ; in fact, in two or three places not above eighteen
inches wide—a foot of it serving as parapet, six inches
of sloping rock forming the path.  From one of these
craggy spots a noble landscape is spread before us,
eighty miles of coast-line, with all the intervening
country being visible at once.  With one or two exceptions, plains skirt the sea-shore, then an undulating
country, gradually rising to ranges varying from two
to three thousand feet, with glimpses of silvery streams
flowing among them. The waters of the Mengkabong

and Sulaman, swelling to the proportions of lakes, add a diversity to the scene.

It is fortunate that the ridge is not often so narrow as at these spots; for on one side there is a sheer descent of fifteen hundred feet, and on the other is very perpendicular ground, but wooded. Two decaying rocks that obstruct the path are also dangerous to pass, as we had to round them, with uncertain footing, and nothing but a bare, crumbling surface to grasp. With the exception of these, the path is not difficult or tiring, until we leave the ridge and descend to the right towards the valleys: then it is steep, slippery, and very fatiguing, and this continues for several miles, until we have lowered the level nearly four thousand feet. The path, in fact, is as vile as path can be.

By the time I reached the hut where I had left Mr. Low, I felt completely exhausted; but a little rest, a glass of brandy-and-water, and a bathe in the dashing torrent that foamed among the rocks at our feet, thoroughly restored me. The water here felt pleasant after the bitter cold of that near the cave. My companion had employed his time collecting plants, though his feet were not at all better.

Next morning we manufactured a kind of litter, on which Mr. Low was to be carried, and then started along a path that skirted the banks of the Kalupis, that flows beneath the village, and is, in fact, the source of the Tampasuk. We passed through several fields of tobacco, as well as of yams and kiladis; the first is carefully cultivated, and not a weed was to be observed among the plants. Leaving the water, we pushed up the steep bank to the lower houses of the

village, and made our way on to Lemoung's, to
reach it just as a drenching shower came on.

Here we found one of our Baju guides, who had been
sent back to construct rafts for the return voyage.  I
was not sorry to find that some had been prepared,
as it appeared otherwise necessary that Mr. Low
should be carried the whole way.

The villagers said they were at war even during
the time we were at their houses with a neighbouring
tribe, which induces them to bear arms wherever they
may go; but the whole affair must be very trifling, as
they sleep at their farms, and we saw, totally unpro-
tected, troops of girls and women at work in the
fields.

We thought it better to make some complaints of
the dishonesty shown, before we ascended the mountain; they were profuse in apologies, but they had
evidently enjoyed the sausage.

We spent the afternoon and evening in settling
all claims against us, and having completed that
work, ordered the rest of our baggage to be packed up
ready for an early start next morning.  Among the
undistributed goods was about twenty pounds weight
of thick brass wire.  While I was away bathing,
Lemaing coolly walked off with it; but on my return
Mr. Low informed me of what had occurred.  Knowing
that if we permitted this to pass unnoticed, it would
be a signal for a general plunder, we determined to
recover the wire.  As Mr. Low could not move, I
went by myself in search of Lemaing, and soon heard
his voice speaking loudly in the centre of a dense
crowd of the villagers.  I forced my way through,
and found him seated, with the brass wire in his

hand, evidently pointing out its beauty to an admiring audience. I am afraid I very much disconcerted him, as with one hand I tore the prize from his grasp, and with the other put a revolver to his head, and told him to beware of meddling with our baggage. I never saw a look of greater astonishment; he tried to speak, but the words would not come, and the crowd opening, I bore back the trophy to our end of the village house.

The Bajus told us we should find the Ida'an of the plains dishonest, while those of the hills had the contrary reputation. We lost nothing in the plains; here we had to guard carefully against pilferers.

We noticed that as we gradually receded from the sea, the clothing of the inhabitants became less—on the plains all the Ida'an wore trousers and jackets; at Koung and Kiau very few, and we were assured that those in the interior wore nothing but bark waist-cloths.

An incident occurred the evening before our departure, which showed how the Ida'an distrust each other. Among the goods we paid to our guides were twenty fathoms of thick brass wire; the coils were put down before them; they talked over it for two hours, and could not settle either the division, or who should take care of it until morning; at length one by one all retired and left the wire before us, the last man pushing it towards Musa, asking him to take charge of it. Not relishing this trust, he carried it to Li Moung's house, and placing it in the midst of the crowd, left it, and they then quarrelled over it till morning.

We thought last night every claim had been settled,

but this morning they commenced again, anxious to
prevent any goods leaving their village. We ourselves did not care to take back to our pinnace anything that was not necessary to enable us to pay our
way. We made liberal offers to them if they would
carry Mr. Low to the next village, but they positively
refused to assist us farther. We therefore collected
our Malays outside the place, and prepared to start ;
and were on the point of doing so, when shouts in the
village house attracted our attention, and a man ran
out to say that they were plundering the baggage left
in charge of the Buñgol Ida'an. As this consisted
of our clothes and cooking utensils, it was not to be
borne, and I ran back into the house, where I found
a couple of hundred men surrounding our Ida'an followers and undoing the packages ; they were startled
by the sight of my rifle, and when they heard the rush
caused by the advance of Mr. Low and our Malays,
they fled to the end of the house, and soon disappeared
through the opposite door. The panic seemed to
cause the greatest amusement to the girls of this
house, who talked and laughed, and patted us on the
shoulders, and appeared to delight in the rapid flight
of their countrymen. None of their own relatives,
however, had joined in the affair.

Mr. Low's rapid advance to my support surprised
me ; but I found that with the assistance of a servant
he had hopped the whole of the way, revolver in
hand. Our men behaved with remarkable resolution,
and would have driven off the whole village had it
been necessary. One Malay got so excited, that he
commenced a war dance, and had we not instantly
interfered, would have worked himself up to run a

muck among the Ida'an.    Though we wished to
frighten them into honesty towards us, we were most
anxious that not the slightest wound should be given,
and I may here remark, that in none of our journeys
have we ever found it necessary to use our weapons
against the inhabitants.    We discovered that showing ourselves prepared to fight, if necessary, prevented
its being ever necessary to fight.

We pushed on to Koung by a path that led below
Labang Labang, Mr. Low suffering severely from the
necessity of having to walk six miles over stony
country with suppurating feet.

At Koung we vainly endeavoured to obtain a
buffalo, on which Mr. Low might ride; but the
villagers showed no inclination to assist.    So next
morning we pushed on through heavy rain to the
village of Tambatuan, where the Tampasuk becomes
a little more fit for rafts.    I was glad to see Mr. Low
safely there, and then, as the rafts would not hold us
all, I walked on with the men.    The heavy rain had
caused the river to swell, and the walking and the
fording were doubly difficult, but we continued our
course, and in two days reached the village of
Ginambur, and joining Mr. Low on the raft, pursued
our journey to the Datu's house.

Next day to the Abai; but contrary winds prevented our reaching Labuan for five days.

We were not quite satisfied with the results of this
expedition, and determined to start again, but
choosing another route, the same followed by Mr.
Low in 1851.

# CHAPTER IX.

## SECOND ASCENT OF KINA BALU.

IN June, 1858, the cholera which had been slowly
advancing towards us from the south, suddenly burst

upon Brunei with extreme violence, and laid the city
in mourning.   From day to day the deaths increased
in number; every house flew white streamers, which
showed cholera was there present; pious processions
paraded the town, the mosques were crowded, all
merriment at an end, though religious chants were
heard from every boat; there was fear, but no panic,
and the sick were cared for by their relations.   The
deaths were awfully sudden, one of my servants at
work at five, was dead by eleven.   My house was
crowded by anxious parents seeking medicine, which
was soon all distributed, and no one thought of
business, attention being only given to this fearful
scourge.

Mr. Low and I had determined to make another
attempt to ascend Kina Balu in August, but fearing
that if the cholera spread along the coast before we
reached our point of debarkation, the Dusuns and
Ida'an might prevent our passing through their villages, we resolved to anticipate the appointed time,
and sailed from Labuan early in July, and in a few
hours passed Tanjong Kubong, near the northern
point of the island, where the best coal seams are
situated.   The view from the sea is very picturesque :
two hills, grass-covered, with the dark outlines of the
forest in the rear, and a valley between, sloping upwards, showing, at one glance, the works of the coal
company.   On a bold rocky bluff is the manager's
house, overlooking the open sea, with a clear view of
the great mountain.   It is to be regretted that there
is no good anchorage in the north-east monsoon off
this point, as it necessitates a railway of seven miles
being carried through the island to the splendid

harbour of Victoria. However, should this work be
undertaken, it is very possible it may be the means of
opening out the other veins which are known to
exist in the centre of the island. The coal seams of
Tanjong Kubong are perhaps as fine as any in the
world; and it is probable that the failures in develop-
ing them have arisen from applying the same means
of working the mine as are used in England,
forgetting that the fall of rain is four times as
great. Labuan ought to supply all the farther
East with coal, and may yet do so, under judicious
management.

Passing on, we steered clear of the Pine shoals, and
directed our course to Pulo Tiga, an island so called
from the three undulating hills that form its surface.
It is quite uninhabited, except occasionally by a few
fishermen or traders, seeking water there. On its
broad sandy beaches turtle are said to congregate,
and here we have picked up some very pretty shells,
particularly olives. The coast between Labuan and
Nosong point, at the entrance of Kimanis Bay, consists of low hills only partly cleared. At one place
there are some bluff, red-looking points called Tanah
Merah, or Red Land, and near it are many villages of
Bisayas, who are engaged in planting pepper. Their
gardens are said to be very neatly kept, and the
system, which has descended to them from the former
Chinese cultivators, is far superior to that pursued in
Sumatra. There the Malays allow the vines to twine
round the quick-growing Chingkariang tree, whose
roots must necessarily absorb much of the nourishment; but here they plant them in open ground, and
train them up ironwood posts, thus preserving to them

all the benefit of the manure they may apply to enrich the soil. Although the Bisayas are not careful cultivators, yet they prepare heaps of burnt earth and decaying weeds to place round the stems of the vines before they commence flowering.

Along this beach, herds of wild cattle are often seen wandering, particularly on bright moonlight nights, in search, most probably, of salt, which they are so fond of licking. All the natives declare that the species found here is smaller than those monsters I saw up the Limbang and Baram. It is very likely there may be two kinds.

A pleasant S.W. breeze carried us rapidly along this coast. Our craft, though not famous for its sailing qualities, ran well before the wind. It was a small yacht, belonging to the Eastern Archipelago Company, the same which we used when we went to Abai in the spring. Dr. Coulthard had put himself to some inconvenience in lending it to us, as he was obliged to content himself with a native-built boat of mine, that was called by the ominous name of the "Coffin," and on one occasion nearly proved to be one to the obliging doctor. I myself had great faith in that boat, as it had taken me safely through many a hard blow.

Rounding Nosong Point, we crossed the broad Bay of Kimanis, which here runs deep into the land, and receives the waters of numerous rivers. Just round the point is Qualla Lama, or the Old Mouth: entering this, a large boat can pass through an inner channel, and reach the mouth of the Kalias, opposite Labuan. It is often used by the Malays to avoid the heavy sea, which, during the height of the south-west

monsoon, breaks upon this coast. The shores of
Kimanis Bay are rather low, yet have an interesting
appearance, from the variety of tints to be observed
among the vegetation.

There runs into this bay a pretty little river of the
same name—Kimanis, from *kayu manis*, "sweetwood."
Its forests are famous for the large amount of cassia
bark which used to be collected there, but which has
now all been exhausted near the banks by the continued requisitions from the capital. This district is
the appanage of one of the sons of the late Sultan, the
Pañgeran Tumanggong, and he used every year to
send up several trading prahus to be loaded with
cassia,—paying to the aborigines tenpence for every
133 lbs., and selling the same amount for nine
shillings. As long as the bark could be easily
obtained from the trees near the banks of the river,
the people were content to work for the low price;
but as soon as it required a long walk from their
villages, the Muruts declared the whole forest was
exhausted. I am assured, however, by trustworthy
men, that ship-loads might be obtained, if the
aborigines were offered fair prices; but the noble and
his followers do their utmost to preserve a strict
monopoly. And this is the case in most of the
districts near the capital. Though they cannot themselves obtain much from the people, they have still
sufficient influence to paralyze trade.

Kimanis, like most of the other rivers north of
Labuan, is obstructed by a bar; in fact, though I
could see its mouth from my boat, yet I could not
find the channel, till a Malay canoe led the way by
coasting south about three hundred yards: then,

pulling straight for the shore over the boiling surf, we soon found ourselves in the smooth river. The scenery, though not grand, is very lovely, and consists generally of the variety to be observed in the groves of cocoa-nuts and fruit-trees which line its banks, and the cultivated fields stretching inland. I 'always remember my visit to Kimanis with pleasure, as it was on turning a wooded point I had my first view of Kina Balu. A straight reach of the river stretched before us, overshadowed on either side by lofty trees, and the centre of the picture was the precipices and summit of the massive mountain.

On the left-hand bank is the grave of Pangeran Usup, who, flying from the capital, met his death, under orders from the Government, at the hand of the chief of this river. I have heard the story told several ways, but the one the Orang Kaya relates himself is a curious illustration of Bornean manners. The Pangeran, flying from his enemies in the capital, came to Kimanis, which was one of his appanages, and asked its local chief whether he would protect him. The Orang Kaya protested his loyalty, but, a few days after, receiving an order from the Government to seize and put his guest to death, he made up his mind to execute it. He imparted the secret to three of his relations, whom he instructed to assist him. Pangeran Usup was a dangerous man with whom to meddle, as he was accompanied by a devoted brother, who kept watch over him as he slept or bathed, and who received the same kind offices when he desired to rest. For days the Orang Kaya watched an opportunity—tending on his liege lord, holding his clothes while he bathed, bringing his

food, but never able to surprise him, as he or his
brother were always watching with a drawn kris in
his hand. The three relations sat continually on the
mats near, in the most respectful attitude. The
patience of the Malay would have carried him
through a more difficult trial than this, as I think
it was on the tenth day Pañgeran Usup, while standing on the wharf, watching his brother bathe, called
for a light. The Orang Kaya brought a large piece
of firewood with very little burning charcoal on it,
and the noble in vain endeavoured to light his cigar.
At last, in his impatience, he put down his kris, and
took the wood in his own hand. A fatal mistake!
The treacherous friend immediately threw his arms
round the Pañgeran, and the three watchers, springing up, soon secured the unarmed brother. Usup
was immediately taken to the back of the house, and
executed and buried on the hill, where his grave was
pointed out to me.

We continued our voyage along the coast till about
four in the afternoon, when heavy clouds rising in
the south-west warned us that a squall was coming
up. We, therefore, resolved to take shelter under
the little islet of Dinaman, to the north of the Papar
River. At first, we thought of running in there, as
I had not yet seen this district, so famous for the
extent and beauty of its cocoa-nut groves, and for the
numerous population which had rendered the river's
banks a succession of gardens.

Our anchorage sheltered us tolerably well from the
storm which now burst over us, but we rolled heavily
as the swell of the sea came in. Drenching rain and
furious blasts generally pass away quickly, as they

did that evening, and left us to enjoy the quiet, starlight night.

We always endeavour to start on an expedition a
few days before full moon, having a theory that the
weather is more likely to be fine then, than during
the days which immediately follow a new moon.

Next morning we set sail for Gaya Bay, and in a
few hours a light breeze carried us over a rippling
sea to the deep entrance of this spacious harbour, in
which all the navy of England could, in both monsoons, ride in safety. It is formed by numerous
islands and an extended headland, which make it
appear almost land-locked. The harbour is surrounded by low hills, some cleared at the top, presenting pretty green patches, others varied with
bright tints, caused by exposed red sandstone; the
rest covered with low thick jungle.

When I last visited this place, Pañgeran Madoud
lived up the Kabatuan river, which flows into the bay,
but had now removed to the shore, and established
there a village called Gantisan. I had twice visited
this Malay chief, and on both occasions had disagreeable news to impart to him, as I had to remon-
strate against his system of taking goods from English
traders and forgetting to pay them when the price
became due. The banks of the Kabatuan, except
near the entrance, were entirely of mangrove-swamp,
until we arrived within a short distance of the
scattered village of Menggatal, but from our boat
we could see the sloping hills that rose almost immediately behind the belt of mangrove.

The first buildings we saw were those in which the
natives were making salt. I have already described

the process pursued in the Abai, but here it was somewhat different, as they burnt the roots of the mangrove with those of the nipa palm, as well as wood collected on the sea-beach, and therefore impregnated with salt.  In one place, I noticed a heap, perhaps fifteen feet in height, sheltered by a rough covering of palm-leaves, and several men were about checking all attempts of the flames to burst through by throwing salt-water over the pile.  This, doubtless, renders the process much more productive.  In one very large shed, they had a kind of rough furnace, where they burnt the wood ; and suspended around were many baskets in which the rough remains of the fire are placed, and the whole then soaked in water and stirred about till the salt is supposed to have been extracted from the charcoal and ashes.  The liquid is then boiled, as at Abai, in large iron pans purchased from the Chinese.

The village of Menggatal contained about a hundred houses scattered among the trees, and in the centre was the residence of Pañgeran Madoud, tolerably well built of thick posts and plank walls. We found chairs and tables had already penetrated to this secluded spot, and the Pañgeran was not a little proud of being able to receive us in European fashion.  He was at the period of our first visit about forty, tall, and with rather a pleasant, quiet countenance ; but having little strength of character, was willing to enter into intercourse with the pirates, if by so doing he could gain anything.  He had, in fact, just purchased from them a trading prahu, which they had captured north of Labuan, after having killed two of the Bornean crew, who were his

own countrymen.    Like all the other chiefs, he
attempts to monopolize the trade of his district, and
thus reduces it to a minimum.

While we were conversing, there came in a party
of the Ida'an, whose young chief had a very intelligent countenance, broad-shouldered, with his waist
drawn in as tightly as he could ; over his breast
he wore strings of cowrie shells, and round his loins
neatly-worked rattan rings, and on his neck a brass
collar open at the side, enabling him to take it off
with ease.    Their baskets were filled with hill
tobacco for the Pañgeran, who is said subsequently
to have so oppressed the neighbouring villages of
Ida'an, that they threatened to attack him, and being
rather timid, he retired before the storm.    Building
their houses at Gantisan on freshly cleared jungle,
the Malays suffered severely from fever ; the whole
population is said to have been attacked, of whom
many died.

We found anchored at Lokporin, in the north-west
part of the bay, a Spanish brig, belonging to Monsieur
Cuarteron, the Prefect Apostolic of the newly-arrived
Roman Catholic mission.    He had built a hut and a
chapel of palm stems and leaves, as a commencement
of what he hoped would be a prosperous mission ; but
he had his attention too much directed to temporal,
to take proper care of spiritual affairs.*

We paid a visit to the Chief Pañgeran Madoud
and settled to leave our pinnace under his care, and
start next morning, as the cholera had already invaded
this place, and eight deaths were reported.

* A short account of this mission will be found at the end of the
second volume.

Having distributed our luggage among our followers, we landed and walked over to the waters of
the Mengkabong, a low. ridge only separating them;
from it we had a good view of this extensive salt
lake, filled with islands, and on the inland side bor-
dered by hills.    At the landing-place we met the
nominal ruler of Mengkabong, Pañgeran Duroup,
who had kindly provided canoes to take us to the
point where our walking journey would. commence.
We stopped to breakfast at his house, and Monsieur
Cuarteron, who was with us, pointed out an intelligent lad, the son of Duroup, whom he intended to
raise to power over the surrounding countries, and
be himself the boy's Prime Minister.

A Spaniard has many temptations to intrigue in
these districts, as there are here numerous inhabitants
of the Philippines, originally captured by the Lanun
and Balignini pirates, and sold into slavery.   They
have married and intermarried with the inhabitants,
and forming a part of the regular population, are
most unwilling to leave the country.   Some have
risen to respectable positions, and nearly all have
turned Mahomedans.   Still they have a respect and
a fear of the Spanish priests, and are much open to
their secular influence, though very few will re-enter
the Roman Church.   As might be expected, the
priest's political intrigues did no good, but, instead,
diffused suspicion and dislike among the natives.

We started again after breakfast, and passed the
entrance from the sea, through the chief town, and
by the numerous villages scattered about.   Nearly
all the houses are built on the water.   We estimated
the population at above 6,000.   A glance at the

accompanying map will explain the kind of place Mengkabong is, but I may observe that this salt-water creek or lake is very shallow, in many places dry, or but a few inches deep at dead low-water, so that it must be rapidly filling up, and all the plains skirting the sea had probably a similar origin. To the south and south-east it is surrounded by hills, none of which exceeds eight hundred feet in height.

Mengkabong is the head-quarters of the Bajus on the north-western coast of Borneo; and being the only population to be found in the villages scattered over the lake, they are more tempted to pursue their old habits than those of the northern rivers, who have the Lanuns between them and the sea. They are bold seamen, and will venture anywhere in search of wealth. When the *Fiery Cross* was wrecked on a shoal far out in the China Seas, the captain and crew made for Labuan. The news soon spread along the coast that a ship with a valuable cargo was on shore, and a small squadron of native prahus was immediately fitted out at Mengkabong to look for her. They boldly put forth to sea, visiting all the reefs with which they were acquainted, and even pushing their researches so far as to sight the coast of Cochin China, known to the Malays under the name of Annam. Their exertions were for them unfortunately unavailing; but they often pick up a prize, as when a Bombay cotton ship was wrecked at Meñgalong; and during the last China war, they found a large French vessel deserted on a reef to the north of Borneo, but which, to their infinite disgust, proved to have only a cargo of coals. The Baju prahus may gene-rally be known by their tripod masts, which consist

19—2

of three tall bamboos, the two foremost fitted on
a cross beam, the last loose; so that when a heavy
squall threatens, they can immediately strike their
masts. Their sails are not handsome; for being
stuck out on one side, they look ungainly.

I have mentioned, in my account of our first expedition to Kina Balu, the Baju attack on a village in
Banguey; they themselves often suffer from the fleets
of Balignini pirates, who return home from their
cruises in Dutch waters along the north-west coast of
Borneo, and pick up the fishermen they find at sea.
During the last few years they have seldom appeared
off the coast more than once during a season, and
then only touching at Sirik Point, and afterwards
giving our colony of Labuan a wide berth, to fetch
the coast again about Pulo Tiga.

The Balignini used to be the terror of the Indian
isles, but their pursuits have been interfered with
and their gains much curtailed since the introduction
of steamers into the Archipelago. The Spaniards,
with heavy loss to themselves, drove them from their
haunts on the islands of Tongkil and Balignini in the
Sulu Archipelago, since which time they have never
again assembled in positions so strong. These two
small islands are low, surrounded with mangrove
swamps, and appear very similar to the eighteen
others we could count at the same time from the
deck of a ship. But behind the swamps were erected
formidable stockades, and the garrison made a stub-
born defence, although most of their fighting men
were away.

I heard a Spanish officer who was present give an
account of the attack: three times the native troops

charged, and three times they were driven back, till
the Spanish officers and artillerymen put themselves
in a body at the head of the force, and led the
storming party, and, with severe loss, won the inner
stockade.   One of my Manilla followers on our
present expedition was a captive at the time, and had
concealed himself among the mangrove trees till the
fighting was over.   He said it was a fearful sight to
see the slaughter which had occurred—one hundred
and fifty of the Spanish force fell, and many more of
the pirates, as they had commenced killing their
women and children, till promised quarter.

I never saw a more savage set of fellows than those
who escaped from this attack.   The Sultan of Sulu
had given them an asylum, and they were quartered
near the spot at which ships usually water.   It is
about a mile from the capital, Sugh; is on the
beach; and the clear spring bubbles up through
the sand, where a pool is easily formed, at which the
casks are filled, or whence the hose is led into the
boats.   The place is well marked by a tree, that, in
the distance, looks like an oak: its trunk is of enormous thickness, but low, as the spreading branches
stretch out from the stem about ten feet from the
ground, but afford shelter to a considerable space,
and under its shade a market is held several times a
week.   I measured its stem: it was above forty feet
in circumference at a man's height above the ground,
and considerably more close to the earth, where the
gnarled roots were included.

The Bajus of Mengkabong are, as I have said, a
very lawless people, and the following anecdote, told
me by Signor Cuarteron, will assist to prove it.   He ·

was anchored opposite his chapel in Lokporin, when
he heard that there was fighting in Mengkabong,
and, on inquiry, found that a boat, returning from
Labuan to Cagayan Sulu, had put into that place for
water, and was being attacked by the Bajus. He
instantly manned his boats and pulled round to the
salt-water lake. On arriving near the first village,
he saw several hundred men assembled in prahus,
round a detached house, near which a trading-boat
was fastened, and guns were occasionally discharged.
He inquired the reason, and the Bajus declared they
were going to revenge the death or captivity of some
of their countrymen who had disappeared a few
months before, and whom, they had heard, people
from Cagayan Sulu had attacked. It was immaterial
to them whether these were the guilty parties or not,
if they came from the same country. Signor Cuarteron then pulled up to the detached house, to find
from its beleaguered inmates who they were. He soon
discovered they were peaceful traders, not concerned
in the outrage of the spring; upon which, by dint of
threats and persuasion, he was enabled to rescue
them from the Bajus, and escort them to the mouth
of the Mengkabong—a very creditable action of the
priest. The lawlessness of the Bajus is notorious,
and they are now seldom employed, since the murder
of some Chinese traders, who trusted them to form
the crew of their boat.

Pañgeran Duroup, the nominal ruler of this place,
always kept aloof from these things, as the Bajus
despised any order he gave; in fact, their open
defiance of his authority had induced him to remove
from the town to a little island nearly facing the

mouth, whose low land was formed of mud on a bed
of water-worn pebbles.

A very barbarous custom exists on this coast—that
wrecks and their crews belong to the chief of the
district where they may suffer their misfortune. The
Bajus used to give us much trouble on this account,
though they would now assist the distressed, if they
belonged to an English vessel, as they are well aware
of our power to reward or punish.

As an instance of the above practice, I may relate
an incident which took place whilst I was in Brunei.
A large prahu sailing from Palawan to the Spanish
settlement of Balabak was caught in a violent storm,
and the captain noticed that his canoe, which, according to custom, he was towing behind, was rapidly
filling with water; he therefore anchored, and ordered
three men to get into and bail it out. The storm
continued, and driving rain and mist rendered every
object indistinct, when suddenly the towing rope
parted, and the canoe drifted away. The three men,
having no paddles, soon lost sight of their prahu, and
continued driving before the wind.

The north-east monsoon was blowing, and the current sets down the coast, and, after a few days, this
canoe was seen drifting towards the shore at Tutong,
at least 150 miles from the spot where it had parted
with its companion. The fishermen put off, and, on
reaching the boat, found the three men lying in it,
utterly exhausted from want of food and water, and
from the daily and nightly exposure. They were sent
on to the capital, and in a short time recovered,
when they found they were considered as slaves of
the Sultan.

In this emergency they came privately to my house and laid their case before me: so, in the evening, I went to the Sultan to hear the wonderful story from his own lips; and, when he had concluded, I congratulated him on the excellent opportunity he had of renewing friendly relations with the people of Palawan, by sending these men back in a prahu which was to sail for Maludu the following day. He hesitated at first, but after a little persuasion agreed to do so, and I had the satisfaction of seeing them safely out of the river. The Sultan did not regret sending them away; but he had been so accustomed to consider he had a right to these godsends, that he would certainly have kept them, had he not been asked to let them go.

I have noticed, in my account of our first expedition to Kina Balu, how mixed in breed were many of the Bajus with whom we conversed; but, although there is occasionally some Chinese blood found among them, yet it has rarely left a trace on their features. They appear to me to be very much like the Orang Laut, who frequent the small islands to the south of Singapore and about the Malay peninsula; they are generally, however, smaller, and their voices have a sharper intonation than that of the Malays.

I think, however, that the bold spirit shown by these men, their love of the seas, and their courage, might be turned to good account under a steady Government.

Leaving the lake we pushed up a narrow creek to a house inhabited by Pañgeran Sirail, who politely requested us to spend the night at it, adding that in the morning a bazaar would be held close at hand, at which we should meet all the Dusuns of the Tawaran river; among others the Datu of the village of Tamparuli, the chief who escorted Mr. Low in his journey undertaken in 1851. We were happy to accede to his request, and finding his house very comfortable, took up our quarters in a charming little audience hall or smoking-room which extended in front, and was neat and clean.

Our baggage being heavy, we hired some Bajus to assist our men, and then lighting our lamps, sat down to dinner. Our host, while declaring that his religion prevented him joining in a glass of whiskey and water, was suddenly seized with such severe spasms in the stomach as to require medicine; we unsmilingly administered a glass of warm whiskey and water, which our host drank with evident gusto, but it required a second to complete the cure. As the evening advanced, and his utterance became more indistinct, he kept assuring us that a Mahomedan should never drink, except when spirits were taken as medicine.

We were sorry to find that the cholera had already reached Mengkabong, and that several deaths had taken place. In the night we were disturbed by piercing shrieks and mournful wails from a neighbouring house; we thought it was another victim of the epidemic, but it proved to be a young girl sorrowing for the loss of a sister, who died in the night from abscess.

Early in the morning the market-people began to assemble, and Bajus and Dusuns crowded round the house; the former brought salt, salted fish, iron, and cloth, to exchange for rice, vegetables, and fruit.

These markets are very convenient, and, as at Brunei, are held daily at different points, in order to accommodate the various villages scattered around the lake. To-day there was a very great gathering, as many disputes had to be settled.

The old Datu of Tamparuli came, and at first appeared uninterested and scarcely noticed us, his eye-sight was weak, and he appeared dull and stupid. A glass of whiskey and water revived his energies and his recollection, he shook Mr. Low warmly by the hand, and then turning to the assembly told them in an excited voice of the wonderful feats he had performed in the old journey, and how he had actually reached the summit of Kina Balu.

This fired the ambition of Pañgeran Sirail, who, as long as he was under the influence of whiskey, declared it would be dishonour to allow the white men to do this difficult task alone, and pointing to the craggy summits now clearly visible above the trees, swore he would reach them, but his courage soon oozed out at his fingers' ends. The Datu, however, considered himself as too old again to attempt the journey, but said he would send his son-in-law and a party of followers.

When the market was over we started, most of our baggage being placed on light bamboo sledges drawn by buffaloes, which appeared to pass over the soft soil with great ease. The path, nearly due east, lay over a pretty plain for the most part under cultivation; men were ploughing, harrowing, and sowing in various fields, that were carefully divided into small squares with slight embankments between them. The ploughing was better than at Tampasuk, deeper, and the ground more turned over; each section of these fields is as much private property as any in England, and in general so much valued as to be rarely parted with.

In crossing this cultivated plain we had the finest view of Kina Balu that could be imagined, it was just before we reached the Tawaran river; we were standing where the young rice was showing its tender green above the ground: on either side were groves of tall palms, and in front, the hills rose in successive ranges till Kina Balu crowned the whole. Its purple precipices were distinctly visible, and broad streams of water, flashing in the bright morning sun, were flowing down the upper slopes to disappear in mist or deep ravines, or to be lost in the shadows of the great mountain.

About three miles walking brought us to the Tawaran, whose banks were lined with groves of cocoa-nut and other fruit-trees; interspersed among which were Dusun villages and detached houses. We observed also a plantation of sago palms, which the inhabitants said were plentiful, but certainly not in the parts we had traversed.

There were also gardens here as neatly fenced in and as carefully tended as those of the Chinese; and this rich soil produced in great perfection sugar-cane, Indian corn, yams, kiladis, and other vegetables. The whole had a very civilized appearance, the neatness was remarkable, and about the houses were cattle, buffaloes, and goats, in great numbers. On reaching the Tawaran, Monsieur Cuarteron left us to visit a Manilla man, who, though formerly a captive sold into slavery, had now become the chief of a Dusun village.

We continued our course inland along the banks of the Tawaran until we reached Tamparuli, prettily embowered in extensive groves of fruit-trees: we took up our quarters for the night at the old Datu's house, which was very similar to those of the Sea Dayaks.

The Tawaran, where we first joined it, was about sixty yards broad, and the stream was rapid, swollen by the late rains, and muddy from recent landslips. It is a river very unimportant in itself, as here, not perhaps ten miles from the sea, there are already rapids that can only be passed by very small native craft.

The old Datu of Tamparuli is the proud possessor of the famed sacred jar I have already referred to. It was a Gusi, and was originally given by a Malau chief in the interior of the Kapuas to a Pakatan Dayak, converted, however, to Islam, and named Japar. He sold it to a Bornean trader for nearly two tons of brass guns, or 230*l.*, who brought it to the Tawaran to resell it, nominally for 400*l.*, really for nearly 700*l.* No money passes on these occasions, it is all reckoned in brass guns or goods, and the old Datu was paying for his in rice. He possesses another jar, however, to which he attaches an almost fabulous value; it is about two feet in height, and is of a dark olive green. He fills both the jars with water, and adds flowers and herbs to retail to all the surrounding people who may be suffering from any illness. The night we were there they little thought that a scourge was coming upon them which would test to the utmost the virtue of the sacred jars.

Perhaps, however, the most remarkable jar in Borneo, is the one possessed by the present Sultan

of Brunei, as it not only has all the valuable properties of the other sacred vases, but speaks. As
the Sultan told this with a grave face and evident
belief in the truth of what he was relating, we
listened to the story with great interest. He said,
the night before his first wife died, it moaned sorrow-
fully, and on every occasion of impending misfortune
it utters the same melancholy sounds. I have sufficient faith in his word to endeavour to seek an explanation of this (if true) remarkable phenomenon, and
perhaps it may arise from the wind blowing over its
mouth, which may be of some peculiar shape, and
cause sounds like those of an Æolian harp. I should
have asked to see it, had it not been always kept in
the women's apartments.

As a rule, it is covered over with gold-em-
broidered brocade, and seldom exposed, except when
about to be consulted. This may account for its
only producing sounds at certain times. I have
heard, that in former days, the Muruts and Bisayas
used to come with presents to the Sultan, and obtain
in return a little water from this sacred jar, with
which to besprinkle their fields to ensure good crops.
I have not known an instance of their doing so during
late years, as the relations between monarch and
people are now of the most unsatisfactory kind.

In looking over Carletti's *Voyage*, I find he mentions taking some sacred jars from the Philippine
Islands to Japan, which were so prized there, that
the punishment of death was denounced against them
if they were sold to any one but the Government.
Some, he says, were valued as high as 30,000*l.* The
Sultan of Brunei was asked if he would take 2,000*l.*

for his; he answered he did not think any offer in the world would tempt him to part with it.

The Datu possessed a daughter, the loveliest girl in Borneo. I have never seen a native surpass her in figure, or equal her gentle, expressive countenance. She appeared but sixteen years of age, and as she stood near, leaning against the door-post in the most graceful attitude, we had a perfect view of all her perfections. Her dress was slight indeed, consisting of nothing but a short petticoat reaching from her waist to a little above her knees. Her skin was of that light clear brown which is almost the perfection of colour in a sunny clime, and as she was just returning from bathing, her hair unbound fell in great luxuriance over her shoulders. Her eyes were black, not flashing, but rather contemplative, and her features were regular, even her nose was straight.

So intent was she in watching our movements, and wondering at our novel mode of eating, with spoons, and knives and forks, that she unconsciously remained in her graceful attitude for some time; but suddenly recollecting that she was not appearing to the best advantage in her light costume, she moved away slowly to her room, and presently came forth dressed in a silk jacket and new petticoat, with bead necklaces and gold ornaments. In our eyes she did not look so interesting as before.

Pañgeran Sirail now approached us to say that he felt he was too old and weak to ascend the great mountain, but had brought three of his people to supply his place. We were not sorry, as his devotion to whiskey would have sadly reduced our little stock. Although it was but three months after the harvest, yet we could obtain no supplies of rice; they had it in the form of padi, but were unwilling to part with it, so we sent back some of our followers to procure sufficient for a few days.

Next morning we made but little progress, as we had to wait for the men who had gone in search of rice. However, we reached the village of Bawang, our path lying among the fruit groves that skirted the river's banks. As it was now unfordable, we had to cross it by a boat, and this was a slow process with our large party.

Bawang, a Dusun village, consists of scattered dwellings, like those of the Malays, while the others we have seen resemble the houses of the Sea Dayaks. A family very hospitably received us, and gave up half their accommodation to us and our immediate followers. The Datu who had accompanied us to this place now returned, handing us over to Kadum, his son-in-law, a very dull-looking man; we were also joined by ten others. One, a Malay named Omar, who was to act as interpreter and guide, was a willing but a stupid fellow; he came originally from the Dutch settlement of Pontianak, and had been married five years to a Dusun girl, yet he could scarcely manage to act as interpreter, not so much from ignorance, as from a confusion of ideas.

Started soon after six for a cleared spot about a quarter of a mile above the village, where we stopped to introduce some order in our followers: we divided the packages among them, and found each of the forty-one men had sufficient to carry.

About two or three miles above Bawang the Tawaran divides—one branch running from the south, the other from the S.E. by E. We soon reached the foot of the sandstone range, which bounds the low land, and like all heights composed of this rock, it was very steep to climb. For a thousand feet it was abrupt, and severe work to those unused to such toil. The path then led us along the top of the ridge to a peak about 1,500 feet high, from which I was enabled to take compass bearings. A fine view was to be had a few feet from the summit, the coast line being quite clear from Gaya Bay to Sulaman Lake, and the distant isles scattered on the sea were distinctly visible. A wide plain stretches below us, mostly rice fields, with groves of fruit-trees interspersed among them, and the Mengkabong waters appearing extensive, form a pleasing feature in the scene.

We continued our course to the village of Si Nilau, passing over a hill of a similar name, about 1,800 feet high. The village, if village it can be called, where a number of little detached hamlets are scattered about the slopes of the hills, amid groves of palms, is a good resting-place. We brought up here to give time for our followers to join us, as they felt the climbing more than we did, who carried nothing but our weapons. We were three hours, exclusive of stoppages, advancing four miles of direct course E. by S. Most of the ranges run nearly E. and W., though occasionally there is some divergence.

After breakfasting, we started, hoping to reach the next village of Kalawat, but our guide making a mistake, led us in a totally wrong direction, so that after wandering about two hours in a scorching sun without shelter, we returned to Si Nilau.

Heavy masses of clouds were now driving over the

sky, threatening a deluge of rain, so we determined to
spend the night here, and told our guide that we
would distribute our men among the houses.    Omar
presently returned, saying the villagers refused us entrance into their dwellings.  As now heavy drops began
to fall, I went down from the fruit grove, where our
party was assembled, and approaching a house which
appeared the neatest and the cleanest, I found the
door shut.  There were evidently people inside, while
all the other houses were empty.  It is an universal
custom in Borneo to afford shelter to travellers, but
they very rarely like to enter houses whose owners
are absent.    Hearing some whispering going on
inside, I knocked and directed the interpreter to ask
for shelter; there was no answer, and as the heavy
drops were coming down faster, I gave a vigorous
push to the door.    The fastening gave way, and an
old woman fell back among a crowd of frightened
girls, who, at the sight of a white man, shrieked
and sprang to the ground through an opposite window.
They did not run far, but turned to look if they were
followed.    We went to the window, and, smilingly
beckoned them to come back, and as the rain was
now beginning to descend with violence, they did so.
We apologized for our rough entry, but the high wind
that drove sheets of water against the house was our
best excuse.  We promised to pay for our accommodation, and in five minutes they were all busily
engaged in their usual avocations.    On the return of
the men from their farms, we told them what had
occurred, at which they laughed heartily as soon as
they found we were not offended by having had the door
shut in our faces, and we then made many inquiries

concerning the lake of Kina Balu, and whether either
branch of the Tawaran ran from it; but all the
Dusuns were positive that the river had its sources in
the hills, which we could see farther east.  Of the
lake itself they had never heard.

The Nilau tribe is very scattered, none of the
hamlets having above a dozen small houses; but
in personal appearance Mr. Low found them much
improved since he saw them in 1851.  It is impossible
even to guess at the population; but judging from the
cleared appearance of the country, it must be tolerably
numerous.   There is little old forest, except on the
summit of the highest ridges, all the land being used
in succession.   Rice, however, is the principal cultivation, there being few kiladis, and we observed no
tobacco plantations.

The girls of this village wore black cloths over
their shoulders, and brought down so as to conceal
their bosoms.

Started early for Kalawat in an E. by S. direction.
A sharp ascent led us to the top of the heights
of Tangkahang, from which we had a very extensive
view, reaching from Mantanani to Mengkabong.
Ranges of hills, nearly parallel to our walk, occurred
on either side, with feeders of the Tawaran at their
feet.   After an hour's walk, reached the Kalawat
hills, nearly 3,000 feet high.   The path passed, after
a few hundred yards, to the south of the range, perhaps 200 feet from its summit, and after a mile turned
to the S.E.   Then the walk became very tiring, up
and down the steepest of ravines, with slippery clay
steps or loose stones.   I was not sorry, therefore, to
reach the village of Kalawat, a cluster of about ten

houses, containing upwards of eighty families. The village was dirty and so were the houses.

We stopped here to breakfast, and to wait the arrival of our straggling followers, and heard of the desertion of one of them. He was a negro, of great size and power, and, in muscular development, equal to two or three of our other men. Our overseer had chosen him to carry our edibles, as tea, sugar, salt, and curry stuffs; but had unfortunately trusted him also with half a bottle of whiskey. He had complained bitterly of the exhausting nature of the walk, and no sooner were our backs turned than he slipped into the brushwood, and devoted himself to the bottle; he was found there by the overseer, who, after extracting a promise that he would follow when sober, left him with all our condiments. These very heavy muscular men have generally proved useless in jungle work. In all our arrangements we now greatly missed Musa, my head boatman, who had stayed behind at Brunei, to look after his family during the cholera.

Starting again, a very trying climb took us to the top of a hill, from which a long but easy descent led to the Tinuman, a feeder of the Tawaran. We observed, both yesterday and to-day, many villages scattered over the face of the country, as Tagau, Bañgau, and others. Though there was no plain at the foot of the hills, yet many of the slopes were easy, occasionally almost flat.

At the little stream of Tinuman, we came upon a party of Dusuns, belonging to the village of Buñgol, who led us by a very winding path to their houses, situated on the left-hand bank of the Tawaran. We had scarcely reached it when rain came on, as

it appears generally to do about three o'clock in the
afternoon in the neighbourhood of Kina Balu and
other lofty mountains.

Buñgol is a large village, and contained, in 1851,
according to their own account, about 120 families; but
this time (1858), they appeared uncertain how many
there were. I estimated, from the length of the
different houses that there were above 160 families.
It is situated on grassy, undulating land, about fifty or
sixty feet above the level of the stream; yet the
inhabitants are exposed to floods, that reach their
houses and damage the crops on the low lands.

In our first expedition up the Tampasuk, we rested
at some houses of the Buñgol Ida'an, but we could
discover no more connection between these communities of the same name than between the others.
Notwithstanding the pouring rain, we walked through
the village, and bathed in the rushing torrent that
ran beneath the houses, the Tawaran now deserves
no other name.

Next morning, Omar, the guide, came to say that
all the bridges of the regular path had been washed
away, and that it would be necessary to take us by
another, with which he was unacquainted. We
suspected that this announcement was merely to serve
a friend who was hired as guide; but we gave way
to their assurances that the old path was impassable,
and had reason to repent it, as, instead of taking
us by the direct route, only four miles in an east
direction, he led us first north, then north-east,
ending in east-north-east, and after wandering over
numerous pathless ranges, at last, after eight hours'
walking brought us to the Tampasuk, about three

miles below the village of Koung. The dividing ranges are very much broken up, and run in all directions. A tributary of the Tawaran, to the north of us, came within a mile of the Tampasuk, running direct towards Sulaman, and then turning to the eastward.

We had beautiful views to-day of the surrounding country, both towards the sea and towards the mountains; but had scarcely reached the Tampasuk when heavy rain came on, totally obscuring the prospect, and although we pushed on resolutely for an hour, fording the swelling stream and climbing the slippery banks, were at last obliged to stop at a hut amid a field of kiladis, and give up our intention of reaching Koung.

We thought ourselves completely exhausted, until we saw the bungling attempts of our men to set up the tents. The Malays were very tired, and were shivering in the drenching rain and cold wind which swept down from the mountains, so we determined before taking off our wet clothes to see our men comfortable. Under our directions, and with our active assistance, the tents were soon raised, as the men, encouraged by our example, worked with a will. But it was a fatiguing day—nine hours of continued climbing and descending.

On the following morning we proceeded to Koung. There were few farms in sight that day, though yesterday we saw immense clearings, some extending over a whole hill-side, and all were working hard to increase them.

On reaching Koung, we found the villagers assembled, and crowds occupying the chief's house. We had intended, if possible, to reach the summit of

Kina Balu from this village, as on the last occasion, we were disgusted with the conduct of the Kiau people; but soon ascertained. it was not to be done, as the western spurs did not reach above half way up the mountain side; nor was there any rice to be procured in this village. We were also very much astonished to hear the kind old chief asking for black-mail; it did not appear to come from his heart, so we looked round to find who was his prompter, and, at the first glance, discovered the ugly face of Timbañgan, a wall-eyed man—the very chief who had tried to prevent our passing through Labang Labang, in the spring. To give way would have been absurd, as we should have had black-mail demanded of us at every village, and increasing in a progressive ratio. So we called up all the interpreters and made them carefully explain what were our motives in travelling and the objects we had in view; that we would pay for everything we required, or for any damage done by our followers, but not for permission to travel through their country. We then reminded them how their great enemies, the Lanuns of Tampasuk and Pandasan, had been defeated by the English, and how impossible it would be for the Ida'an to fight with white men. A revolver was then discharged through a thick plank, to show the effect of that small instrument, and how useless a defence their shields would prove; and I handed the chief my heavy double-barrelled rifle to examine, that he might reflect on its great power.

The effect of the explanations and of the conical balls was immediate, and we heard no more of black-mail; on the contrary, the most friendly relations

were established. To show what a curious people
they are, and how we appeared to have hit the hidden
springs of their actions, I may mention that we now
felt the utmost confidence in them, and asked the
chief to take care of a fever-stricken servant, and of
all such portions of our baggage as we did not wish
to carry on with us. He cheerfully agreed to do all
we wished, and proved most friendly and useful. We
then made presents to his wife to a greater extent
than his demand for black-mail, trying to convince
them by our actions that the better they behaved
to us, the more kindly and liberally we should behave
to them.

Next morning we started for Kiau. We noticed,
the previous day, that Timbañgan had disappeared
immediately after the pistol was discharged, which was
a demonstration especially intended for him, and one
of our guides told us he was about to collect his tribe
to dispute our further passage, and advised us to
make a detour round his village; but, if hostilities
were intended, it was better to face them, as, by the
lower path, we might easily have been surprised at a
ford or in some deep ravine. At the foot of the hill
we halted till all our force was collected, and then
marched up to the village. To our great surprise,
we found it deserted by all except Timbañgan, who
offered his services as a guide; though we knew the
way as well as he did, we cheerfully accepted his
services, and well rewarded them.

We followed the same path as during our last expedition, and reached Kiau without difficulty, to find
all our old acquaintances merry-making at a wedding.
We were rather anxious about our reception, after

the lively scene that had closed our last visit, and
had determined to put ourselves in the hands of the
old man, Li Moung, as we were very dissatisfied with
the conduct of Li Maing, our former guide. We
entered the almost deserted house we had formerly
occupied, but were soon surrounded by the wedding
guests, who came flocking down to meet us, and welcomed us in the most friendly and hearty manner.
And these were the very men with whom, on our last
visit, we were apparently about to exchange blows.
I say apparently, because I do not believe they ever
really intended to fight. They had been accustomed
to parties of Baju traders arriving at their village,
whom they could frighten into compliance with their
demands, and thought they might do the same with
us; but finding from their former experience they
could not, they did not attempt it this time, and we
ourselves placed the fullest confidence in them. The
Bajus, however, now seldom visit these distant villagers, who are thus compelled to take their own
produce to the coast, to be cajoled or plundered in
their turn, which is one of the reasons why cloth and
iron are so rare among them.

Li Moung was delighted with our determination to
leave all arrangements in his hands; and Li Maing
was not very much dissatisfied, as a huge boil almost
prevented him walking. We made our beds under a
large window which opened from the public room, as
the only spot where fresh air could be obtained. This
house was better arranged than the ordinary Sea Dayak
ones. Instead of having the whole floor on a level
with the door, they had a long passage leading through
the house: on one side the private apartments; on

the other, a raised platform on which the lads and unmarried men slept. We found this very comfortable, as the dogs were not permitted to wander over it.

The wedding guests were very excited, having drunk sufficient to loosen their tongues; the men were talkative, while the women pressed in crowds round the foot of our mats. The great difficulty was, as usual—no rice to be had.

Next day we sent our men through the village to find if it were possible to procure provisions, but they only obtained sufficient for a day's consumption. This determined us to send back to Mengkabong all our followers but six to procure supplies. We told the Ida'an of our resolve, and I think this proof of our confidence had a great effect on them; in fact, we always treated them in the same way, whether we were backed by a large force or not, and we never had to repent of our conduct towards them.

# CHAPTER X.

SECOND ASCENT OF KINA BALU—*Continued.*

Return of the Men for Rice—Readiness to assist us—New Kinds of
Pitcher Plants—The Valley of Pinokok—Beautiful Nepenthes—
Kina Taki—Description of the *Nepenthes Rajah*—Rocks Coated
with Iron—Steep Strata—The Magnolia—Magnificent Sunset
Scene—Fine Soil—Talk about the Lake—Change of Fashions
—Effect of Example—Rapid Tailoring—Language the same
among Ida'an, Dusun, and Bisaya—Reports—Start for Marei
Parei—The Fop Kamá—Prepare Night Lodgings—Fragrant
Bed—Stunted Vegetation—Appearance of Precipices—Dr.
Hooker—Botanical Descriptions—*Nepenthes Rajah*—Manner of
Growing—Great Size—Used as a Bucket—Drowned Rat—
*Nepenthes Edwardsiana*—An Account of it—Beautiful Plants
—Botanical Description of *Nepenthes Edwardsiana* — Exten-
sive Prospects—Peaked Hill of Saduk Saduk—Noble Buttress
—Situation for Barracks—Nourishing Food—Deep Valleys—
Familiar Intercourse with the Villagers—Turning the Laugh—
Dirty Faces—Looking-glasses—Their Effect—Return of our Fol-
lowers—Start for the Mountain—Rough Cultivation—The Moun-
tain Rat used as Food—Our Old Guides—Difficult Walking—
Scarlet Rhododendron—Encamp—Double Sunset—*Nepenthes
Lowii*—Botanical Description—*Nepenthes Villosa* — Botanical
Description—Extensive View of the Interior of Borneo—The
Lake—The Cave—Ascend to the Summit—Its Extent and Pecu-
liarities—Distant Views—North-western Peak—Severe Storm
—Injured Barometer—Useless Thermometers—Dangerous De-
scent—Accidents—Quartz in Crevices—Clean and Pleasant
Girls—Friendly Parting—Ida'an Sacrifices—Return by Koung
—Kalawat and Nilu—Death of Sahat—A Thief—Cholera—
Incantations and Method of Treatment—Arrival at Gantisan—
Fine Wharf—The Pangeran—Bad Weather—Heavy Squall—
Little Rice to be had—Sail—Anchor at Gaya Island—Curious
Stones—Fish—Description of a magnificent Kind—Poisonous

KADUM and the men of Tamparuli, together with the
overseer and most of our followers, started on their
journey, while we amused ourselves in collecting
vocabularies, and trying to make ourselves understood
by the people.  They showed a great readiness to
assist us, particularly the girls, who made us repeat
sentences after them, and then burst into loud
laughter either at our pronunciation or the comical
things they had made us utter.

All the lads of the village were rejoiced at our
arrival, as we purchased the plants they brought in,
particularly those with variegated leaves, and they thus
obtained brass wire and cloth.   One evening, a man,
who had been visiting another village of this tribe,
produced from his basket specimens of two new kinds
of nepenthes, or pitcher-plants, which were wondrous
to behold, so we determined to make a visit to the
spot where he found them.

As the man assured us it would be a very long
walk, we provided ourselves with blankets, to enable
us to sleep out a night, if necessary.  We passed over
a hill at the back of the village, which, where the
path crosses it, is about five hundred feet above the
houses, and is a continuation of a spur of Kina Balu.
We then descended into a ravine, and, crossing over
a subspur, had a fine view of a valley about three
miles broad.  A stream ran on either side of it, and
between was a fine space almost flat, at the lower end
of which was the village of Pinokok.  Having de-

scended and crossed two streams called Haya Haya, which soon joined, however, into one to form the Pinokok, we traversed the plain, and rested on the banks of the Dahombang, or Hobang Stream, to breakfast on sweet potatoes and sardines, the worst things that can be imagined for a morning meal. Crossing the Hobang, a steep climb led us to the western spur, along which our path lay; here, at about 4,000 feet, Mr. Low found a beautiful white and spotted pitcher-plant, which he considered the prettiest of the twenty-two species of nepenthes with which he was then acquainted; the pitchers are white and covered in the most beautiful manner with spots of an irregular form, of a rosy pink colour. On each leaf is a row of very soft downy hairs running along its edge, and a similar brown pubescence grows on the cups. It is a climbing plant, and varies from fifteen to twenty feet in length. Its leaves are about nine inches long in the blade, and have winged petioles which are carried down the stem to the next leaf below, each of which bears a pitcher on a prolonged petiole about fifteen inches in length.

We continued our walk along the ridge until we had reached an elevation of 4,500 feet, when the path descended to the pleasant stream, or rather torrent, of Kina Taki, in which greenstone was the principal rock. All the rivulets we have passed to-day fall into the Dahombang, which continues its course until, winding round the bluff point of Labang Labang, it joins the Tampasuk. Another steep climb of 800 feet brought us to the Marei Parei spur, to the spot where the ground was covered with the magnificent pitcher-plants, of which we had come in search. This one

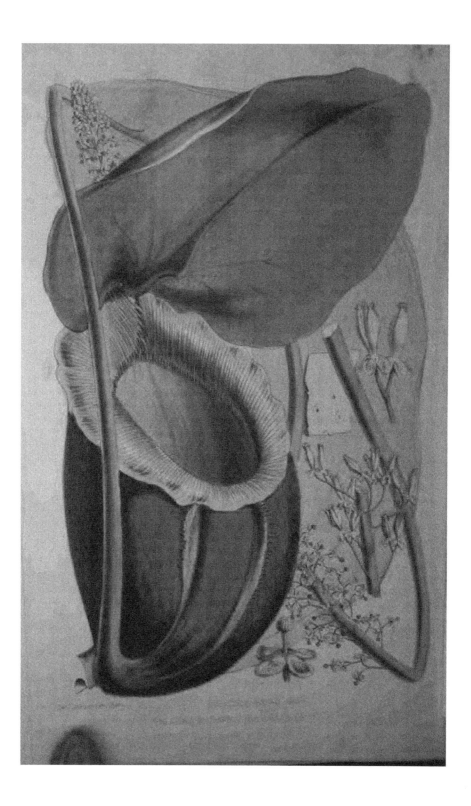

... the *Nepenthes Rafflesia*, which is a plant
... in length, with level leaves stretching
... having the great pitcher ... on
... circle about it. It is said ...
... will give ...

Charles ...
... numerous ti...

has been called the *Nepenthes Rajah*, and is a plant about four feet in length, with broad leaves stretching on every side, having the great pitchers resting on the ground in a circle about it. Its shape and size are remarkable. I will give the measurement of a small one, to indicate the form : the length along the back was nearly fourteen inches ; from the base to the top of the column in front was five inches ; and its lid was a foot long by four inches broad, and of an oval shape. Its mouth was surrounded by a plaited pile, which near the column was two inches broad, lessening in its narrowest part to three-quarters of an inch. The plaited pile of the mouth was also undulating in broad waves. Near the stem the pitcher is four inches deep, so that the mouth is situated upon it in a triangular manner. The colour of an old pitcher was a deep purple, but was generally mauve outside, very dark indeed in the lower part, though lighter towards the rim; the inside is of the same colour, but has a kind of glazed and shiny appearance. The lid is mauve in the centre, shading to green at the edges. The stems of the female flowers we found always a foot shorter than those of the male, and the former were far less numerous than the latter. It is indeed one of the most astonishing productions of nature.

Mr. Low set to work enthusiastically to collect specimens, while I tried to procure some compass bearings; but the mist kept driving over the country, so that I had only one good opportunity. I rested the compass on a rock, and was surprised by its pointing in a very different direction from what the position of the sun showed it should. On raising

it in my hands, it pointed correctly.   I found, on
examination, that the rock was covered with a thick
coating of iron, and all in the neighbourhood were
in a similar state.   To-day we reached an elevation
of 5,400 feet.   The path we followed was tolerably
good; we were told that it led to the village of
Sayap, a branch of the Kiau tribe.

The sandstone near the mountain is almost perpendicular, being at an angle of 80°: lower down the
sides it lessens.   It appears as if the molten granite
had been forced up through the sandstone.   Along
the sides of the spurs were huge boulders of granite,
left, doubtless, by the streams ere they cut their way
deeper in the earth.   Mr. Low having finished collecting, we returned, and during the walk were continually regaled with the rich perfume of the flowers
of the magnolia, but could not find one of them,
though the plant was a common shrub.   After a
tiring descent, we reached the plain about five, and
made preparations to pass the night at a hut belonging to Limoung, in the valley of Pinokok.

We never had a finer view of Kina Balu than this
evening.   A white cloud in the form of a turban,
its edges richly fringed with gold, encompassed most
of the highest peaks, while the brightness of the setting sun rendered every other portion of the mountain
distinctly visible, except those dark valleys cut deep
in its sides, where the Dahombang and the Pinokok
have their rise; and even here a succession of cascades
reflected back the sun's rays from the shadowy gloom.

We were standing opposite its western face, and
having no high buttress between us and the mountain, we could observe the great precipice, which is

t
n
in

eve
its e
of tl
ting
distin
in its
have th
reflectec
We w
having n
tain, we c

here nearly perpendicular from the sloping summit
down to an elevation of about 5,000 feet.  As we
stood there admiring the extreme beauty of the scene,
a double rainbow began to appear, and apparently
arching over the mountain, formed, as it were, a
bright framework to the picture.  We stayed there
until the sun setting beyond the distant hills threw
the valley into shade, but left its brightness on the
craggy peaks above.  Gradually the wind rose
and drove the clouds over the heavens, and the
form of the mountain and the brilliant rainbows
vanished.

The land in this valley is of the richest description—far superior, Mr. Low thought, to that used in
Ceylon for coffee plantations.  The hut where we
stayed the night was 3,000 feet above the level of the
sea, and the hills around about 4,000 feet.

Next morning we returned to the houses by the
same path, and rested on the summit of the hill overlooking the village.  Here we sat for some time,
making inquiries about the great lake.  They speak
of it as undoubtedly existing, saying we could reach
it in three days.  One who had traded with the
villages on its banks asserted that standing on the
beach, he could not see the opposite side.  The first
village on the road is Tuhan, and the next Inserban:
they all call the lake Ranau, a corruption of the
Malay Danau.  We could scarcely make any connected inquiries, on account of the indifference or
stupidity of our interpreter; but seriously discussed
the possibility of our being able to combine the two
journeys, but found our means insufficient.  With
our party we should have taken a long time, parti-

cularly as the villagers refused to furnish us with guides until their rice-planting was over.

We noticed the great change that had taken place in the ways and tastes of these people. When Mr. Low was here in 1851, beads and brass wire were very much sought after. When we came last April, the people cared nothing for beads, and very little for cloth ; their hearts were set on brass wire. We, however, distributed a good deal of cloth, at reasonable rates, in exchange for food and services rendered. We now found that even brass wire, except of a very large size, was despised, and cloth eagerly desired. Chawats were decreasing, and trousers coming in. This is a taste very likely to continue, as the weather at Kiau is generally very cool, and it might also stimulate their industry. At present, although they keep their plantations very clean, they use no instrument to turn up the soil, merely putting the seed in a hole made by a pointed stick. In size, their kiladis, sweet potatoes, and rice are very inferior and their crops scanty, though the flavour of their productions is excellent, but with their tobacco they appear to take much pains. Thinking that potatoes might flourish here, Mr. Low, in 1856, sent some by Mr. Lobb to be given to the villagers to plant; next morning, however, he found the little boys playing marbles with them.

Even the more civilized Javanese cared little for the seeds of European vegetables which were distributed freely by the Dutch Government. It at last struck some shrewd officer that if the natives saw the results of cultivating these vegetables, they might be induced to turn their attention to them. He therefore obtained permission to establish a model garden, and the result was satisfactory. The Javanese, who had despised the seeds, could not overlook the profit to be derived from the sale of the crops of potatoes, cabbages, and other esculents, displayed for their imitation, and were then grateful for seeds. Nothing but some such scheme will ever induce the Dayaks to alter their present slovenly system of cultivation.

Among those who accompanied us to Marei Parei was a young lad, who was paid for his services in gray shirting and thin brass wire. As soon as he had received them, he cut off three inches of the wire, and began beating out one end and sharpening the other: it was to make a needle. His sister brought him some native-made thread; then with his knife he cut the cloth into a proper shape, and set to work to make a pair of trousers; nor did he cease his occupation till they were finished, and by evening he was wearing them.

We were so pleased with our visit to the Marei Parei spur that we determined to move thither for a few days with our servants, and live in tents. In the meantime we continued our collection of Kiau words, which was difficult work with our interpreters.

It has been thought that the tribes living around Kina Balu speak different languages, but we found, on the contrary, that the Ida'an, Dusun, and even the Bisaya, can converse freely with each other. We had with us, during our different expeditions, Bisayas from the river Kalias, opposite Labuan, an interpreter who had learnt the language from the people in the interior of Membakut, Malays who had learnt it at Kimanis, Dusuns from Tamparuli, on the Tawaran, and Ida'an from the plains of Tampasuk; and yet, after a few days, to become accustomed to the differences of dialect, all these men conversed freely with the Kiaus.  If they are asked whether they speak the same languages, they will answer, "No," and give as an example—" We say *iso*, when the Kiaus say *eiso*, for ' no ';" but these are only localisms.  I must add, that none of these people had ever visited the Kiaus until they accompanied us.

In making vocabularies here we found the villagers very careless of their pronunciation: for instance, the word " heavy " was at different times written down, *magat, bagat, wagat,* and *ogat;* for "rice," *wagas* and *ogas;* for "to bathe," *padshu, padsiu,* and *madsiu,* and indifferently pronounced in these various ways by the same people.  Many years previously, when I was at Maludu Bay, I collected a few words of the Ida'an, and they were essentially the same as those of the aborigines of Tampasuk; and the Malays tell me that the Ida'an of the north-eastern coast speak so as to be understood by them, who have acquired their knowledge on the western coast.  I may here observe that the same people are indifferently called Dusun and Ida'an.  The term Dusun, the real meaning of which is villager, is applied to these northern inhabitants of Borneo by the Malays, while the Bajus generally call them Ida'an.

While we were making preparations for our short visit to Marei Parei, we noticed some agitation among the Kiaus, and found it arose from a report that a large party of Europeans had arrived at Bawang, on the Tawaran, on their way to the mountain, and it was added, heavy guns had been heard at sea.  We could

not, of course, offer any explanation, but thought
there was very little likelihood of any one coming to
join us, and suggested, what proved to be the truth,
that the news of our own arrival at Bawang had been
reaching them by a circuitous route. We treated the
report with so much indifference as to satisfy their
suspicious minds.

The next morning, the men who had agreed to
carry our bedding refused to fulfil their contract
unless paid double wages; so we started with our own
servants, but were quickly followed by the Ida'an,
who eagerly shouldered the heaviest burdens. They
were only trying how far they could succeed in im-
posing on us. The Fop also took a load. That name
was affixed to him, on our first visit, from his great
attention to dress, and the favour shown him by all
the young girls, more due to his evident good-nature
than to his good looks; he was, however, an active,
powerful man. When we were here in April, he had
just married a fine girl, named Sugan, and used
always, when the crowd surrounded us, to be seen
standing behind her with his arms folded round her
neck. He was better mannered than any of his
neighbours, and never annoyed us by begging. He
it was who told us he had been to the lake, and
. followed the route through Tuhan, Inserban and Bar-
bar. His name is Kamá. I mention him, as he
might prove useful as a guide to the lake, should
any traveller be induced to try that journey.

We followed the same path we used on the former
occasion—across the Pinokok valley, and up the
buttress, till we reached Marei Parei, and encamped
on a rocky, dry spot near the place where the

21—2

*Nepenthes Rajah* were found in the greatest abundance.

Knowing that the cold would be severely felt by our followers, accustomed all their lives to the heat of the plains, we tried to induce them to take precautions, but without avail. We, however, took care of ourselves by cutting enough brushwood to raise our bedding a foot above the damp ground, to fill up the end of our tent and cover it over with bushes, grass, and reeds, to prevent the cold piercing through. Around us were thickets of magnolias, but without flowers, and among the other shrubs which grew near was one which we selected for our beds, as when bruised it emitted a myrtle-like fragrance.

The temperature was very pleasant in the afternoon, being 75° in the shade; but this was partly caused by the refraction from the rocky soil around. In the water the thermometer marked 66·5°, but at sunset it fell to 60° in our tent, and the men, too late, began to repent of their idleness.

The vegetation around is very stunted, though above the trees are large-sized: the former is due to the stony nature of the soil and the great amount of iron that renders all compass bearings untrustworthy. It is, I believe, decomposed serpentine, containing a large quantity of peroxide of iron. Above the vegetation the mountain presents nothing but rough precipices impossible to ascend. On their face we observed broad white patches and white lines running across, similar to those I observed on the summit during my former ascent. On the top of the north-west peak we noticed a heap of stones, which, through a good telescope, looked like a cairn, and we were full of conjectures as to the possibility of a traveller in ancient times having made the ascent. This apparent cairn was afterwards explained by similar heaps of granite piled up as if by man, but being simply the harder portions of the rock remaining when the rest had crumbled away.

At sunrise the thermometer marked 55°, and the air felt very chilly; so, after a cup of chocolate to warm our blood, we started to explore the slopes above us.

Dr. Hooker having kindly allowed me to make use of his descriptions of the wonderful pitcher-plants discovered during these expeditions, I shall avail myself of the permission, and introduce here his notes on the Bornean species of *Nepenthes*, as well as the botanical account of the ones found on the Marei Parei spur.

The largest was the *Nepenthes Rajah*. The plates, copied from those published in the *Linnean Transactions*, merely give the form, as it has been found necessary to reduce them to the size of the volume.

" The want of any important characters in the flowers and fruit of *Nepenthes* is a very remarkable feature of these plants. The leaves differ considerably in insertion, and in being more or less petioled. The pitchers of most, when young, are shorter, and provided with two ciliated wings in front; more mature plants bear longer pitchers, with the wings reduced to thickened lines. The glandular portion of the pitcher remains more constant than any other, and the difference between the form of old and young pitchers is often chiefly confined to the

further development of the superior glandular portion into a neck or tube."*

" *Ascidia magna, ore mediocri, annulo latissime
explanato, dense lamellato v. costato.*

"Nepenthes Rajah, H. f. (Frutex, 4-pedalis, *Low*).
Foliis maximis 2-pedalibus, oblongo-lanceolatis petiolo
costaque crassissimis, ascidiis giganteis (cum operculo
1-2-pedalibus) ampullaceis ore contracto, stipite folio
peltatim affixo, annulo maximo lato everso crebre
lamellato, operculo amplissimo ovato-cordato, ascidium
totum æquante.—(*Tab.* LXXII).

" *Hab.*—Borneo, north coast, on Kina Balu, alt.
5,000 feet (*Low*). This wonderful plant is certainly
one of the most striking vegetable productions
hitherto discovered, and, in this respect, is worthy of
taking place side by side with the *Rafflesia Arnoldii*.
It hence bears the title of my friend Rajah Brooke,
of whose services, in its native place, it may be com-
memorative among botanists. . . . I have only
two specimens of leaves and pitchers, both quite
similar, but one twice as large as the other. Of
these, the leaf of the larger is 18 inches long,
exclusive of the petioles, which is as thick as the
thumb and 7-8 broad, very coriaceous and glabrous,
with indistinct nerves. The stipes of the pitcher
is given off below the apex of the leaf, is 20 inches
long, and as thick as the finger. The broad
ampullaceous pitcher is 6 inches in diameter, and
12 long : it has two fimbriated wings in front,
is covered with long rusty hairs above, is wholly
studded with glands within, and the broad annulus

* *The Transactions of the Linnean Society of London.* Vol. XXII.,
Part IV., p. 419.

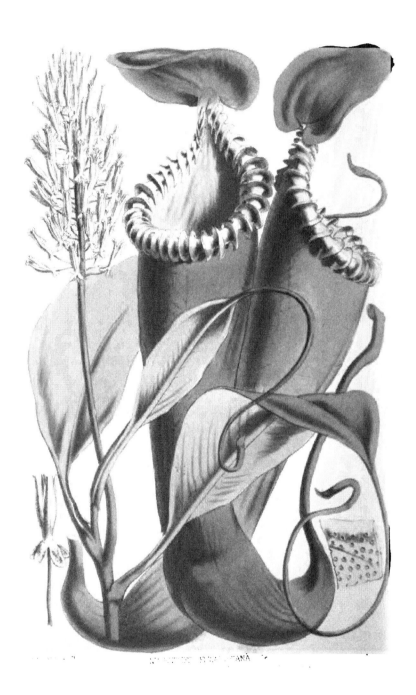

is evened, a... l... l...l.
shortly expire... ... Les [

... ... ... ... harc

r... ... ... ... ... ...

ny... ... ... ... ... llov...

v... ... ... ... ... lancie

... ... br l... l...

... les lo...

... ... ...

...

Th...

... gr...

... ...

...

...

... ...

... ...

... ... w... l...

... ... ... ...

na... ... ... made w... ... r...

search ... ... in w... ... a

drow... ...

As... ... ... ... ... ... red

a t... l... ... ... ... ... l..., and

... ... ... ... ... ... w. some-

... ... ... ... ... p... ... gr... v

... ... ... by... ... ... ... the

V... ... ... l... times... i... was

... ... ... d... ng the spar, but con-

... ... to... ... r of a mile in length,

* ... ... ... ... ... V... XXII.,

Part l... ... p. 1...

is everted, and 1–1½ inch in diameter. Operculum shortly stipitate, 10 inches long and 8 broad.

"The inflorescence is hardly in proportion. Male raceme, 30 inches long, of which 20 are occupied by the flowers; upper part and flowers clothed with short rusty pubescence. Peduncles slender, simple or bifid. Fruiting raceme stout. Peduncles 1½ inches long, often bifid. Capsule, ¾ inch long, ⅓ broad, rather turgid, densely covered with rusty tomentum."*

The pitchers, as I have before observed, rest on the ground in a circle, and the young plants have cups of the same form as those of the old ones. This morning, while the men were cooking their rice, as we sat before the tent enjoying our chocolate, observing one of our followers carrying water in a splendid specimen of the *Nepenthes Rajah*, we desired him to bring it to us, and found that it held exactly four pint bottles. It was 19 inches in circumference. We afterwards saw others apparently much larger, and Mr. Low, while wandering in search of flowers, came upon one in which was a drowned rat.

As we ascended, we left the brushwood and entered a tangled jungle, but few of the trees were large, and the spur of the mountain became very narrow, sometimes not much wider than the path, and greatly encumbered at one part by the twining stems of the *Nepenthes Edwardsiana*. This handsome plant was not, however, much diffused along the spur, but confined to a space about a quarter of a mile in length,

* *The Transactions of the Linnean Society of London.* Vol. XXII., Part IV., p. 421.

and grew upon the trees around, with its fine pitchers
hanging from all the lower boughs.  We measured
one plant and it was twenty feet in length; it was
quite smooth, and the leaves were of a very acute
shape at both ends.  It is a long, cylindrical, finely-
frilled pitcher, growing on every leaf; one we picked
measured twenty-one inches and a half long, by two
and a half in breadth.  They swelled out a little
towards the base, which is bright pea green, the rest
of the cylinder being of a bright brick-red colour.
Its mouth is nearly circular, the column with the
border surrounding the mouth being finely formed of
thin plates about a sixth of an inch apart, and about
the same in height, and both were of a flesh colour;
the handsome lid is of a circular shape.  The dried
specimen forwarded to Dr. Hooker only measured
eighteen inches.  The plant is epiphytal, growing
on casuarinas (*species nova*).  The pitchers of the
young creepers precisely resembled those of the older
ones, except in size.

Whilst examining these, and vainly searching for
their flowers, Mr. Low came upon a small species of
a bright crimson colour; its pitchers were three
inches long, and one and a half broad at the widest
part, and the mouth was oblique.  Another, but
which may be the same in a more mature state, was
green, with irregular spots of purple, having stems of
the latter colour; it was a low plant, not reaching
above four feet in height.

A very handsome plant of a trailing habit also
grew on this spur; it had large bunches of beautiful
flowers of the colour of the brightest of the seedling
scarlet geraniums, and while endeavouring to obtain

a view to the eastward, my eye fell upon something of a beautiful white, which proved to be a lovely orchid. Of these Mr. Low made a great collection; I fear, however, it is not a new one.

The following is the botanical description of the *Nepenthes Edwardsiana* :—

"*Ascidia magna, ore lamellis latis disciformibus annularibus remotis instructo.*

"Nepenthes Edwardsiana, Low. MSS. — Foliis (6″ longis) crasse coriaceis longe petiolatis ellipticis, ascidiis magnis crasse pedunculatis cylindraceis basi ventricosis 8–18″ longis, ore lamellis annularibus distantibus rigidis magnis cristato, collo elongato erecto, operculo cordato-rotundato, racemo simplici, rachi pedicellisque ferrugineo-tomentosis. (*Tab.* LXX.)

"*Hab.*—Kina Balu, north side; alt. 6,000–8,000 feet (*Low*).

"The leaves, ascidia, and pitchers sent by Mr. Low are all old, and nearly glabrous; but the young parts —rachis, peduncles of the panicle, and the calyx— are covered with ferruginous tomentum. One of the pitchers sent is eighteen inches long from the base to the apex of the erect operculum; it is two and a half inches in diameter below the mouth, one and a half at the narrowest part (about one-third distant from the base), and the swollen part above the base is about two inches in diameter. The beautiful annular discs which surround the mouth are three-quarters of an inch in diameter." *

We had occasionally very extensive prospects, and the day being bright and sunny, could obtain

* *The Transactions of the Linnean Society of London.* Vol. XXII., Part IV., p. 420.

almost an uninterrupted view of the whole coast from
Kimanis to Tampasuk, with glimpses of the river
reaches below, winding among the hills, and flowing
through the open plains of Tampasuk, Sulaman, and
Tawaran, and beneath our feet were the sources of
the Peñgantaran, which we crossed on our last expedition.   The only interruption was, in fact, the
double peaks of Saduk Saduk, which is about 6,000
feet high; and as we only ascended 6,200 feet, we
were but beginning to see over them.   One side of
that mountain is almost cleared to its summit for rice
plantations, though the produce could not be very re-
paying.  Mr. Lobb reached its top, but had, I believe,
no instruments to fix its height.   From the north the
two peaks are in a line, it then appears a sharp hill;
and I should judge from its aspect that it is sandstone to the summit.

We carefully examined the noble buttress on which
we were encamped, and were convinced that if ever
the north of Borneo fall into the hands of a European power, no spot could be better suited for
barracks than Marei Parei.  The climate is delightful: at sunrise the average was 56°; midday, 75°;
sunset, 63°; and this temperature would keep European soldiers in good health: there is water at hand,
and up the western spur a road could be easily made
suited to cattle and horses; in fact, buffaloes are now
occasionally driven from Labang Labang to Sayap.

The second day our men were more amenable to
advice, and made great preparations to resist the cold,
as the wind was rising and rain threatening; but after
a heavy shower, it cleared off, and we passed a very
pleasant night.   We found the most sustaining and

warming nourishment on the mountains, was to boil or stew a couple of fowls, with a two-pound tin of preserved soup. As we scarcely ever rested much during the day our appetites were keen, and we retired to our beds very shortly after seven to enjoy an almost uninterrupted sleep from eight till daylight.

Having finished collecting the plants of this spur, we returned to Kiau, and noticed during our walk that the sources of the Hobang and Pinokok cut very deep valleys into the actual mountain, and after the heavy rain last night, foaming cascades were visible in these as yet unlit valleys, for the morning sun had not risen above the mountain tops.

The villagers appeared to be very glad to get us back among them, and the girls became friendly and familiar; they even approached us and sat at the end of our mats, and talked, and laughed, and addressed us little speeches, which were, of course, nearly unintelligible, though we were making progress in the language. They had evidently been very much interested in all our movements; and as our toilettes were made in public, they could observe that every morning we bathed, cleaned our teeth, brushed and combed our hair, and went through our other ordinary occupations.

To-day they had grown more bold, and were evidently making fun of the scrupulous care we were bestowing on our persons while the cook was preparing our breakfast. We thought that we would good-humouredly turn the laugh against them, so we selected one who had the dirtiest face among them—and it was difficult to select where all were dirty—and asked her to glance at herself in the looking-glass. She did so, and then passed it round to the others; we then asked them which they thought looked best, cleanliness or dirt: this was received with a universal giggle.

We had brought with us several dozen cheap looking-glasses, so we told Iseiom, the daughter of Li Moung, our host, that if she would go and wash her face we would give her one. She treated the offer with scorn, tossed her head, and went into her father's room. But, about half an hour afterwards, we saw her come in to the house and try to mix quietly with the crowd; but it was of no use, her companions soon noticed she had a clean face, and pushed her into the front to be inspected. She blushingly received her looking-glass and ran away, amid the laughter of the crowd of girls. The example had a great effect, however, and before evening the following girls had received a looking-glass. I mention their names as specimens : — Ikara, Beiom, Sugan, Rambeiong, Iduñgat, Tirandam, Idoñg, Sei, and Sinéo. Among the males near were Kadsio, the trouser-maker, Bintarang, Lakaman, and Banul, who had lent his kitchen to us.

We spent a couple of days quietly at the village, waiting the arrival of our party : reports often reached us that they were not far off, and at last they came in, but sadly reduced in numbers. Seven had deserted, while one had stayed behind to look after his companion Sahat, who had been stricken with cholera while passing through Si Nilau. However, they brought sufficient rice to last us during the ascent of the mountain, as well as a few condiments for ourselves. We heard, also, to our satisfaction that the chief of Gantisan had seized Kamis the negro, and had confined him for theft and desertion.

All our preparations being completed, we started for our expedition to the summit of the mountain, following a path along the side of the valley, which ran below the houses, and was crossed by miniature torrents at various places. The ground was all under cultivation, principally tobacco and kiladis. Being in admirable walking condition from our regular exercise, we soon passed the hut where Mr. Low had rested during my former ascent, and crossing the stream, found ourselves in freshly-cleared ground, where crowds of women and children were planting rice. The ashes from the burning of the trees and brushwood must assist greatly to fertilize the soil, otherwise we could scarcely conceive that seed placed in a little hole driven in the hard-baked ground could produce a crop. It was a burning-hot day, and our men appeared to suffer severely in passing along this unsheltered path, so it was a relief to enter the forest.

We advanced by the same way I followed on the previous occasion; it was steep, and but rarely traversed, except by the rat snarers. The farther we advanced, the more numerous were the traps, but during our ascent none were caught. In fact, these wary animals are seldom taken, except when trying to escape from the active village curs. We heard the shouts of the hunters below, and the bark of the dogs, but we had passed on before they reached the path. The mountain-rat seems a favourite article of food among the Kiaus, though they do not eat those

which frequent the houses.    The edible animal is
about the size of the grey Norway rat, and is of the
Bandacoot species.

At 4,400 feet elevation we pitched our tents; and
here Li Moung and Li Maing, who had accompanied
us so far, handed us over to the younger men, headed
by Kamá, and returned home.   We hired both these
leaders, as we were unwilling to . be the cause of a
feud arising in the tribe, and by following this course
we kept friends with both parties.

We started early next morning, and after three
hours climbing of the sub-spurs, which were occasionally very steep, we reached the ridge of the great
buttress, and the walking became easier.   We passed
to-day the hut that I had constructed on the former
occasion.   As I have before observed, this ridge is
occasionally very narrow, and where it has been
exposed to the full force of the monsoons, the trees
bent over us, so as often to necessitate our crawling
beneath their overhanging trunks; for those who
carried burdens it was tiresome work, particularly as
the ground and trees were covered with soppy moss,
cold and unpleasant to the touch.   Where we did
not crawl, we had often to advance in a stooping
posture.   Occasionally we passed between fine forest
trees, with thickly-growing bamboo beneath them,
but these were only to be found in deep or sheltered
spots.   When we joined the first ridge, we came
upon numerous flowers of a rhododendron scattered
over the surface of the ground, and it was some time
before we could find the plant, but Mr. Low's quick
eye at last discovered it.   It looked gorgeous, being
completely covered with bunches of flowers of a

brilliant scarlet, and in masses of colour, as forty-two blossoms were counted growing in one of the bunches.

We at last reached a narrow, rocky ridge, covered with brushwood, but with thousands of plants of the beautiful *Nepenthes Lowii* growing among them. As water was to be had near, at a little marshy spot, we determined to pitch our tents here, and spend the evening collecting specimens. Our guides, however, strongly objected to this, and declared we must reach the cave to-night; but as this involved a climb of nearly 3,000 feet more, we declined, disregarding their threats that they would leave us where we were and return to their houses. Our coast men appeared totally unfit for such an exertion, though the cold weather had an invigorating effect upon ourselves.

There was another great objection to this rapid ascent: it prevented our seeing anything, or enjoying the views that this lovely weather promised to afford. It was true that day the scenery had been obscured by the blinding columns of smoke rising in every direction from the burning felled forest, but that objection might not hold another day. To the eastward, we had glimpses of high mountains, and of a river running through a plain.

I have seldom witnessed any of those beautiful phenomena of which I have read—as double sunsets —but that evening we witnessed one. A dark cloud hung over the horizon, and beneath it we saw a sun, clear and well-defined, set in vapour: we hurried on our preparations for the night, for fear darkness should overtake us, when the true sun, suddenly bursting from behind the concealing cloud, restored the day. I never saw men so astonished as were our followers, and we were as completely deceived as they were, though we did not give the same explanation, that we had fallen among jinn and other supernatural creatures.

We sent our men on next morning to wait for us at the cave, while we stayed behind to collect specimens of the *Nepenthes Lowii* and the *Nepenthes Villosa*. The former is, in my opinion, the most lovely of them all, and its shape is most elegant. I will give Dr. Hooker's botanical description of both.

"*Ascidia magna, curva, basi inflata, medio constricta, dein ampliata, infundibuliformia; ore maximo, latissimo, annulo O.*

" Nepenthes Lowii, H. f.—Caule robusto tereti, foliis crasse coriaceis, longe crasse petiolatis lineari-oblongis, ascidiis magnis curvis basi ventricosis medio valde constrictis, ore maximo ampliato, annulo O, operculo oblongo intus dense longe setoso. (*Tab.* LXXI.)

"*Hab.*—Kina Balu; alt. 6,000–8,000 feet (*Low*).

"A noble species, with very remarkable pitchers, quite unlike those of any other species. They are curved, 4–10 inches long, swollen at the base, then much constricted, and suddenly dilating to a broad, wide, open mouth with glossy shelving inner walls, and a minute row of low tubercles round the circumference; they are of a bright pea green, mottled inside with purple. The leaves closely resemble those of *Edwardsiana* and *Boschiana* in size, form, and texture, but are more linear-oblong.

"I have specimens of what are sent as the male flower and fruit, but not being attached, I have not ventured to describe them as such. The male raceme

a.d we were as completely deceived as they were,
th... ... c..i not ...ive the same explanation, that
. ... ...a a...... jinn and other supernatural

... ... ... on next morning to wait for us
... ... ... .e stayed behind to collect speci-
me... ... *athes Lowii* and the *Nepenthes*
*I... ...* ...er is, in my opinion, the most
lov.ly ... ... ...'. i's shape is most elegant.
I will ... ... th. .. .'s botanical descripti... of
both.

"... *..* ... ... ..., *basi inflata, medi.* ...
*su.* ... ... ... ...*cyl.* ..., *baliformia; ore maxime,*
... *... dum* ...

... ... ..., H. f.—Caule robusto tered-
... ...nge crasse petiolatis linear.
... ...urvis basi ventricosis medi
... ... ampliato. annulo O, ...-
... ... ...e setosо. (*Tab.* LXXI
... ... ...—K... ... ... ... 6,000–8,000 feet (*L.* ...
...A n.." sp... ... w.th very remarkable pitcher-
...'... like those ... ... other species. They are
... ..., 4–10 in.es long, swollen at the base
... much con.ricted, and suddenly dilating to a
...' ...'... ...n mouth with glossy shelving inner
... ... ...ute row of low tubercles round the
... ... ...: ... are of a bright pea green, mottled
in ... ... p.'.e.. The leaves closely resemble those
of *Edwar'siana* and *Baschiana* in size, form, and
texture, but are more linear-oblong.

"I have specimens of what are sent as the male
flower and fruit, but not being attached, I have not
...tured to describe them as such. The male raceme

is eight inches long, dense flowered. Peduncles simple. Perianth with depressed glands on the inner surface, externally rufous and pubescent. Column long and slender. *Female* inflorescence : a very dense oblong panicle ; rachis, peduncles, perianth, and fruit covered with rusty tomentum. Capsules, two-thirds of an inch long, one-sixth of an inch broad." *

The outside colour of the pitchers is a bright pea-green, the inside dark mahogany ; the lid is green, while the glandular are mahogany-coloured. A very elegant claret jug might be made of this shape.

" *Ascidia magna, ore lamellis latis disciformibus annularibus remotis instructo.*

" Nepenthes Villosa, H. f. (Hook, Ic. Pl. t. 888). —Ascidia magna turgida late pyriformia coriacea, 5″ longa, 3½″ lata, alis anticis mediocribus grosse dentatis, ore aperto annulo maximo ! lamellis annularibus distantibus disciformibus rigidis, 1″ diam., cristatis posticis in spinas rigidas ½″ longas, fundum ascidii spectantibus productis, collo elongato erecto, operculo orbiculato intus densissime glanduloso dorso basi longe cornuto. (*Tab.* LXIX.)

"*Hab.*—Borneo (*Lobb*), Kina Balu, alt. 8,000– 9,000 feet (*Low*).

" . . . The whole inner surface of the pitcher is glandular, except a very narrow area beneath the mouth at the back." *

The pitchers of the young plant resemble the old, and their colour looks like that of a downy peach skin, with a great deal of dark crimson in it. The circular

* *The Transactions of the Linnean Society of London.* Vol. XXII., Part IV., p. 420.

annulus is like flesh-coloured wax, its lid dull green, with red shading in the centre.

The *Nepenthes Villosa* continued to skirt our path for the next two thousand feet; and among the most extraordinary shrubs was the heath rhododendron.

At an open space about 7,500 feet above the level of the sea, we had a fine view of the south and south-east part of Borneo, which stretches away to the great river of Kina Batangan. Numerous mountain ranges and lofty peaks, some estimated as high as 7,000 to 8,000 feet, were clearly visible. Between us and the mountains bearing south-east by east, and apparently eighteen miles off, there was a grassy plain, perhaps three miles by two, in which were many villages; and through this there flowed a rather large river. We could trace its course as far as the third spur that springs from the main buttress of Kina Balu, on which we now stood. There, a line of hills appeared to obstruct it; but beyond we could again trace the course of a stream which may probably be its source. This river, our guide stated, fell into the lake of Kina Balu. It runs from south-west to north-east. With the exception of the plain above mentioned, and a marsh, whose commencement we could observe north-east of the plain, all the country appeared hilly. Most of the land was cleared, and either under cultivation, or showing the remains of former farms. We could observe in the second valley two villages: the first called Tuhan; the next, Inserban. At both cotton is stated to be cultivated. Many more distant villages and detached houses could be seen to the south-east, whose names our guides had forgotten.

The road to the lake is by the above-mentioned villages. The names of those beyond are Penusuk, Tambian, Paka, and Koporiñgan. These are either on the route, or close to the lake.

We sat looking at this extensive view, and enjoying the refreshing breeze and the bright sun. Kamá was in a communicative mood to-day, and we had a long talk about the great lake. We could clearly perceive that it was not in the position assigned to it in all the maps, as the whole country from east-south-east to the western coast was distinctly visible, and the Ida'an expressly stated that it was farther to the north and east of the little plain I have before noticed. Its size would, I believe, entirely depend on the season it was visited, as the heavy rains would cause it to overflow the country, and probably add the marsh and plain we saw to its extent, and the native travellers would naturally give different accounts.

We now continued our ascent to the cave by the same path I followed before, and found it quite sufficient for a day's journey. The cave proved to be above 9,000 feet above the level of the sea; and although we tried by fires and hanging up oiled cloths before the entrance to keep out the raw night air, yet the men felt it very cold.

We started early next morning for the summit, with a clear sky and a brilliant sun, through thickets of the scarlet and rosy-purple rhododendrons which extended for nearly a thousand feet above the cave, and soon reached the granite slopes, which, by the clinometer, we found to have an angle varying from 35° to 39° at the steepest parts. Leaving Low's Gully on the right, where the purple or rather

blood-coloured rhododendron flourishes, we pushed
on for the terrace lying between the southern and
northern peaks.

As I spent very little of my time in looking for
plants, I reached it some time before my fellow-
traveller, and was surprised to find the great ease with
which we could converse, although more than a
quarter of a mile apart.   It really required no effort,
and the air appeared so transparent as to render it
difficult to judge of distances.   From Low's Gully to
the north-western peak does not exceed two miles ;
and we were struck by a remarkable feature in the
granite rocks, which run in a broken line along
the northern face of the summit.   It appeared as
if they were lying in strata, which partly accounts
for the angular granite we observed in the streams
below.

When I first reached the terrace the sun was shining brightly on the landscape below, and my first im-
pulse was to turn to look for that lofty mountain
of which I had obtained a glimpse during my former
ascent, but the southern peak shut in that view, and I
had to content myself with the still extensive prospect.
Looking over the valley of Pinokok, I could distinctly
trace the coast line down even to Labuan, which, though
somewhat hazy, was yet visible, near the great mountains of Brayong and Si Guntang.   The Bay of
Kimanis was to be seen in all its distinctness, and,
with Nosong Point, Pulo Tiga, and Papar Headland, looked at this distance almost land-locked.
Gaya island was there visible, but the bay was shut
in by its surrounding hills.   Mengkabong and Sulaman waters showed clear, and I could occasion-

ally observe some reaches of the Tawaran glistening among the fruit groves of the plain. The horizon was perhaps distant a hundred miles, showing a broad expanse of ocean. We stood looking at this prospect with great pleasure; but at last, being joined by the man who carried the barometer, I left Mr. Low to prepare the instrument, and started for the north-western peak, from which I hoped to have the most extensive view to be seen in all Borneo, and to have the satisfaction of examining that heap of stones which looked like a cairn from below.

It was easy to get to its base. On the northern side of it were heaps of broken but angular granite, which appeared to have fallen from its sides, leaving a perpendicular face, a little overhanging at the summit. The slabs of granite, which peel off its western and southern sides, roll on a sharp slope, and must glide down to fall over the great precipice overlooking the valley of Pinokok. The heaps I observed to the south move more slowly onward towards the cliff, as the incline is less.

I tried to reach the summit of this peak by a narrow edge of rock abutting from its southern front; but after following it with my face towards it, and moving sideways with my arms stretched out on either side, till it narrowed to about eight inches, I thought it prudent to return; but at a spot where I had secure footing, I pitched a stone on the summit, which was about forty feet above the highest point I reached.

I had scarcely regained the base, when I saw a thick white cloud suddenly sweep up from the north, and heavy rain and gusts of wind soon wetted us

through and chilled us to the bone. I hurried along
the huge natural wall which skirts the northern edge
of the summit, and is the termination of the great
terrace, to join Mr. Low, and then heard that last
night's rain had wet the leather of Adie's barometer,
and it would not act. We tried the boiling-water
thermometers, but in this storm of wind, rain, and
hail, though we managed to light the spirit-lamp, we
could not read the number of degrees, the apparatus
appearing defective. We waited for nearly two hours,
hoping it would blow over; but it only increased in
violence, and enveloped in this rain-cloud, we could
not see fifty yards.

Unwillingly we now attended to the remonstrances
of our shivering followers, and commenced descending. The wind veered round suddenly to the east,
and drove the sleet and hail into our faces, while
torrents formed in every direction, and rushed over
the smooth surface of the granite. To descend was
a work of danger, as the streams of water crossed
our path in every direction; and had we lost our
footing while passing them, we should have been
sent gliding down to the precipices. It was bitterly
cold, the thermometer at two P.M. falling to 43°.
As we approached the steeper incline, the velocity
of the running water increased, and in one place, even
Kamá appeared at fault, as the granite was as slippery
as glass, being reduced to a fine polish, as it formed
the course down which the rains always ran; but
at last finding a crevice, into which we could insert the
sides of our feet, we managed to pass the momentarily
swelling torrent. One of our Malays was seized with
fever and -ague at this most difficult part of the

descent; but he behaved manfully, and managed, by his own exertions, to get down the granite slopes. My Chinese boy, Ahtan, fell, and rolled over several times, but escaped with a slight wound, but heavy bruises. One Malay's feet slipped from under him, and he fell heavily on his back, but his head escaped, as he was carrying on his shoulders a large basket full of flowers.

During both ascents, I observed the men carefully examining the crevices of the granite in search of little pieces of very transparent quartz, which were to be found there. I picked up, during the former trip, a little of them, that were greatly prized by the ladies of the capital, who had them inserted into rings.

After three hours' hard work, we reached the cave, in company with our invalids. The poor fever-stricken Malay looked in a woful plight, but we gave him immediately ten grains of quinine in a glass of whiskey, and by evening the fit was over. We found many of our men were injured by falls, but not seriously. Though Mr. Low made a fine collection of herbaceous and other plants, yet we were greatly disappointed with the result of our ascent, as the injury to the barometer was caused by our own carelessness.

We determined, however, to reascend to the summit next morning; but on trying the boiling-water thermometers, they did not act properly, and varied five degrees: the barometer also continued useless. We therefore gave up our intention, particularly when we found that all the Ida'an guides were making up their packets, declaring nothing should induce them to go through such exposure as they

suffered yesterday, and as we found many of our men
were ailing, we unwillingly, therefore, commenced
our descent, collecting plants by the way, and spent
the night at the hut I had erected during my first
expedition.

Next day we reached the village of Kiau, and had
a very different kind of settling day from the last.
Lemoung was civil and obliging, and all appeared
sorry at our leaving them, and begged us to return
again as soon as possible, promising to take us to the
lake, or wherever we might choose to go.

The girls now presented a very different appearance
from before: they thronged round us, most of them with
carefully-washed faces, and requested us to remember
their commissions.   Some wanted thread and needles,
others looking-glasses and combs.   As we did not
intend to re-ascend the mountain, we, in return for
the neat little baskets of tobacco with which they
presented us, made a distribution among them of all
our surplus warm clothing, and their delight was
great; and Lemoung's daughter took so great a fancy
to my comb and brush that, though unwilling, I was
obliged to part with them.

When we started next morning, crowds of friendly
faces were around, and a troop of girls walked with us
part of the way; and on our leaving them at the crown
of the hill, they insisted upon our repeating the
promise to visit them again.   The good impression we
made upon these villagers may be of service to future
travellers.   We stopped at Koung for the night, as
many of our followers were ill, or suffering from falls
received on that unlucky day on the summit of Kina
Balu.   We made the old chief's heart glad by pre-

senting him with one of our tents, and such goods as
we could spare.

A hundred years ago, it was reported that the Ida'an
were in the habit of purchasing Christian slaves of the
pirates, in order to put them to death for the sake of
the heads. If it were ever true, I believe it is not so
now, as we never noticed dried skulls in any of their
houses, except at Tamparuli; and if they had been
given to any such practice, the Bajus, who never
missed an opportunity to malign them, would have
mentioned the subject to us.

As we were anxious to get our large collection
of plants as fast as possible to the vessel, we pushed
on next morning by the direct route to Buñgol and
breakfasted there; and, notwithstanding heavy rain,
continued our journey to Kalawat.

Next day we reached Si Nilau, to find that poor
Sahat was dead of cholera, and that his companion had
disappeared. We inquired about him, but could hear
nothing. We asked for the rice that they had left
here, but the owner of the house denied having any;
though one of our guides discovered hidden away in
a corner all the goods belonging to Sahat and the
missing man. The thief finding himself discovered,
ran into a neighbouring house and began to beat the
alarm signal on a drum, and in a very short time the
neighbouring villagers were seen collecting in arms;
but hearing the cause of the disturbance they dispersed, saying the English might settle with the old
thief as they pleased. However, on inquiry, finding
our missing follower was safe, we merely warned the
villager and continued our journey.

On arriving at Bawang we heard the distressing

intelligence that cholera was in possession of all the villages. We met processions on the river: old women, dressed up like the priestesses among the Land Dayaks of Sarawak, were chanting and beating gongs, and on the banks of the stream were erected altars, round which gaily-dressed women were dancing with a slow, measured step.

We were surprised at the wealth displayed by the family of the old Datu of Tamparuli. There were silks, and gold brocade, and a large amount of gold ornaments. We arrived late, having walked in one day what had taken us three in our advance to the mountain.

During the night we were disturbed by the cries of some of the inmates of our house, three of whom where suffering from attacks of cholera, and the only remedy they appeared to apply was water from the sacred jars, though they endeavoured to drive away the evil spirits by beating gongs and drums all night. Three people had died the previous day, but when we left in the morning the sufferers I have before mentioned were still alive. We had no medicines, not even a glass of spirits, to give them.

Next morning we walked over to Pañgeran Sirail's to breakfast, as our friends at Tamparuli were so much taken up with the awful visitation which had come upon them as to be unable to attend to anything else. In fact, though exceedingly hungry after our hard walking, we could not last night purchase anything for our dinner, and had to content ourselves with plain boiled rice. The Malay chief, however, was very hospitable, and soon procured us fowls, and sent off to Pañgeran Duroup for canoes to take us

across the lake.	On our arrival at Gantisan we
found the cholera had left it, though not before it
had carried off thirty-seven victims.

Signor Cuarteron came to visit us, and we kept him
to dinner; but, in the evening, the south-west monsoon
commenced blowing so heavily, that it was impossible
for him to return to the vessel, and this was merely
a commencement of what we had to expect.	In the
morning, however, it cleared up a little, and we
landed to visit Pañgeran Madoud.	He was erecting
a very substantial-looking wharf, nearly a hundred
yards in length, to enable people to get ashore at all
times of tide, and he intended it partly to give protection to very small trading prahus during the south-west
monsoon.	It was a grand work for a Malay to con-
ceive, and, although not constructed in a way likely
to be very lasting, it was a good commencement.
The Pañgeran had established himself in a very comfortable house, and in his audience hall had a large
table and many chairs.	He was very curious to hear
everything connected with the great mountain, and
begged, laughingly, for a single seed of the lagundi
fruit, that his youth might be restored to him.	We
found Kamis, the negro, looking very sad in the
stocks, but he got off with a very slight punishment;
but, as a warning to others, we refused to receive
the deserters on board, and let them return in a
native prahu.

We did not attempt to sail, as heavy clouds were
driving across the horizon, promising unsettled
weather; and, in the afternoon, so heavy a squall
arose, that our anchor could not hold, and we began
drifting towards the shore.	We hauled in the chain, but

when it was nearly all on board, we were not ten feet
from the coral reefs opposite Gantisan. With extreme
difficulty, on account of the breaking waves, we got
the smaller anchor into our boat, and sent it out fifty
yards ahead, and hauling in that merely saved us
from striking, as it came home as well as the larger
one. For two hours we continued sending out one
anchor after the other, but it did not keep us clear
of the danger, as during one heavy puff our pinnace
struck the coral, and we thought she would soon go
to pieces; but this blast was followed by a momentary
lull, during which we managed to haul out a hundred
yards, and let go both anchors; and, veering out as
much chain as we could, we felt comparatively safe.
The storm broke on us again with great violence, but
our anchors held.

For three days this dirty weather continued, blowing steadily from the south-west, and we had some
difficulty in procuring supplies of rice for our men.
In fact, the village had but little in store, as all
communication with the Dusuns had been put a
stop to on account of the cholera. It was, therefore, fortunate we had not delayed our expedition till August, for we certainly would have been
turned back, as all the paths were now pamali or
interdicted.

On the fifth day, the wind appearing to moderate,
we set sail from Gantisan, intending to pass through
the broad channel, between Gaya and Sapanggar
Islands; but, when we opened the sea, the waves
were breaking in white foam, and so heavy a swell
came in that our pinnace could not beat against the
wind: we, therefore, ran into a small harbour on

the north of Gaya Island, and anchored in thirteen fathoms. In the evening we landed, but, finding the jungle tangled, did not penetrate far; and, leaving Mr. Low to botanize, I strolled along the beach to the rocky sandstone point.

I came there upon certain stones which appeared to me very curious. On the surface of some were marks, as if huge cups, three feet in diameter, were let into the rock and then filled up with a different kind of sandstone. One only did I see which was detached from the surrounding rock; it was round, with an edge two inches thick, raised three inches above the inner surface.

This little harbour is plentifully supplied with water, as several small rivulets fall into it from the surrounding high land. We could observe the waves breaking on the sands and rocks at the mouth of the Ananam, as the wind drove the sea through the narrow and dangerous passage between Gaya Island and the mainland. At night very heavy rain came on, and the wind moderated.

In the morning, though there was a heavy swell, the wind was moderate, and many fishing-boats were seen scattered over the surface of the bay. We hailed one, and the fishermen coming alongside with a large number for sale, we purchased all he had. Among them were several fish which frequent the coral rocks; one was small, slightly streaked with red, with very prickly fins, which the natives are careful to chop off before attempting to handle them, as, if wounded by one, the effect is as if poison had been injected into the flesh. There are also many others, whose fins are equally to be avoided.

Some of the fish brought alongside were as beautiful as those celebrated in the Arabian tale, where " the fisherman, looking into the lake, saw in it fish of different colours—white, and red, and blue, and yellow;" indeed, they could not have been more beautiful than ours. In fact, all that are caught on coral reefs are remarkable for the great variety of their colours; but I must particularly describe one which bore the palm from all its splendid companions. It was about ten inches in length, and had for the basis of its colours an emerald green, with a head of a lighter shade of the same hue, which was banded longitudinally with stripes of rosy pink, and lines of the same beautiful tint were placed at intervals of an eighth of an inch transversely across its whole body, the scales on which were very small. The two pectoral fins were rosy pink in the centre, surrounded by a broad band of ultramarine. The short dorsal and ventral fins, which were continued to the tail, were of the same colours, the pink being inside. The tail was ultramarine outside, and the centre part of the fin of gamboge yellow: it had no anal fins. There was another extremely beautiful one of a pea-green colour: it appeared to be of the same genus as the former.

The one streaked with red, with the poisonous fins, had firm flesh, and was rather pleasant to the taste; but in general their flavour and quality by no means equalled the brilliancy of their appearance. We placed the lovely emerald fish in a bucket of sea-water, but it soon turned on its back, and showed unmistakable signs of exhaustion. It seemed a sin to dine off so beautiful a creature. However, I suffered for it during the evening : I thought I was seized with cholera, and could scarcely get rid of the pains in the stomach ; but Mr. Low did not feel any ill effects, so the fish may be harmless.

Next morning, there being a slight land breeze at early dawn, we stood out to sea, notwithstanding the heavy swell, as the leaves of our mountain collection were beginning to fade from their long confinement on board, though we had brought proper boxes in which to plant them. We soon got clear of the harbour ; but no sooner did we begin to shape our course down the coast, and get to the leeward of Gaya Island, than the breeze failed us, and the roll of the China seas appeared to be forcing us on the rocky point not half a mile off. We manned our boat, and attempted to tow the pinnace off shore, but our efforts would have been in vain had not the ebb tide gradually swept us beyond the island, and thus restored to us the faint land breeze. Presently it died away, but we were now beyond immediate danger ; and though the heavy swell continued, there were no waves. As the sun was warm and brilliant, we felt sure that in the afternoon we should have a fine sea breeze ; so that we were proportionably annoyed when our head man came to tell us they had forgotten to replenish their casks at Gaya Island, and were now without water. We sent the boat away, as it was impossible to foretel how many days we might be at sea ; but before they returned, heavy clouds began to show on the western horizon, threatening bad weather.

I never saw a more singular sight, as the long line of black cloud gradually gathered above the sea, leaving a clear space below it, and waterspouts began to form. I counted at one time seventeen, either perfect or commencing. I carefully watched the whole process : the cloud appears to dip a little, and the sea below is agitated and covered with foam ; gradually a pillar begins to descend from on high with a gyrating motion, and a corresponding pillar rises from the sea. Sometimes they meet, and the whole object is completed ; at others, they do not, and the water falls back into the ocean with great disturbance. I have watched them trying again and again to meet : sometimes the wind drives the cloud-pillar to an acute angle, and prevents the junction ; at others, vain efforts, as vainly repeated, are made by sea and cloud. I have heard so many stories of danger to ships from these waterspouts that I always felt rather nervous when passing them in a very small vessel. Our boat being still away, we took advantage of the commencement of the sea breeze to run under one of the islets to the south of Gaya and anchor there. Between the larger island and the point of Api Api on the mainland I once attempted to pass, but we grounded on a coral reef ; however, there is a passage, but a difficult one to those accustomed to the coast.

I am not aware who inserted the names in the Admiralty charts, but they are often ill spelt, and incorrectly placed. Loney Island, south of Gaya, is generally called Sinitahan, "Hold here," Island, from the great protection it affords to native prahus in both monsoons ; and our informants insisted that the islands marked Bantok, Baral, and Risa, should be Memanukan, Sulug, and Memutik, and that the

opposite point, called Lutut, or the Knee, should be
Aru. I only mention this, as some of the officers in
Labuan might be requested to furnish the correct
names to the Admiralty, as it is exceedingly inconvenient to voyagers along the coast to ask for places
by names which are not recognized by the inhabitants.
While speaking of these otherwise admirably correct
charts, I would draw attention to the fact, that the
position of Tanjong Baram, or Baram Point, in the
last published general chart of Borneo, differs about
ten miles from that given in the charts recording the
surveys of Sir Edward Belcher and Commander
Gordon. This requires explanation.

Our boat having joined us, we got under way, and
stood towards Pulo Tiga; the weather was squally
and the night proved unpleasant, with strong gusts of
wind and heavy rain, but in the morning we found
ourselves opposite the island for which we were steering. A light land breeze now carried us past Nosong
Point, with its curious detached rocks, but left us in
a calm after we were a few miles from shore.

As usual, the sea breeze sprang up in the afternoon, but it came from the south-west. As we had
been awake most of the previous night, we were dozing
in the afternoon, when a bustle over our heads startled
us, and we went on deck to see what was the matter.
We found we were among the Pine-tree Shoals, with
a large water-washed rock, not marked in the charts,
within fifty yards of us. To let go the anchor and
take in the sail, to meet a heavy squall from the
westward, was the work of a moment. A heavy
squall in a dangerous position is a thing to be remembered: you see advancing upon you an enor-

mous arch of black cloud, with a slightly white
misty sky beneath, called by the Malays the wind's
eye, and when it breaks upon you with a force
almost sufficient to lift you from your legs and
sweep you into the sea, you feel your own nothing-
ness, and how impotent are most of our efforts to
contend against the elements.

That day it blew heavily, and much depended
whether it were good holding ground, but our principal fear was that another water-washed rock might
be astern, on which if our vessel bumped she must go
to pieces. The villagers from the neighbouring coast
saw our danger and thronged to the beach: but we
paid little attention to them, as we kept our eyes on
two points to watch if the pinnace drifted. The
sea as far as the eye could reach was one sheet of
curling waves, crested with foam, which broke upon
our bows and washed our decks; but as the wind became stronger, we veered out cable, though cautiously,
as we were uncertain what hidden dangers there might
be astern of us. It was an anxious time, as the squall
lasted two hours without abatement; but even storms
must have an end, and half an hour before sunset the
wind lessened, as it often does about that time, and
we sent out our boat to sound, and were soon able to
have the pinnace towed clear of the water-washed
rock, and setting sail we stood out to sea in a
north-westerly direction to give us a good offing.
We sat up by turns all that night, and amused
ourselves by watching the hundreds of stars that
fell or shot across the heavens, as is usual in the
month of August; and I saw a brilliant meteor
of a bluish colour, which appeared in the east, and

flashed across the dark sky to disappear almost in a moment. We reached Labuan by daylight the following morning.

I am sorry to say that we did not fulfil our promise to the Kiaus, to go and explore the lake. I fully intended doing so during my last visit to Borneo, but was prevented by my return home. I had not forgotten their commissions, and had provided myself with a large store of needles and thread, which were, however, equally prized by the ladies of Brunei.

I must add a few remarks respecting the plates of the *Nepenthes* which appear in this volume; they are copied, as I have before observed, from the magnificent plates published in the fourth part of the *Transactions of the Linnean Society of London*. It is impossible to obtain a complete idea of these astonishing pitchers from the plates I have inserted, as I have been obliged to reduce them to the size of my work; but I the less regret this, as they have been drawn the size of life in the *Transactions*. With regard to the colouring, I obtained the assistance of Mr. Low, who first saw the plants, and has studied their appearance and growth; and many of the apparent contradictions in describing their appearance arise from the change which takes place in their tints at different ages.

# CHAPTER XI.

THE PHYSICAL AND POLITICAL GEOGRAPHY OF THE
DISTRICTS LYING BETWEEN GAYA BAY AND THE
TAMPASUK RIVER; * WITH A GEOGRAPHICAL
SKETCH OF MALUDU BAY AND THE NORTH-EAST
COAST OF BORNEO.

* I have inserted this chapter, though, in fact, it contains but a
summary of the geographical information collected during our two
expeditions to Kina Balu, and some previous coasting voyages. I
necessarily involves repetition, but I hope will prove useful to geo-
graphers who may be desirous to have the subject presented to
them in one view, and it will help to elucidate the accompanying
map. To render it more complete, I have added a geographical
description of Maludu Bay and the north-east coast of Borneo.

THE coast line, as viewed from the sea, presents the
following appearance: Gaya Island, and the shores
of Gaya, and Sapangar Bays are hilly, and this continues to within a mile of the mouth of the Mengkabong; the land then becomes flat, with the exception
of the Tambalan hill, as far as the mouth of the
Sulaman creek or river. High land then commences,
which continues for a short distance beyond the Abai,
when it again becomes low, and presents the same
appearance for many miles beyond the Tampasuk
river, the coast being fringed by Casuarinas.

The mouths of the rivers Ananam, Kabatuan,
Mengkabong, Tawaran, Sulaman, Abai, and Tampasuk are all shallow, and unfit for European vessels;
the deepest having but nine feet at low water, and
with the exception of the Ananam, Kabatuan, and
Abai, are much exposed during both monsoons,
and are rendered dangerous by the numerous sandbanks that lie off their mouths. The Ananam in
Gaya Bay, and the Kabatuan in Sapangar Bay, are
only suited for native craft. The Abai has more
water, and, its mouth being sheltered, small vessels,
at certain times of tide, might enter; within, the
river deepens to four fathoms, and the surrounding
hills render it a perfectly land-locked harbour.

There are several bays along this coast which
insure complete shelter for shipping. The finest of

these harbours is that composed of the two bays Gaya
and Sapangar, which is large enough to afford protection during both monsoons for every vessel that
trades to the East; it contains within itself minor
harbours, as one on the north-east of Gaya Island,
which has thirteen fathoms, and is perfectly safe;
while abundance of fresh water may be obtained on
its western shore.   Lokporin, in Sapangar Bay, is
also a secure anchorage.   Gantisan, the Malay town
on the north-eastern shore, though good for shipping,
is not so secure for very small craft, as squalls from
the south-west raise rather a heavy sea there.  Several
coral reefs jut out from the northern shore, with deep
water on either side of them.   This harbour is the
most important in Borneo, from its commanding position in the China seas, and from its great security.

Good shelter may also be found in Ambong and
Usukan Bays, but I have not entered them myself.
Ambong is described as running deep into the land,
and surrounded by hills with smooth surfaces and of
gentle ascent; the alternations of wood and cleared
land affording a most beautiful landscape.  The harbour of Ambong abounds in beautiful sheltered little
bays, but barred by coral patches, which rise exactly
from the spots where they disturb the utility of these
snug retreats.*   The next, Abai, affords excellent
shelter during both monsoons, though open to the
north-west; it is, however, of inferior importance,
though fresh water may be obtained in small quantities on the grassy plain at the entrance of the river:
water, however, is rarely absent where the land
is hilly.   Wherever the country is low, and occa-

* *Voyage of the Samarang*, vol. i. p. 190.

sionally elsewhere, there are sandy beaches. The west end of Gaya Island, Gaya Head, and the points between Sulaman and Abai, are rocky; beyond these appear broad sandy beaches.

Passing the coast line, the country presents varied forms; the hills that surround Gaya harbour are low, and cleared at the top, bearing at present a rank crop of grass; others have a reddish tint, from the ferruginous nature of the soil; the rest are covered with jungle. On entering the Kabatuan, the banks are lined with a narrow belt of mangrove, but the hills rise immediately at the back, and this character appears to extend far into the interior both of the Kabatuan and Mengkabong. From the latter river to the Sulaman stretches a plain, perhaps seven miles in width, varied by a few very low hills. The country changes here, and broken ranges extend to the Abai: hill and plain are then intermixed; but, as soon as we approach the Tampasuk, the country opens, and, for Borneo, an extensive plain spreads out, reaching to the foot of the Maludu mountains. It is, however, occasionally diversified by low, undulating sandstone hills.

This flat, level ground is admirably adapted for rice cultivation, as it is grass land, without any jungle. On leaving these plains, ranges of hills commence, rising generally with great abruptness, presenting steep sides and narrow ridges, and running, for the most part, in an eastern and western direction. There are, however, exceptions to the above description: a few of the hills have easy slopes, and many of the ranges are connected by cross ridges running north and south, particularly at the heads of valleys where the waters of the different tributaries flow in opposite directions to join their main rivers. The highest of the hills we measured was under 3,000 feet. The ranges towards the interior are higher, and at the back of these are very lofty mountains, including Kina Balu,* 13,698 feet (Belcher); Saduk Saduk, about 6,000 feet; and others, whose names we could not obtain, estimated at above 7,000 feet. All the hills in these districts that we examined consisted of sandstone until we reached Kina Balu.

With regard to the height of that mountain, various opinions have been entertained; but until some one is fortunate enough to reach its summit with a good barometer, I think we may rest contented with Sir Edward Belcher's measurement by trigonometry. He makes it 13,698 feet. Mr. Low, on his first ascent, had a very inferior barometer; while during the last two expeditions we were provided with magnificent barometers by Adie; but unfortunate accidents rendered them useless. However, sufficient observations were taken to show that the first barometer was incorrect, and, though both inclined, during our first joint expedition, to place the height of the mountain at about 11,000 feet, the last makes us feel assured that we underrated the height. I am, therefore, inclined, from all the observations made, to think that Sir Edward Belcher's measurement is correct.

The summit of Kina Balu consists of syenite granite, which is in many places so jointed as to give it the appearance of being stratified. About ten peaks spring from a line running from east to west, while about half a mile to the southward rises another

* Called Kini by the Dusuns and Ida'an.

detached peak.  Between the latter and the western
portion of the former is an open space, like a broad
terrace, with sloping sides, down which huge slabs are
continually gliding.  The southern peak presents
a very different aspect, according to the point from
which we view it: from the terrace, it looks sharp,
not above a yard in breadth; while from the east
and west it seems quite rounded.  This renders
it comparatively easy of ascent.  On three sides it is
perpendicular, while, on the south, it presents no
material difficulty.  Without careful barometrical
observations it will be impossible to fix on the
highest peak.  From several views, the southern, the
summit of which I gained during the first trip,
appeared as high as the others, while from the terrace
both east and west appeared rather higher.  The
west has a rounded appearance; but we failed to
discover a way of ascending to its summit.  I reached
within perhaps forty feet, when it presented only perpendicular sides.  It is gradually giving way before
atmospheric influences, its northern base being covered
with huge angular stones that have fallen; the
summit is still overhanging, and much of it apparently ready to topple over.  Between the western and
eastern peaks, on the edge of the cliffs which overlook deep chasms below, is a sort of wall, principally
of huge granite rocks, some so perched on the others
that at first sight it appears the work of man—
geologically explained, I suppose, by the wearing
away of the softer portions of the rock around.  Some
of the peaks present the appearance of a thumb, while
others are massive, as those that rise on either side of
the spot where Mr. Low, in 1851, left a bottle.

The summit is above two miles in length; and I observed that, in descending to its N.W. and E. spurs, the rocks assume a perfectly serrated appearance. Kina Balu extends a long distance towards the N.E. or E.N.E., its height varying perhaps from 10,000 to 11,000 feet: but partially divided from the parent mountain by a deep chasm. From the top, we did not see this portion of the mountain; in fact, the mist generally obscured the view, leaving but patches visible. The summit of the mountain, as I have before observed, consists of syenite granite; but every here and there it is crossed by belts of a white rock. For about 3,000 feet below the peaks there is but little vegetation, and the face of granite sweeps steeply up at an angle of $37\frac{1}{2}$ degrees. In the gullies, and in other sheltered spots, are thickets of flowering shrubs, principally of rhododendrons—a few even extending to the base of the peaks, particularly in the " bottle gully."

From what we observed, the summit of the mountain can only be reached by the way we followed— I mean that portion above 9,000 feet. To that spot there are said to be two paths. Kina Balu throws out, on every side, great shoulders, or spurs, which have also their sub-spurs. The principal are the N.W., very steep; the W.N.W., which subdivides. On the western face of the mountain there are but minor spurs, which leave 5,000 feet of precipice above them. From the southward, two huge spurs extend: on one is the village of Kiau. It springs from the left of the southern face, and running S.W., turns to west and by north, and subdivides. The next spur that springs from the eastern portion of the southern face is, in every respect, the most important. It may be called, for the sake of distinction, the main spur. Those to the left we could not observe fully, as we then only saw them from above, but from the north-east coast they appeared to slope very gradually. The main spur runs at first to the S.W. for about five miles; it then follows almost a S.S.W. direction for about twenty miles, throwing off, on either side, many sub-spurs. A glance at the map will best explain my meaning. This is the range that is observed from the sea, and gave the notion of a back-bone to Borneo; but beyond these twenty-five miles it does not appear to extend. In fact, mountain ranges, running to the east and west, are distinctly visible —the first, at not a greater distance than thirty-five or thirty-six miles, appears to cross close to the end of the main spur. If we were disappointed by not obtaining complete views from the summit, we were partially repaid by the clear view we had of the country lying to the S. and S.E. of Kina Balu. We were at an elevation of between 7,000 and 8,000 feet on the main spur, and observed numerous mountain ranges whose bearings I will give.

| | | | |
|---|---|---|---|
| High peaked mountains . | S. ½ E. ...... | 8,000 ft. | ....30 miles distance. |
| „ „ | S.E. by E. . | 7,000 ft. | ....18 „ |
| „ „ | S.E. by E. ¾ E. | 7,000 ft. | ....18 „ |
| A range : highest peak . | S. ............ | 8,000 ft. | ....25 „ |
| „ „ | S.S.W. ...... | — | 70 „ |
| A range : eastern end of a long table range running E. by N. and W. by S. ................. | S.S.E. ...... | — | 60 „ |
| A peak..................... | S.E. ¾ E. ... | — | very distant. |
| A long range (peak) ... | S.E. ......... | — | „ |

The latter is stated to be in the Kina Batañgan country. The distances and heights are estimated.

Between us and the mountains, bearing S.E. by E. eighteen miles, there was a grassy plain, perhaps three miles by two, on which were many villages, and through this there flowed a fair-sized river. We could trace its course as far as the third spur that springs from the main one; then a line of hills appeared to obstruct it; but beyond we could again trace the course of a stream, which is probably its source. This river, it was stated by the people of the country, flows into the lake of Kina Balu. It runs from the S. W. to the N.E. With the exception of the plain above-mentioned and a marsh, whose commencement we could observe north-east of the plain, all the country appeared hilly, and most of the land was cleared, and either under cultivation, or showed the remains of former plantations. We could observe in the second valley two villages—the first called Tuhan, the next Inserban, and at both cotton is said to be cultivated. Many villages and detached houses were also observed, whose names our guides had forgotten. The road to the lake is by the two above-mentioned villages, while the names of those beyond are Penusuk, Tambian, Paka, and Koporiñgan—these are stated to be on the route, or close to the lake. A few words concerning this mythic sheet of water, as it has generally been considered : that it exists to the east of the mountain appears from inquiry to be almost certain. Its size it is unnecessary to estimate, though our informants stated that, standing on one bank, it was not possible to see the opposite one. It cannot, however, be of the great size marked

in the old maps, or in the situation assigned
to it, as the whole country, from E.S.E. to the
western coast, was distinctly visible, and the Ida'an
expressly stated that it was farther to the north and
east of the plain I have before noticed. Mr. Low
made many inquiries during our first trip, and we
jointly questioned the Ida'an, on many occasions during our long stay at the Kiau village, and they spoke
of it as a certainty, many affirming that they themselves had been on trading expeditions to it. I may
add that Mr. De Crespigny, who lived some time at
Maludu Bay, heard that the lake was to the south of
Kina Balu, where it certainly is not. Peterman's map
is entirely incorrect as to the position of the lake.

I must now make a few remarks on the vegetation
which covered the mountain. Cultivation extends, in
a few places, to the height of 3,500 feet, but beyond
that there is a fine jungle, on the main spur, to the
height of 6,000 feet; it then begins to degene-
rate, and in the exposed portion of the ridge the
trees are bent across the path, inferior in size and
covered with moss. But above this height, in sheltered spots, the trees again increase in size; beyond
7,000 feet, however, there are few fine trees, the
vegetation changing its character, most of it consisting of flowering shrubs, varying in height from ten to
twenty feet. The trees, however, on the sides of the
spurs continued of a comparatively large size until we
had passed 9,000 feet; at 10,000 feet the shrubbery
became very straggling, and above that it was only
scattered among the granite rocks. On the W.N.W.
spur, called the Marei Parei, the vegetation even at
4,500 feet was exceedingly stunted in many places;

rymple's story, which has been often repeated, of the
Tawaran rising in the lake; it evidently springs from
the main spur of Kina Balu.

The Abai is a salt-water creek, but preserving
more the appearance of a river; much of both banks
are mangrove until we approach the houses. Its
depth varies: on the bar it is but one fathom, while
inside it deepens to four, and it has a channel to the
villages of about two fathoms. It is a favourite
anchorage for native prahus, being admirably adapted
for them. Two small rivulets join the Abai; the
Gading, and the Paka Paka, both inhabited by the
Ida'an.

The Tampasuk is essentially a fresh-water river,
very similar to the Tawaran, of no importance to European ships, except that in wet seasons its waters run
unmixed half a mile out to sea. It differs from the
Tawaran, in having occasionally immense granite
boulders in the stream; while the latter drains only
a sandstone country; but, like the Tawaran, it
divides into two branches; the eastern one flows
from the northern portion of Kina Balu. We
could observe its direction for above ten miles, as it
ran through the low land, and its course was E.S.E.
from the junction. The Pengantaran, that drains a
portion of the north-west of Kina Balu, bringing
down immense quantities of blocks of serpentine, is
the only other stream worth noticing. The natives
seldom make use of the Tampasuk beyond the spot
where the river divides, though above it rafts are occasionally used; but it evidently is not a general practice,
as the river is filled with fish traps, which require the
stream to be dammed across with loose stone walls.

The hills do not press closely to the river's banks; if they do so on one, side, the other is certain to have a strip of low land, along which the path is carried; in fact, from the sea to Koung village there is but one steep hill to cross. Sometimes there are small plains, that skirt the banks; at others, gently sloping fields. The steep hills commence a few miles below Koung, on the left bank, and continue, with few exceptions, to the base of Kina Balu. The village of Labang Labang, on a spur of Saduk Saduk, has an easy slope from Koung, while towards the great mountain it is very steep. Near Labang Labang the river divides and assumes different names: the principal branch is called the Kalupis; the other, the Dahombang, or Hobang, and this receives the Kini Taki and the Pinokok. Between the Hobang and Pinokok streams is a sort of table-land, about a couple of miles across, by perhaps four in length; it is not absolutely flat, but the ground swells very gently. The Kalupis has its source at the very summit of the hill, and we could trace its course from the time it was but an inch deep, till collecting all the drainage of the top, it dashed past our resting-place (at 9,000 feet) a fair-sized mountain torrent. About 1,000 feet below, at the head of the Kalupis valley, it throws itself over the rocks, forming a fine cascade of perhaps 1,500 feet in height.

I may notice that off the coast between Gaya Bay and the western point of Maludu Bay there is often a very heavy ground swell, and the rollers occasionally are so dangerous as to prevent vessels attempting to communicate with the shallow rivers. I was once very anxious to visit the Pandasan, but when we arrived off its mouth, the rollers looked so dangerous, that the captain of the steamer decided it would be unsafe for the ship's boats to venture in, and I scarcely regretted his determination. The ground swell was so great, that it was almost impossible to stand on deck.

Having noticed the principal features connected with the physical 'geography, I will add a few notes on what Mr. Hamilton correctly calls political geography.

The population of these districts consists principally of three classes—the Lanun, the Baju, and the Ida'an or Dusun.

The Lanuns were formerly numerous, having populous settlements on the Tawaran and the Tampasuk, as well as on the Pandasan and Layer Layer farther west. They originally came from the large island of Magindanau, which is considered as the most southern island of the Philippine group. They have formed settlements on various points as convenient piratical stations, particularly on the east coast at Tungku and other places.

As I have elsewhere observed, not only did they pirate by sea, but they created an unappeasable feud with the Ida'an, by stealing their children. No race in the Archipelago equals the Lanun in courage; the Ida'an therefore considering it useless to make regular attacks, hung about the villages, and by destroying small parties, forced the Lanuns to leave Tawaran, who then joined their countrymen at Tampasuk. Sir Thomas Cochrane attacked both Pandasan and Tampasuk, which induced the most piratical portion to retire to the east coast. At present but few remain in Tampasuk; they are not considered to have more than 150 fighting men; they are essentially strangers, and unpopular. They seldom form regular governments, but attach themselves to certain chiefs, who are partial to high-sounding titles, particularly those of sultan and rajah. These chiefs are independent of each other, and unite only for defence, or for an extensive expedition. They, however, are gradually leaving these districts. Although Mahomedans, their women are not shut up; on the contrary, they freely mix with the men, and even join in public deliberations, and are said to be tolerably good-looking. The men I have seen are better featured than the Malays or Bajus. Our slight knowledge of the Lanuns partly arises from the jealousy of the Bornean Government, which used to employ all its influence to prevent their frequenting Labuan in order to trade. This partly arose from a desire to prevent the development of our colony, and partly from an absurd idea that they could thus monopolize their trade; but the Lanuns, though often deterred from visiting our settlement, seldom cared to meet the Bornean nobles.

The Bajus are scattered along the coast, their principal settlements being at Mengkabong and Tampasuk. At Mengkabong they appear numerous, and perhaps could muster 1,000 fighting men; at Tampasuk, they estimate their own number at 600; at Pandasan, 400; at Abai, Sulaman, and Ambong, there are a few. Their origin is involved in obscurity: they are evidently strangers. They self-style themselves Orang Sama, or Sama men. They principally occupy themselves with fishing, manufacturing salt, and with petty trade. Some

24—2

breed cows, horses, and goats, while a few plant rice, and have small gardens.

They profess the Mahomedan religion, and keep the fast with some strictness ; though, like the Malays, are probably but little acquainted with its tenets. The Bajus are not a handsome race—they have generally pinched-up, small faces, low fore-heads, but bright eyes. The men are short and slight, but very active ; the women have a similar appearance to the men, and are slighter than the Malay. They wear their hair tied in a knot on the fore part of the crown of the head, which is very unbe-coming. The women appeared to have greater liberty than among the Malays, and came and sat near us and conversed. We saw many men that differed totally from the above description ; but on inquiry, we found they were of mixed breed : one, Baju, Lanun, Malay, and Chinese ; the next, Baju, Sulu, Lanun, and Malay. In fact, many intermarry, which renders it difficult to give a particular type for one race. The Bajus of Tampasuk nominally acknowledge a Datu as their chief, who receives his authority from Brunei ; but they never pay taxes to the supreme Government, and seldom send even a present. They are individually very independent, and render no obedience to their chief, unless it suits their own convenience. They are, therefore, disunited, and unable to make head against the few Lanuns, with whom they have con-tinual quarrels. Every man goes armed, and seldom walks. If he cannot procure a pony, he rides a cow or a buffalo, the latter generally carrying double. Their arms consist of a spear, shield, and sword. Their houses are similar to those of the Malays, being built on posts, sometimes in the water, sometimes on the dry land. In Mengkabong, they are all on the water, and are very poor specimens of leaf-huts. The Tampasuk not affording water accommodation, the houses are built on shore. The only good one was the Datu's, which consisted of a planked house of two stories; the lower, occupied by the married portion of the family, consisted of one large room, with broad enclosed verandahs, occupied by the chief, his wife, and his followers, while the upper was reserved for the young unmarried girls and children. Of furniture there is little—mats, boxes, cooking utensils, and bed places being the principal. In these countries there are no public buildings, no offices, jails, or hospitals, or even a fort or stockade; and the houses being built of but temporary materials, there are no ancient buildings of any description. The Bajus are very fond of cock-fighting, and in order to indulge in this sport with greater satisfaction, carefully rear a very fine breed of fowls, which are famous along the coast. I have seen some of the cocks as large as the Cochin Chinese. It is probable they are descended from those brought by the early immigrants from China, as they no way resemble the ordinary Bornean breed found in every Malay and Dayak village. They fatten readily, and the hens bring up fine broods.

Mixed with the Bajus are a few Borneans; in Gantisan they form the bulk of the village; in Mengkabong they are not numerous; while in the northern districts there are few, if any. Of strangers, an occasional Indian, African, or Chinese may be seen, but they are petty traders, who return to Labuan after a short residence.

The principal inhabitants of these districts consist of the Ida'an or Dusun, the aboriginal population.* They are essentially the same in appearance as the Dayak, the Kayan, the Murut, and the Bisaya; their houses, dress, and manners are very similar, modified, of course, by circumstances. In the Kabatuan, Mengkabong, Sulaman, and Abai are some tribes of Ida'an, but I have not visited their villages; I shall, therefore, confine myself to those I observed on the Tawaran and Tampasuk.

On the banks of the Tawaran, where it flows through the plain, are many villages of Ida'an, which are often completely hidden by groves of fruit-trees. These men have a civilized appearance, wearing jackets and trousers. As you advance into the interior, these gradually lessen, clothes being seen only on a few, as at Kiau, near Kina Balu; beyond, they are said to use the bark of trees. Some of the tribes in the Tawaran have followed the Malay fashion of living in small houses suitable for a single family; while others occupy the usual long house, with the broad verandah, and separate rooms only for the families. The house in which we lodged, at Ginambur on the Tampasuk, was the best I have ever seen among the aborigines. It was boarded with finely-worked planks; the doors strong and excellently made, each also having a small opening for the dogs to go in and out; the flooring of bamboos, beaten out, was very neat and free from all dirt, which I have never before noticed in a Dayak house, where the dogs render everything filthy. The Ginambur Ida'an are good specimens of the abori-

* Ida'an is the name given them by the Bajus, Dusun by the Borneans.

gines; they are free from disease, and are clear-skinned; they have good-tempered countenances. None of the women are good-looking; still they are not ugly. All the girls and young women wear a piece of cloth to conceal their bosoms: it was upheld by strips of coloured rattans: their petticoats were also longer than usual, and the young girls had the front of the head shaved, like Chinese girls. I did not notice that any of the men of that village were tatooed, but in our walk we had met parties of men from the interior who were so: a tatooed band, two inches broad, stretched in an arc from each shoulder, meeting on their stomachs, then turning off to their hips, and some of them had a tatooed band extending from the shoulder to the hand. Many of their villages are extensive, as Koung, which is large, scattered on a grassy plain, with a portion on the hill above. It is a very pretty spot, the greensward stretching on either side of the river's bank, where their buffaloes and cattle graze. This tribe has the appearance of being rich; they possess abundance of cattle, pigs, fowls, rice, and vegetables, while the river affords them fish. Kiau is also an extensive village, but the houses and the people are very dirty.

None of these Ida'an pay any tribute, though many chiefs on the coast call them their people; but it is merely nominal, no one daring to oppress them. Each village is a separate government, and almost each house independent. They have no established chiefs, but follow the councils of the old men to whom they are related. They have no regular wars, which would induce them to unite more closely; their feuds are but petty quarrels, and in but one house did I observe heads, and that was at the village of Tamparuli, in the Tawaran plain.  The very fact of troops of girls working in the fields without male protection would prove the security that exists, though every male always walks armed.  We had no opportunity of observing any of their ceremonies, and it is very unsafe to trust to the information of interpreters.

The aborigines, in general, are so honest that little notice is taken of this good quality; however, to our surprise, we found that these Ida'an were not to be trusted.  We were warned by the Bajus to take care of our things, but we felt no distrust.  However, at Kiau they proved their thievish qualities, which, however, we frightened out of them, as during our second residence we lost nothing there.  At the village of Nilu one made an attempt, which we checked.

The Ida'an are essentially agriculturists, and raise rice, sweet potatoes, the kiladi (*Arum*—an esculent root), yams, Indian corn, sugar-cane, tobacco, and cotton.  The sugar-cane is only raised for eating in its natural state, while the cotton is confined to certain districts.

I first saw the natives ploughing in the Tampasuk; their plough is very simple, and is constructed entirely of wood; it serves rather to scratch the land than really to turn it over.  The plough was drawn by a buffalo, and its action was the same as if a pointed stick had been dragged through the land to the depth of about four inches.  After ploughing, they use a rough harrow.  In the Tawaran they ploughed better, the earth being partially turned over to the depth of about six inches.  The Ida'an have divided the land into square fields with narrow banks between them, and each division being as much private property as English land, is considered very valuable, and the banks are made to keep in the water. Their crops are said to be very plentiful. Simple as this agriculture is, it is superior to anything that exists south of Brunei, and it would be curious if we could investigate the causes that have rendered this small portion of Borneo, between the capital and Maludu Bay, so superior in agriculture to the rest. I think it is obviously a remnant of Chinese civilization. Pepper is not grown north of Gaya Bay, and is confined to the districts between it and the capital.

The Ida'an use a species of sledge made of bamboos, and drawn by buffaloes to take their heavy goods to market. The gardens on the Tawaran are well kept and very neatly fenced in. On the hills the plough is not used, the land being too steep; and there the agriculture presents nothing remarkable, beyond the great care displayed in keeping the crops free from weeds. The tobacco is well attended to, and these districts supply the whole coast, none being imported from abroad. When carefully cured, the flavour is considered as good, and the cultivation might be easily extended. Of the cotton I can say little, as I did not find that any of the tribes through whose country we passed cultivated it, though they assured me they purchased their supplies from the villages near the lake. The Tuhan and Inserban districts produce it, they said, in considerable quantities; and I observed the women, in several places, spinning yarn from the cotton. The Bajus obtain their supplies from a tribe

near Maludu Bay.  Among the hills the implements
of agriculture consist of simply a parang chopper and
a biliong, or native axe, and the ground is, therefore,
no more turned up than what can be effected by a
pointed stick ; in fact, the steepness of the valley
sides is against a very improved rice cultivation ; it is
better adapted for coffee.    Mr. Low, who has much
experience, pronounces the soil, a rich orange-coloured
loam, to be superior to that of Ceylon, and, Kina
Balu being but twenty-five miles from the sea-coast,
there are great advantages there.    The plains are
alluvial and very fertile.

With regard to the amount of population, all
estimates would be mere guess work ; but it
must be considerable, as little old forest remains,
except at the summits of lofty hills ; the rest being
either under cultivation or lying fallow with brushwood upon it.   The tribes on the Tampasuk estimated their own numbers at five thousand fighting-
men ; the Tawaran tribes were equally numerous ;
but reducing that estimate, and putting together the
various information received, I should be disposed
to place the entire population of these districts at
above forty thousand people.   This is under rather
than over the amount.

The five thousand fighting men who are stated by
the Ida'an to live in the Tampasuk are, they say, thus
divided :—

| | | | | |
|---|---|---|---|---|
| The Piasau Ida'an | ... | ... | ... | 500 |
| Ginambur | ... | ... | ... | 1,000 |
| Bungol... | ... | ... | ... | 1,000 |
| Koung ... | ... | ... | ... | 500 |
| Kiau  ... | ... | ... | ... | 2,000 |
| Total | ... | ... | ... | 5,000 |

It is impossible to verify this statement, but we may
test it slightly by the observations made. The Piasau
Ida'an, so named from the extensive groves of cocoa-
nuts that surround their villages (*piasau*, a cocoanut),
are spread over the Tampasuk plain, and I think
I am understating, when ·I say we noticed above
fifteen villages, and I should have myself placed their
numbers much higher that five hundred. The
Ginambur was a large village, and there was
another of the same Ida'an about a mile off among
the hills, which I passed through on our return.
Buñgol is also stated at a thousand men. Our
Malays, who visited it, said that it was very large;
while the extensive village of Tambatuan, Peñgantaran, and Batong, with numerous others among the
hills, have to be included in the Ginambur and
Buñgol tribes. Koung is placed at five hundred,
which is not a high estimate, there being about
three hundred families in the village. Kiau is stated
to contain two thousand fighting men; in this number
are included the village of Pinokok (small), of
Labang Labang (large), of Sayap, which we did not
see. I should be inclined to reduce the Kiaus by
five hundred men, though we understood them to say
that their tribe was numerous beyond the north-
western spur, in the neighbourhood of Sayap. I
think we shall not be over-estimating the population
by placing it at four thousand fighting Ida'an, or
sixteen thousand inhabitants. Rejecting the women
and children, both male and female, and the aged,
one in four may be taken as the combatants. There
were many villages on the eastern branch, some of
Piasaus, others probably of Buñgol. The great extent

of country cleared shows the population to be comparatively numerous. I may make this observation,
the result of many years' experience, that I have
seldom found the statements of the natives with
regard to population above the truth. In Sarawak
and the neighbouring rivers, where we had better
means of ascertaining the correctness of the accounts
rendered, I have always found it necessary to add
a third to the numbers stated.

The Tawaran, perhaps, contains a population nearly
equal to that of the Tampasuk. The villages between
the mouth and Bawang are numerous, but much
concealed by groves of fruit-trees. Tamparuli was
an extensive village, and Bawang of fair size. The
Nilau tribe was scattered over the sides of the hills.
Kalawat was a large village, with perhaps eighty
families. Buñgol contains, perhaps, over one hundred
and fifty families. The Tagoh, Bañgow, and other
villages, were observed on sub-spurs; and beyond
Buñgol the tribes must be numerous, if we may
judge from the extensive fires made by them to clear
their plantations. On the right-hand branch are
also many villages, but we had no opportunity of
examining them. By native accounts, the Tawaran
district is more populous than the Tampasuk.

Of Anaman I know nothing; of Kabatuan I
saw little beyond the Malay town; but I was informed
that the Ida'an were numerous in the interior of this
river, as well as on the hills that surround Mengkabong. I have placed them at two thousand, which
is not a high estimate.

Mengkabong contains also an extensive Baju population, and in estimating them at six thousand, it is,

I believe, much below the number. The villages are numerous, and the chief town large. It is possible that there are not more than a thousand fighting-men, but the Bajus are holders of slaves, and there are also many strangers settled among them.

Sulaman is placed at a thousand, which includes both Baju and Ida'an, and may be a little over the mark; for it I have nothing but vague native testimony.

Abai contains about thirty houses, perhaps not above two hundred people; while on the hills are a few small villages of Ida'an. I have put them at one hundred and twenty-five fighting-men, or five hundred in all.

Tampasuk contains about one hundred and fifty Lanun men, or seven hundred and fifty population. Bajus, five hundred, or two thousand five hundred people. I have multiplied the Lanun and Baju fighting-men by five, as they have many slaves both male and female.

Gaya Bay contains about three hundred people.

The population of these districts may therefore be entered as follows:—

| | | |
|---|---|---|
| Gaya Bay | 800 | Malays and others. |
| Kabatuan | 1,000 | Ida'an. |
| Mengkabong | 6,000 | Bajus and others. |
| ,, | 1,000 | Ida'an. |
| Tawaran | 10,000 | Ida'an. |
| Sulaman | 1,000 | Ida'an and Bajus. |
| Abai | 200 | Bajus. |
| ,, | 500 | Ida'an. |
| Tampasuk | 2,500 | Bajus. |
| ,, | 750 | Lanuns. |
| ,, | 16,000 | Ida'an. |
| Total | 45,250 | |

The only figures in the above which I think may possibly be overstated, are the Bajus of Tampasuk. We may fairly reckon the population of the districts between Gaya Bay and Tampasuk at forty-five thousand, being quite aware, at the same time, that it is founded on very loose data; but it may serve as a guide to future inquirers.

There are but trifling manufactures carried on. The Bajus are much occupied in preparing salt for the inland tribes. The only other manufacture that is worth noticing, is that of cloths from native cotton, and the most esteemed are those of the Lanuns. The cloth is generally black, with a few white lines running through it, forming a check. It is strong and more enduring than any other I have seen, and fetches a high price—varying from 1*l*. 5*s*. to 2*l*. 10*s*. for a piece sufficient for a single petticoat. They are, however, deteriorating since the introduction of cheap English yarn, which is superseding the carefully-spun native. No minerals have as yet been discovered in these districts beyond the coal in Gaya Island, though tin has been found to the north of Kina Balu, near one of the streams flowing into Maludu Bay.

There is but little trade carried on: the only articles of export are tobacco, rice, a little wax, cattle, and horses, or rather ponies; the imports consist of cloths, iron, gongs, and earthenware, with occasionally a valuable jar. Little beyond tobacco is brought from the interior, as everything is carried on men's shoulders, none of their paths being as yet suited for loaded beasts.

It is a great drawback to this country, having

no navigable rivers, nor on the hills have they good
paths. The latter are easily made, the country
presenting no natural difficulties, while in the plains
very fair roads already exist, fit for their sledges.
The tribes in the interior are at present far beyond
any commerce ; in fact, the people near the lake
have never been visited by the coast population, and
trust to exchanging with the other Ida'an. But
as the taste for cloth is evidently on the increase, it is
possible the trade may improve. Englishmen travelling in that country do great good by spreading a
taste for European manufactures.

With respect to the languages spoken, I will at
present make but few remarks. The Lanun and
Baju are entirely different from the language of the
Ida'an. I have made several vocabularies and many
inquiries. At Kiau, we collected above 400 words ; at
Blimbing on the Limbang, 300 ; and whilst in Maludu
Bay, seven years ago, I likewise made a short vocabulary. These three agree so far that I may say that
the Ida'an and Bisaya have two out of three words
in common ; and on further inquiry, I think that the
remaining one-third will gradually dwindle away,
as at present many of the words in my Bisaya
vocabulary are Malay, for which they have their
native word. The result of my inquiries is that
all the Ida'an speak the same language with slight
local differences. We found all the tribes on the
Tampasuk and Tawaran spoke fluently to each other,
and one of our interpreters, who had never before
visited these countries, but had been accustomed to
the aborigines to the south, conversed freely with
them. The Bisayas live on the rivers in the neigh-

bourhood of the capital, and their language differs but little from that of the Ida'an.

The Ida'an contains but few Malay words, these generally referring to imported articles and domestic animals. Some are similar to those of the Land Dayaks of Sarawak.

I will add a few remarks on the geology of these districts, premising them, however, by the observation that I am ignorant of the science. Wherever the rocks protruded through the hills, we noticed they were decomposing sandstone; and this character continued until we reached the great mountain. Occasionally, as in Gaya island, the rocks were of a harder texture; and here a Mr. Molley is said to have been shown a vein of coal. In the districts to the west and south of the Tampasuk, we noticed no signs of primitive rock; while in the Tampasuk river, huge boulders of granite are met with a little above Butong, while the debris extends as far as the junction; but the rocks of the hills are sandstone, and this character continues to the base of the mountain. At Koung, the rocks dipped to the south-west by south, at an angle of 45°. On the Marei Parei spur, we could trace the sandstone to the height of about 4,000 feet, the dip about 80° to the south-west; greenstone immediately after protruded, and appeared to form the chief rock. On the Marei Parei spur, the compass was so affected by the peroxide of iron which formed a sort of coating to the rocks, that it would not act. The main spur consists at first of sandstone; then of shale, almost as hard as stone; and of various rocks which I could not recognize; then of decomposing granite, above which commences the massive outline of the summit. We found in our collection a piece of limestone that was broken off somewhere near the base of the mountain in the Kalupis valley.

The country presents the appearance of having been originally of sedimentary rocks, through which the granite has forced its way, upheaving the sandstone to an angle of 80°.

With regard to the climate, I made a few notes. The plain and low hills are much the same as the rest of Borneo, or other tropical countries; but in the neighbourhood of Kina Balu it is of course different. We found at the village of Kiau that the thermometer never marked above 77° during the day, and varied from 66° to 69° during the nights. The mean of all the observations gave a shade below 68°. The Marei Parei spur offered a fine position for a sanitarium, at any height between 4,000 feet and 5,000 feet. Our tent was pitched at about 4,700 feet, and we found that the thermometer marked 75° (mean) in the mid-day shade, 56° at six A.M., and 63° (mean) at six P.M. This would be a delightful climate in a well-built house. The cave at 9,000 feet was very cold—at two P.M. 52° mean; and during the three nights I slept there on my first expedition, it was 40° 33' (mean); ranging between 36° 5' and 43°. In my last expedition, in the cave, the thermometer marked: 6.30 A.M., 43°; 9.15 A.M., 48°; 3.30 P.M., 51·250°; 6 P.M., 45·750°. Night, registering thermometer: 41·250° and 41°. On the summit, during mist and rain, it marked 52°; while exposed to a strong wind and a storm of sleet and hail, it fell to 43°. On a fine day, however, it marked 62° in the shade, there being much refraction from the rocks.

I think it most probable that water would freeze on the summit during a similar storm of hail and sleet to which we were exposed, were it to occur during the night-time, as at two P.M. the thermometer fell to 43°, though held in the hand: and at the cave it fell to 36·5° during a very cold night, though partly protected by the tent, and when I went out, I found a sort of hoar-frost on the rocks and leaves.

I must add a few remarks on the map. The sea-line is taken from the Admiralty chart, while the interior I have filled up from the observations and rough plans made during the journey. It may afford some idea of the country, and serve until a traveller with greater advantages makes a better.

I will add a few remarks on that great indentation of the land to the north of Kina Balu, called Maludu Bay, but more correctly Marudu. Steering from the westward, there are two channels by which the northern point of Borneo may be rounded: they are to the north and south of the little island of Kalampunuan. A sweeping current often renders the latter dangerous, as it would drive a vessel on a reef of rocks that runs off the island. Just before the extreme point is reached there is a small river or creek of Luru, which is also known by the name of Simpang Mengayu, or the Cruising Creek, the Sampan Mangy of the Admiralty charts. Round the point there is another, named Karatang, and both are well known to the natives as the spots where the Balignini and

Lanun pirates lurked to catch the trading prahus which passed that way.

An incident occurred to a Bornean acquaintance, named Nakodah Bakir, who had accompanied me on my visit to the Baram River. He had found, from experience, the inutility of arming his prahus, with brass swivels of native manufacture; as, though they carry far, they seldom hit anything; so he changed his plan and armed his men with English muskets. Early in the autumn of 1851, he was on a trading voyage to Maludu Bay, and having secured a good cargo, was returning to the capital. As he rounded the northern point, five Lanun boats dashed out of Luru, and pulled towards him, firing their brass swivels, whose balls passed harmlessly through his rigging. He kept his thirty men quiet till the first pirate boat was within fifty yards, when his crew jumped up and fired a volley of musketry into it. This novel reception so astonished the pirates that they gave up the pursuit.

Maludu Bay extends nearly thirty miles inland. The western shore, near the point, is rather flat, but soon rises into a succession of low hills; and as you penetrate deeper into the bay they swell to the proportion of mountains on both shores, and Kina Balu and its attendant ranges form a fine background to the end of the bay, which, for nearly four miles from the shore, shallows from about two fathoms to scarcely sufficient water to float a boat. By keeping the channel, however, the principal river may be reached. The land is quite swampy on both banks, mangrove jungle reaching to within a mile of the town, then nipa palms, mixed with a few forest trees; in fact, the whole of the

25—2

head of the bay appears gradually filling up : the land
obviously encroaching on the sea, the nipa palm
gaining on the mangrove, which is spreading far out
in the salt water on the flat muddy bottom.    The
rush of the current from these rivers is sometimes so
great that we have found the whole head of the bay
for five miles completely fresh, and the amount of
earth held in suspension renders it of a white appearance.    The houses are built on a narrow creek on
the right-hand bank of the river ; near the country is
flat, but the mountains soon skirt the plains.    The
population of the bay is sufficient to render it a valuable commercial settlement for native traders, if security
for life and property could be established, and if the
monopolies of the chiefs could be destroyed.    To
show the insecurity, I may mention that in 1859 the
Sultan of Brunei sent a trading prahu there with a
valuable cargo.    On the return voyage, just as they
were leaving the mouth of the river Panchur, the
vessel commenced leaking, and they had to land a part
of the cargo.    The supercargo returned to the town
for assistance, and during his absence, a large party of
men came into the river, drove away the crew, and
carried off all the goods.    They were not regular
pirates, but a band of Sulus, who could not resist the
temptation to plunder.

The monopolies of the chiefs, however, prevent any
intercourse with the producing classes, and thus prevent the possibility of a large increase of trade.

I made many inquiries as to the amount of population which dwells in the districts bordering on this
deep bay.    I obtained from Sherif Hasan, the son of
Sherif Usman, who formerly ruled these districts with

a strong hand, a list of the number of Ida'an families
who paid tribute to his father. I then inquired
of the chief Datu Budrudin, of Sherifs Musahor,
Abdullah, and Houssein, and of a number of traders,
and their accounts do not greatly vary.

Sherif Usman received tribute from the following
districts :—

| | | |
|---|---|---|
| Udat ... ... ... ... | 200 families of Ida'an. | |
| Milau ... ... ... ... | 200 ,, | ,, |
| Lotong ... ... ... ... | 150 ,, | ,, |
| Anduan ... ... ... ... | 50 ,, | ,, |
| Metunggong ... ... ... | 300 ,, | ,, |
| Bira'an ... ... ... ... | 100 ,, | ,, |
| Tigaman ... ... ... ... | 250 ,, | ,, |
| Taminusan ... ... ... | 50 ,, | ,, |
| Bintasan... ... ... ... | — | — |
| Bingkungan ... ... ... | 60 ,, | ,, |
| Panchur ... ... ... ... | 500 ,, | ,, |
| Bungun ... ... ... ... | 800 ,, | ,, |
| Tandek ... ... ... ... | 1,500 ,, | ,, |
| | 3,660 families. | |
| Add a third ... ... | 1,220 families not paying revenue. | |
| Total ... ... ... | 4,880 families. | |

At six to a family, this would give nearly 30,000
people.

Comparing this statement with those given by the
assembled chiefs, I find they slightly differ. They
reckoned the population at 36,000 people; and I
account for it, first, by Sherif Hasan not having given
the population of Bintasan; and, secondly, by his only
mentioning the number of families on the Buñgun
who paid tribute to his father, there being above a
thousand families who did not.

They all represented the district of Bengkoka,
not included in the above list, as the most important

and populous of all; it is on the eastern coast of
the bay, and the river, though barred at the entrance,
is reputed deep inside. Its population is stated at
16,000 Ida'an. The Malays and Sulus residing in
all these districts are represented as not very numerous; in fact, as under 5,000, of whom 1,500 are at
Panchur, 1,500 at Bengkoka, and the rest scattered
at the various other villages. If the above figures
represent the numbers, there are about 52,000 Ida'an
on the banks of the rivers flowing into the bay, and
about 5,000 strangers. They all, however, explained
that, when they enumerated the Ida'an, they only
spoke of those villages which were under the influence
of the people of the coast, and that there were many
tribes among the mountains with whom they had
little intercourse.

I once met a party of these Ida'an; they were
a dark, sharp-featured race, intelligent-looking, and
appeared in features very much like the Land Dayaks
of Sarawak. They were dressed in their war costume,
consisting of heavy, padded jackets, but wore the
chawat or cloth round their loins. They were slight
and short men.

The productions of these districts consist of rattans, wax, camphor, tortoise-shell, tripang or sea-slug,
and kaya laka, a sweet-scented wood. Large quantities of rice and tobacco are grown, and, if encouraged,
these cultivations would greatly increase. The only
minerals as yet discovered are coal in the Bengkoka
River, and tin in some stream at the foot of the Kina
Balu range. I saw specimens of the latter, but no
one has ventured to work it yet. The insecurity
would prevent the Chinese succeeding.

Starting from the head of Maludu Bay, and skirting the eastern shore, it is found to be shoal off
Mobang Point, and on the next inlet, Teluk Mobañg,
Sherif Usman endeavoured to establish a village ;
but while his people were clearing the forest, they
were seized with severe vomitings, many dying; all
arising, the Malays, confidently believe, from the
machinations of the evil spirits who had been disturbed in their homes. Leaving the points of Taburi
and Si Perak, we pass through the straits formed
by the island of Banguey and the mainland. That
Island is inhabited in the interior by Ida'an, but on
the shore many Bajus assemble, collecting tortoise-
shell and sea-slug, and they have built many houses
near the peak. It was they who pillaged and burnt
the *Minerva*, wrecked off Balambañgan, in November,
1848. I have mentioned the Mengkabong people
having treacherously plundered a village on Banguey; the inhabitants consisted of their own race,
mixed with a few Sulus and others. The islets to
the south-west of Banguey are named Padudañgan
(by the Sulus it is called Palarukan), and Patarunan.
Indarawan is the name of a small river at the south
of Banguey, where, it is said, sufficient good water
may be procured to supply vessels. Passing between
Mali Wali and a rock off the coast, the soundings
are very variable, and the sea appears filled with
sandbanks and shoals ; in fact, for a frigate, the sea
is not sufficiently clear of reefs till we arrive opposite
Sandakan Bay.

Commencing from the north-eastern point of
Borneo, we first come to a little bay called Batul
Ayak, the only inhabitants of which are Bajus, who

entirely reside in their boats. Then there is a small
river called Kina (China) Bañgun: there are but
few people residing there, wanderers with no settled
dwellings. After that there is Kang Karasan, where
there are probably not more than a couple of hundred
Mahommedans, but the Dusuns in the interior are
numerous: my informants knew of villages containing above three hundred families. The river Paitan
is large and deep, and there are above a thousand
Islams living here, and the Ida'an in the interior are
represented to be as numerous as the leaves on the
trees, and the slopes of the hills are covered with
great forests of camphor-trees. I may observe that
boxes made of camphor-wood prevent any insects
meddling with woollen cloths, and are therefore very
useful. Camphor has so powerful an aromatic smell,
that it will drive every insect from its neighbourhood.
Passing the stream of Babahar, which is small, and
without inhabitants, we arrive at Sugut, to the
north of the commencement of Labuk Bay; but it
has also a small entrance to the south of it. The
Islam population is represented as numerous, while
seven thousand families of Ida'an reside in the interior; in consequence of their great superiority of
numbers, their chiefs have great influence in those
districts. A few elephants are caught here, but the
principal exports are rattans, wax, and camphor.
The north-east coast of Borneo, as far as the entrance
of the Sugut River, is rather flat, only a few low hills
occasionally diversifying the scene; but no sooner do
you round the point, and enter Labuk Bay, than it
presents a different aspect: the low hills gradually
swell into mountains, one range of which is remark-

ably peaked—as jagged, from one view, as the edge
of a saw. Kina Balu is visible along this coast, and
from the eastern side the ascent appears feasible. A
vessel steering along the shore finds it difficult, from
the numerous shoals, while pretty islets are scattered about in every direction. If the Benggaya be
approached in a direct line, the water gradually
decreases from three to one and a half fathoms; but,
keeping close into the front, it deepens to five, seven,
and no bottom with a ten-fathom line. The country,
as viewed from the mouth of this river, presents only
mangrove jungle, with an occasional glimpse at the
distant mountains: its entrance is very shallow, not
deep enough at low tide to float a ship's cutter. To
reach the village of Benggaya, it is necessary to keep
to the left-hand branch, avoiding the broad stream
which stretches away to the right; but after ten
miles the stream divides, and it is necessary to pass
by the left-hand branch, and continue for about
twenty miles farther up a most extraordinarily winding river before the houses are reached. This out-of-
the-way situation is chosen to avoid the attacks of
pirates. The banks of this river present a continued
succession of mangrove and nipa swamp for many
miles, only occasionally varied by dry land and fine
forest trees. The stream winds in a most extraordinary manner, and at one place the reaches had met,
and nothing but a fallen tree prevented a saving of
two miles of distance. The inhabitants consist of a
few Islams, called men of Buluñgan, doubtless fugitives from the Malay State of that name a couple
of hundred miles farther south. There is an overland communication between Sugut and Benggaya,

prepared by the latter in case of being suddenly
surprised, as they have no interior to fly to, and consequently no Ida'an population.

The largest river which runs into this bay is the
Labuk, which gives its name to the place. It has
three entrances—Kalagan, small; Labuk, large; Sabi,
small. Off its mouth is a place called Lingkabu,
famous for its pearl fishery. The productions of this
district are principally camphor, wax, rattans, and
pearls, and the interior is reported to be well inhabited by the Ida'an. Next to it there is an insigni-
ficant village of Islams on the river Sungalihut, and
is only inhabited on account of the edible birds' nests
found in the interior.

Between the eastern point of Labuk Bay and the
islands there is a three-fathom channel. The coast
is low, with no marked features until we round the
point, and the bluff islands of Sandakan Bay are
visible. Then the land appears to rise gradually
into pretty hills, presenting beautiful slopes for cultivation; but as we approach the entrances of the
Kina Batangan, the land again becomes low. Sandakan Bay itself is a splendid harbour, with a good
supply of fresh water. It used to be well inhabited,
but on one occasion the villages were surprised by
the Balignini pirates, and sacked and burnt by them.
The inhabitants who escaped the attack dispersed
among the neighbouring communities, but every year
strong parties of the surrounding people assemble
there to collect the valuable products of the place,
which consist of large quantities of white birds' nests,
pearls, wax, sea-slug, and the best kind of camphor.

About four or five years ago, Pangeran, or Datu

Mahomed, the ruler of Atas, became so unbearably tyrannical that a large section of the population determined to abandon their country, and hearing of the English settlement of Labuan, resolved to remove there.   One of their principal men proceeded first to make arrangements for the others, who in the meantime made temporary dwellings in Sandakan Bay.   He sailed round to the north-west coast, and unfortunately put into the Papar river for water. The chief of that district, Pañgeran Omar, detained him and forced him to send up his family to his house. Week after week passed, and they were still kept there, till information reached our colony, when the governor sent an officer to try and release these people, but his representations were treated with contempt, as he had no material force at his back; and the next thing I heard was that the Bornean chief had put the Atas man to death, on pretence that he was about to run amuck, and taken the wife and daughters into his harim, reducing the followers to slavery.   When this intelligence reached Sandakan Bay, it is not surprising the fugitives did not venture on the inhospitable north-west coast. The whole affair might have been better managed on our part, and had proper representations been made to the admiral on the station, there is little doubt he would have considered himself authorized to interfere.

Passing this bay, we arrive at the many mouths of the Kina Batañgan river; the first, named Bala-batang, is said to connect the river with the bay; the second is Trusan Abai, by which the first village may be reached in seven days.   The deepest entrance

is Tundong Buañgin, and in certain months, perhaps
after the rainy season, it is said there is a channel
with three fathoms; but in the dry weather the sand
again collects and spoils the passage. It is seldom
used, except by very large trading prahus, as it takes
them thirty days to reach the first village. Judging
by the time required by the Bornean boats to reach
the town of Lañgusin, on the Baram river, during
the rainy season, we may calculate that with the
windings of the river, the first village must be about
a hundred miles from the mouth. The Sulu prahus
being heavier built, the Bornean ones used in the
Baram trade would move a third faster. The first
village on the banks is called Bras Manik. There
are numerous hamlets beyond ; in fact, the Kina
Batañgan river is always spoken of as one of the
most populous, and by far the most important on
the north-eastern coast, and it is the one the Datus
of Sulu watch with the most jealous attention. As
this is the only country in Borneo where the elephants
are numerous, it is the only one where ivory forms an
important article of trade in the eyes of the natives.
But the most valuable articles are the remarkably
fine white birds' nests and the camphor, which is
collected in large quantities in the old forests which
clothe the lofty mountains seen in the interior. Wax,
sea-slug, very fine tortoise-shell, and also pearls, are
the articles that render this trade so sought after.
The tortoise-shell is collected on the many islands
with broad sandy beaches that stud this quiet sea.
My servant once found a packet ready prepared for
sale left by some careless collector near the remains
of a deserted hut. Turtle also frequent these islands ;

and one day, while walking along the beach with a
blue-jacket, we saw a fine animal in shoal water.
He sprang in, and after a vigorous struggle, in which
his companions partly assisted, he turned the beast
on his back and towed him ashore, to afford, next
day, excellent turtle soup for the whole ship's company. The natives generally despise rattans as articles
of export, on account of their great bulk, otherwise
they might collect sufficient to load many ships. The
principal articles of import into these countries are
gray shirtings, chintzes, red cloth, iron, steel, brass
wire, beads, and powder and muskets. With opium,
they say themselves, they are sufficiently supplied by
the Lanun pirates, who obtain it from the prahus
they capture among the Dutch islands.

Sigama is the next river, and has but a small
population of Islams, though there are many Ida'an
in the interior.

Cape Unsang is low and marked by few characteristic features, but on rounding the point becomes
steadily prettier until we reach the Tungku river,
when it presents a beautiful succession of low hills
with the mountain of Siriki to the left, which is a
good mark to discover the pirate haunt of Tungku.
All the small rivers on the southern shore of Cape
Unsang are barred, not admitting a ship's barge at
low-water—at least, we did not find deeper channels.
I saw here a shark, the largest I have ever noticed :
it swam to and fro in the shallow water, eyeing the
English seamen who were dragging their boats over
the sands, but it did not venture near enough to
be dangerous. We were sitting in the gig a little
to seaward and it passed and repassed within a few

yards of us, and I thought it must have been fifteen
feet in length, but the imagination is apt to wander
on such occasions, and as it swam in very shallow
water, it appeared to show more of its back than
usual. As the officers and men were on particular
service, no one attempted to put a ball into it.
Tungku appeared a type of the neighbouring districts: near the sea it is flat, occasionally varied by
a low hill. I walked several hours through this
country, and never before saw more luxuriant crops;
the rice stalks were over our heads, the sugar cane
was of enormous girth, and the pepper vines had
a most flourishing appearance: the soil must be of
the very finest quality.

I have visited none of the districts on the east
coast to the south of Tungku, but I heard that the
people of Tidong, as of old, are troubling the neighbouring countries, as the Dayaks of Seribas and
Sakarang did the north-west coast when I first
reached Borneo. In sight of Cape Unsang, are
many islands, at present the resort of the Balignini,
as Tawi Tawi and Binadan. A chief from the
former captured a Spanish schooner in 1859, and
was reported to have found the daughter of the
captain on board. The Spanish Government made
many efforts to recover her; but by native report she
still lives with her captor, Panglima Taupan, who
treats her with every attention and considers her his
principal wife. I heard last year she had borne
a child to him, and was now unwilling to leave
him.

The inhabitants of the north-east coast may be
divided into Pagan and Mahomedan. The former

are Ida'an, no doubt exactly similar to their countrymen found on the opposite coast; but at Sugut the
natives affirm there is a tribe who have a short tail.
I have elsewhere mentioned that my informant declared he had felt it: it was four inches long, and
quite stiff; and that at their houses they were provided with seats with holes for this uncomfortable
prolongation of the spine; the poorer people contented themselves with sitting on simple logs of wood,
allowing the tail to hang over. It is quite possible
there may have been some instances in a tribe, as I
have heard that this deformity has been known in
Europe; and from one or two would soon arise the
story of the tribes with tails. I do not think I have
mentioned elsewhere that I have seen Dayaks who
carry little mats hanging down their backs, fastened
to their waistcloths, on which they sit: they always
have them there, ready to be used. I at first thought
that the story of the men with tails arose from the
method of wearing the waistcloth adopted by some
of the tribes: they twist it round their loins, and
have one end hanging down in front, the other
behind, but some so manage it that the resemblance
to a tail at a little distance is remarkable, particularly when the men are running fast.

The Mahomedan population consists of Sulus,
Bajus, and a few Lanuns, together with slaves, consisting of captives made by the pirates during their
cruises among the various islands of the Archipelago,
and sold at that great slave-mart, Sugh. The
districts of the north-east coast are nearly all governed
by chiefs from Sulu, or by the descendants of the
Arab adventurers who all assume the title of Serib,

or, more correctly, Sherif. They do their utmost to monopolize the trade, and do not hesitate to cut off any native prahus who may venture on that coast; and Europeans have avoided all connection with it for many years; the last attempt was made by a Mr. Burns, who lost life and ship in Maludu Bay in 1851.

END OF VOL. I

London: Printed by SMITH, ELDER & Co., Little Green Arbour Court, Old Bailey, E.C.

# HISTORY

## OF THE

# FOUR CONQUESTS OF ENGLAND.

### By JAMES AUGUSTUS ST. JOHN.

In Two Volumes.

---

" Gives evidence of the courage and learning which enable a man to form and assert his own opinions."—*Westminster Review*.

" A history, and a very able history of England, from the earliest times to the death of the first Norman monarch. . . . We have no hesitation in saying, that it is in our estimation the best history of the Anglo-Saxons for the general reader we possess. . . . Mr. St. John is a writer of great talent as well as a zealous investigator of historical truth: and his language possesses always the attraction of vigour and elegance, while it is often poetical, and in his descriptions extremely picturesque. He displays, moreover, an intimate and a quick appreciation of individual character, as well as of the causes and motives of political and social action among our Anglo-Saxon forefathers, which we find in none of his predecessors. . . . In conclusion we can only repeat the high opinion we entertain of Mr. St. John's labours. He has given us the best history of the Anglo-Saxons we now possess; and what is more, he has known how to clothe the truth of history with the attractions of romance."— *Literary Gazette*.

" Here are two volumes which reflect credit on the patience, research, industry, and learning of the author. The story of the Four Conquests has never been narrated more lucidly or less drily. The one is not made

to succeed to the other as an independent narrative; but each is shown
to have been a natural and inevitable consequence of the one by which it
was preceded; and thus to the four divisions in which the series of wars is
portrayed is given the interest and the warmth of a continuous history.
Mr. St. John has done his work well and honestly."—*Athenæum.*

" Mr. St. John writes as a patriot; he recognizes no period in the
history of his country when its population deserved the character of un-
civilized savages, which so many writers have attributed to the aboriginal
Britons. . . . As we approach the period of the Norman Conquest,
there is more historical light, and far less room for conjecture than in the
earlier times. . . . All this is well told, and the account of the battle
of Hastings which crowned it with success is one of the most stirring we
have ever read. . . . We heartily accord him our praise for the
thoroughly English spirit in which his history is written, and for the
manliness of the sentiments by which it is pervaded."—*Daily News.*

" Mr. St. John has done a good work. If he has occasionally allowed
his feelings to get the better of his impartiality, he has evidently tried to
arrive at the truth; and we think that his work will ever be regarded as
a worthy addition to English literature, by a more than usually con-
scientious and painstaking historian."—*Critic.*

" The happiest part of this history will be found in the descriptions
of the appearance and products of the island at the various epochs referred
to, and in the sketches of the great men who stand out as light-houses
above the surrounding darkness."—*Globe.*

" Mr. St. John has worthily devoted himself to the production as his
*magnum opus* of a history of that great mingling of races which has
resulted in the growth of the English people. . . . With patient care
Mr. St. John has unravelled the tangled web of the history of these great
events. . . . The result is a history, the best adapted for popular
reading, the most complete and compact narrative of the early history of
this great country, which we possess. And what a history it is! . . .
We are unwilling to lay down the book without a warm tribute to the
author for the research and fairness which distinguish it; and to the
general vigour and picturesqueness of style with which he narrates the
history of the four conquests."—*Weekly Dispatch.*

" The title of this book is in itself very remarkable. . . . The book
itself is as remarkable as its title, which scarcely gives an adequate idea

of its full scope or contents. It is in fact a most masterly history of
England, from the time of Julius Cæsar to the death of the last invader,
William the Conqueror."—*London Review*, first notice.

"What is indisputable is the vastness of the service which Mr.
St. John has done to the history and literature of his country. In
the history of the times to which it refers, these volumes will undoubtedly for the future be the text-book of all historical students;
and the further such students prosecute their investigations, the more
sensible will be their gratitude to the author who has aided their studies
by thus setting before them so vast an amount of valuable information
in so accessible and attractive a form."—*London Review*, second notice.

"His narrative is generally fluent in style and interesting in matter."
—*Spectator*.

"Mr. St. John's two octavo volumes compress an extensive field of
history within a concentrated and distinct view, exhibiting the progress
of our country from the days beyond the Romans, down to the development of the actual English nation after the Norman Conquest.
Mr. St. John is an accomplished and agreeable writer; he has been
a very industrious reader, possesses a clear and graceful pen, and enables
us to travel at a rapid rate through the pages of ancient chronicles and
modern historians. . . . We can heartily recommend his volumes to the
thoughtful student who wishes to learn something more from history
than isolated achievements or barren dates."—*Daily Telegraph*.

"The familiar story is worth reading again in Mr. St. John's vigorous
and precise narrative."—*Examiner*.

"This book is deserving of every praise. Although full of historical
detail, it never wearies; and it has the advantage of being a perfect
history."—*Observer*.

"The work which will entitle Mr. St. John to a proud position
among the historians of this or any other age, written in a chaste and
classic style; the events are truthfully and impartially described, and
the deductions are drawn with logical accuracy."—*Weekly Times*.

"This work, as compared with what passed for history a generation
back, certainly shows what steps historical science has taken. . . .
Mr. St. John throws himself heart and soul into the defence of Godwin
and Harold. He could not take up a better cause. In point of style
Mr. St. John is clear and vivid."—*Saturday Review*.

"Mr. St. John has again taken up his pen to tell the story of the Four Conquests of England in one continuous tale; he has for the first time given a clear and concise account, and described with great vividness and animation the history of the wars to which the separate invasions by Roman, Saxon, Dane, and Norman gave birth. . . . The book is an interesting addition to our historic literature, and will be found by those fond of historical studies to form pleasant and attractive reading."
—*New Quarterly Review.*

"We give words of sincere praise to Mr. St. John's account of England during the period lying between the first invasion of the Romans and the completion of the Norman Conquest. It is not the least of this writer's merits that he does not 'pad' his story of things said and done with too many reflections upon doubtful points. . . . . We should be glad, indeed, if the example set in these volumes by Mr. St. John—the example, we mean, of clear story-telling and intelligent forbearance as to what lies beyond—were likely to be followed by other historians."—*Illustrated Times.*

---

*Preparing for Publication, by the same Author,*

# A LIFE
## OF
# SIR WALTER RALEIGH:

Founded, in great part, on Documents in the State Paper Office, and other Manuscript Collections.

65, *Cornhill, London,*
*May*, 1862.

# NEW AND STANDARD WORKS

PUBLISHED BY

## SMITH, ELDER AND CO.

IMMEDIATELY FORTHCOMING.

### Life in the Forests of the Far East.
By Spenser St. John, F.R.G.S., F.E.S.
Late H.M.'s Consul-General in Borneo, now H.M.'s Chargé d'Affaires to Hayti.
Illustrated with Sixteen Coloured and Tinted Lithographs, and Three
Maps. Two Volumes. Demy 8vo. [*Ready.*

### Reminiscences of Captain Gronow.
Being Anecdotes of the Camp, the Court, and the Clubs,
at the close of the War with France.
With Illustrations. One Volume. Post 8vo. [*Just ready.*

### The Rifle in Cashmere.
A Narrative of Shooting Expeditions in Ladak, Cashmere, &c.
With Hints and Advice on Travelling, Shooting, and Stalking. To
which are added notes on Army Reform and Indian Politics.
By Arthur Brinkman, Late of H.M.'s 94th Regiment. [*Nearly ready.*

### The Port and Trade of London : Historical,
Statistical, Local, and General.
By Charles Capper,
Manager of the Victoria (London) Docks. 8vo. [*Just ready.*

### A Visit to the Suez Canal.
By the Rev. Percy Badger.
8vo. With Map. [*Ready.*

### New Zealand and the War.
By William Swainson, Esq.
Author of "New Zealand and its Colonization." With Map. Post 8vo. 5s. cl.

NEW NOVELS.

### A Loss Gained. In One Volume. [*Just ready.*

### Winifred's Wooing.
By Georgiana M. Craik, Author of "Lost and Won," &c. In One Vol.
[*Nearly ready.*

### Normanton.
By A. J. Barrowcliffe.
Author of "Amberhill," and "Trust for Trust." One Vol. [*Nearly ready.*

## Agnes of Sorrento.

By Mrs. Harriet Beecher Stowe. Post 8vo. Price 7s. 6d. cloth.

## Intellectual Education, and its Influence on the Character and Happiness of Women.

By Emily A. E. Shirreff. Second Edition. Crown 8vo. Price 6s. cloth.

## The Correspondence of Leigh Hunt.

Edited by his Eldest Son.

Two Vols. Post 8vo, with Portrait. Price 24s. cloth.

## Egypt, Nubia, and Ethiopia.

Illustrated by One Hundred Stereoscopic Photographs, taken by Francis Frith, for Messrs. Negretti and Zambra; with Descriptions and numerous Wood Engravings, by Joseph Bonomi, F.R.S.L., and Notes by Samuel Sharpe. In One Vol. small 4to. Elegantly bound. Price 3l. 3s.

## The Wild Sports of India,

With detailed Instructions for the Sportsman; to which are added Remarks on the Breeding and Rearing of Horses, and the Formation of Light Irregular Cavalry.

By Major Henry Shakespear,

late Commandant Nagpore Irregular Force. With Portrait of the Author. Second Edition, much Enlarged. Post 8vo. Price 10s. cloth.

## The Lady's Guide to the Ordering of her Household, and the Economy of the Dinner Table.

By a Lady. Crown 8vo. Price 10s. 6d. cloth.

### MISS MALING'S MANUALS,

## Flowers for Ornament and Decoration; and How to Arrange Them.

With Coloured Frontispiece. Price 2s. 6d. cloth.

## In-door Plants; and How to Grow Them for the Drawing-Room, Balcony, and Green-House.

4th Thousand. With Coloured Frontispiece. Price 2s. 6d. cloth.

## Flowers and Foliage for In-door Plant Cases.

Fcap 8vo. Price 1s.

## Song Birds; and How to Keep Them.

With Coloured Frontispiece. Fcap 8vo. Price 2s. 6d. cloth.

# HISTORY AND BIOGRAPHY.

## History of the Four Conquests of England.
*By James Augustus St. John, Esq.*
Two Vols. 8vo. Price 28s. cloth.

## History of the Venetian Republic:
*By W. Carew Hazlitt.*
Complete in 4 vols. 8vo, with Illustrations, price 2l. 16s., cloth.
*⁎* Volumes III. and IV. may be had separately.

## The Life and Letters of Captain John Brown.
*Edited by Richard D. Webb.*
With Portrait. Fcap 8vo. Price 4s. 6d. cloth.

## Life of Schleiermacher,
As unfolded in his Autobiography and Letters.
*Translated by Frederica Rowan.*
Two vols. post 8vo, with Portrait.
Price One Guinea, cloth.

## The Life of Charlotte Brontë (Currer Bell).
*By Mrs. Gaskell.*
Fourth Library Edition, revised, one vol., with a Portrait of Miss Brontë and a View of Haworth Parsonage.
Price 7s. 6d.; morocco elegant, 14s.

## Life of Edmond Malone,
Editor of Shakspeare's Works. With Selections from his MS. Anecdotes.
*By Sir James Prior.*
Demy 8vo, with Portrait, 14s. cloth.

## The Autobiography of Leigh Hunt.
One vol., post 8vo, with Portrait. Library edition. Price 7s. 6d. cloth.

## Life of Lord Metcalfe.
*By John William Kaye.*
New Edition, in Two Vols., post 8vo, with Portrait. Price 12s. cloth.

## Life of Sir John Malcolm, G.C.B.
*By John William Kaye.*
Two Vols. 8vo, with Portrait.
Price 36s. cloth.

## The Autobiography of Lutfullah.
A Mohamedan Gentleman; with an Account of his Visit to England.
*Edited by E. B. Eastwick, Esq.*
Third Edition, Fcap 8vo.
Price 5s. cloth.

## The Life of Mahomet.
With Introductory Chapters on the Original Sources for the Biography of Mahomet, and on the Pre-Islamite History of Arabia.
*By W. Muir, Esq., Bengal C.S.*
Complete in Four Vols. Demy 8vo.
Price 2l. 2s. cloth.
*⁎* Vols. III. and IV. may be had separately, price 21s.

## Robert Owen and his Social Philosophy.
*By William Lucas Sargant.*
1 vol., post 8vo. 10s. 6d. cloth.

## Women of Christianity
Exemplary for Piety and Charity.
*By Julia Kavanagh.*
Post 8vo, with Portraits. Price 5s. in embossed cloth.

## VOYAGES AND TRAVELS.

### Scripture Lands
in connection with their History:

With an Appendix; and Extracts from a Journal kept during an Eastern Tour in 1856-7.

*By the Rev. G. S. Drew,*

Author of " Scripture Studies," &c.

Post 8vo, with a Map, 10s. 6d. cloth.

### A Visit to the Philippine Isles in 1858–59.

*By Sir John Bowring,*

Demy 8vo, with numerous Illustrations, price 18s. cloth.

### Heathen and Holy Lands;
Or, Sunny Days on the Salween, Nile, and Jordan.

*By Captain J. P. Briggs, Bengal Army.*

Post 8vo, price 12s. cloth.

### Narrative of the Mission to Ava.

*By Captain Henry Yule, Bengal Engineers.*

Imperial 8vo, with Twenty-four Plates (Twelve coloured), Fifty Woodcuts, and Four Maps. Elegantly bound in cloth, with gilt edges, price 2l. 12s. 6d.

### Egypt in its Biblical Relations.

*By the Rev. J. Foulkes Jones.*

Post 8vo, price 7s. 6d. cloth.

### Japan, the Amoor, and the Pacific.

A Voyage of Circumnavigation in the Imperial Russian Corvette "Rynda," in 1858-59-60.

*By Henry Arthur Tilley.*

8vo, with illustrations, 16s. cloth.

### Through Norway with a Knapsack.

*By W. M. Williams.*

With Six Coloured Views. Third Edition, post 8vo, price 12s. cloth.

### Turkish Life and Character.

*By Walter Thornbury.*

Author of " Life in Spain," &c. &c.

Two Vols., with Eight Tinted Illustrations, price 21s. cloth.

### Voyage to Japan,
Kamtschatka, Siberia, Tartary, and the Coast of China, in H.M.S. *Barracouta.*

*By J. M. Tronson, R.N.*

8vo, with Charts and Views. 18s. cloth.

### To Cuba and Back.

*By R. H. Dana,*

Author of " Two Years before the Mast," &c.

Post 8vo, price 7s. cloth.

### Life and Liberty in America.

*By Dr. C. Mackay.*

Second Edition, 2 vols., post 8vo, with Ten Tinted Illustrations, price 21s.

# WORKS OF MR. RUSKIN.

## Modern Painters.

Now complete in five vols., Imperial 8vo, with 87 Engravings on Steel, and 216 on Wood, chiefly from Drawings by the Author. With Index to the whole Work. Price 8*l*. 6*s*. 6*d*., in cloth.

EACH VOLUME MAY BE HAD SEPARATELY.

Vol. I.   6th Edition.   OF GENERAL PRINCIPLES AND OF TRUTH. Price 18*s*. cloth.

Vol. II.   4th Edition.   OF THE IMAGINATIVE AND THEORETIC FACULTIES.   Price 10*s*. 6*d*. cloth.

Vol. III. OF MANY THINGS. With Eighteen Illustrations drawn by the Author, and engraved on Steel.   Price 38*s*. cloth.

Vol. IV. ON MOUNTAIN BEAUTY.   With Thirty-five Illustrations engraved on Steel, and 116 Woodcuts, drawn by the Author. Price 2*l*. 10*s*. cloth.

Vol. V.   OF LEAF BEAUTY; OF CLOUD BEAUTY; OF IDEAS OF RELATION. With Thirty-four Engravings on Steel, and 100 on Wood. Price 2*l*. 10*s*. With Index to the five volumes.

---

## The Stones of Venice.

Complete in Three Volumes, Imperial 8vo, with Fifty-three Plates and numerous Woodcuts, drawn by the Author. Price 5*l*. 15*s*. 6*d*. cloth.

EACH VOLUME MAY BE HAD SEPARATELY.
Vol. I. The FOUNDATIONS, with 21 Plates. Price 2*l*. 2*s*. 2nd Edition.
Vol. II. THE SEA STORIES, with 20 Plates. Price 2*l*. 2*s*.
Vol. III. THE FALL, with 12 Plates. Price 1*l*. 11*s*. 6*d*.

---

## The Seven Lamps of Architecture.

Second Edition, with Fourteen Plates drawn by the Author. Imp. 8vo. Price 1*l*. 1*s*. cloth.

---

## Lectures on Architecture and Painting.

With Fourteen Cuts, drawn by the Author. Second Edition, crown 8vo. Price 8*s*. 6*d*. cloth.

---

## Pre-Raphaelitism.

A New Edition. Demy 8vo. Price 2*s*.

## The Two Paths:

Being Lectures on Art, and its relation to Manufactures and Decoration. One vol., crown 8vo, with Two Steel Engravings.   Price 7*s*. 6*d*. cloth.

---

## The Elements of Drawing

Sixth Thousand, crown 8vo, with Illustrations drawn by the Author. Price 7*s*. 6*d*. cloth.

---

## The Elements of Perspective.

With 80 Diagrams, crown 8vo. Price 3*s*. 6*d*. cloth.

---

## The Political Economy of Art.

Price 2*s*. 6*d*. cloth.

---

## Selections from the Writings of J. Ruskin, M.A.

One Volume. Post 8vo, with a Portrait. Price 6*s*. cloth.

# RELIGIOUS.

## Sermons :
*By the late Rev. Fred. W. Robertson,*
Incumbent of Trinity Chapel, Brighton.
FIRST SERIES.— Ninth Edition, post
8vo. Price 9s. cloth.
SECOND SERIES. — Eighth Edition.
Price 9s. cloth.
THIRD SERIES.—Seventh Edition, post
8vo, with Portrait. Price 9s. cloth.

## Expositions of St. Paul's Epistles to the Corinthians.
*By the late Rev. Fred. W. Robertson.*
Second Edition. One thick Volume,
post 8vo. Price 10s. 6d. cloth.

## Lectures and Addresses.
*By the late Fredk. W. Robertson,*
A New Edition. Fcap 8vo. 5s. cloth.

## The Gospel in the Miracles of Christ.
*By Rev. Richd. Travers Smith, M.A.*
Chaplain of St. Stephen's, Dublin.
Fcap 8vo, price 5s. cloth.

## Sermons :
Preached at Lincoln's Inn Chapel.
*By the Rev. F. D. Maurice, M.A.*
FIRST SERIES, 2 vols., post 8vo, price
21s. cloth.
SECOND SERIES, 2 vols., post 8vo,
price 21s. cloth.
THIRD SERIES, 2 vols., post 8vo,
price 21s. cloth.

## Experiences of an English Sister of Mercy.
*By Margaret Goodman.*
Second edition, Fcap 8vo. 3s. 6d. cloth.

## Tauler's Life and Sermons.
*Translated by Miss Susanna Winkworth.*
With Preface by Rev. C. KINGSLEY.
Small 4to, price 7s. 6d. cloth.

## The Soul's Exodus and Pilgrimage.
*By the Rev. J. Baldwin Brown,*
Author of "The Divine Life in Man."
Second Edition. Crown 8vo.
Price 7s. 6d. cloth.

## "Is it not Written ?"
Being the Testimony of Scripture
against the Errors of Romanism.
*By Edward S. Pryce, A.B.*
Post 8vo. Price 6s. cloth.

## Quakerism, Past and Present :
Being an Inquiry into the Causes of
its Decline.
*By John S. Rowntree.*
Post 8vo. Price 5s. cloth.
\*\*\* This Essay gained the First Prize
of One Hundred Guineas offered for
the best Essay on the subject.

## The Peculium ;
An Essay on the Causes of the Decline
of the Society of Friends.
*By Thomas Hancock,*
Post 8vo. Price 5s. cloth.
\*\*\* This Essay gained the Second
Prize of Fifty Guineas, which was
afterwards increased to One Hundred.

THE BISHOP OF SALISBURY v.
DR. WILLIAMS.

## The Defence of Dr. Rowland Williams ;
Being a Report of the Speech delivered
in the Court of Arches, by JAMES
FITZJAMES STEPHEN, M.A., Recorder
of Newark - on - Trent. Published
from the Shorthand Writer's Notes,
Revised and Corrected. Post 8vo.
Price 10s. 6d. cloth.

# MISCELLANEOUS.

## The Early Italian Poets.
*Translated by D. G. Rossetti.*
Part I.—Poets chiefly before Dante.
Part II.—Dante and his Circle.
Price 12s. cloth.　Post 8vo.

## The Book of Good Counsels:
Being an Abridged Translation of the Sanscrit Classic, the "Hitopadesa."
*By Edwin Arnold, M.A., Oxon.*
Author of "Education in India," &c.
With Illustrations by Harrison Weir.
Crown 8vo, 5s. cloth.

## Education in Oxford:
Its Method, its Aids, and its Rewards.
*By James E. Thorold Rogers, M.A.*
Post 8vo, price 6s. cloth.

## Household Education.
*By Harriet Martineau.*
A New Edition. Post 8vo. Price 5s. cloth.

## Household Medicine; and Sick-room Guide.
Describing Diseases, their Nature, Causes, and Symptoms, with the most approved Methods of Treatment, and the Properties and Uses of many new Remedies.
*By John Gardner, M.D.*
8vo, with numerous Illustrations.
Price 10s. 6d. cloth.

## Ragged London.
*By John Hollingshead.*
Post 8vo, 7s. 6d. cloth.

## The Four Georges:
Sketches of Manners, Morals, Court and Town Life.
*By W. M. Thackeray.*
With Illustrations. Crown 8vo.
Price 5s. cloth.

## Shakspere and his Birthplace.
*By John R. Wise.*
With 22 Illustrations by W. J. Linton.
Crown 8vo. Printed on Toned Paper, and handsomely bound in ornamental cloth, gilt edges, price 7s. 6d.
\*\*\* Also a cheap edition, 2s. 6d. cloth.

## Man and his Dwelling Place.
An Essay towards the Interpretation of Nature.
Second Edition. With a New Preface.
Crown 8vo, 6s. cloth.

## Social Innovators and their Schemes.
*By William Lucas Sargant.*
Post 8vo. Price 10s. 6d. cloth.

## Ethica;
Or, Characteristics of Men, Manners, and Books.
*By Arthur Lloyd Windsor.*
Demy 8vo. Price 12s. cloth.

## The Conduct of Life.
*By Ralph Waldo Emerson,*
Author of "Essays," "Representative Men," &c. Post 8vo, price 6s. cloth.
\*\*\* Also a Cheap Edition, 1s. cloth.

## Bermuda:

Its History, Geology, Climate, Products, Agriculture, &c. &c.

*By Theodore L. Godet, M.D.*

Post 8vo, price 9s. cloth.

---

## Annals of British Legislation:

A Classified Summary of Parliamentary Papers.

*Edited by Dr. Leone Levi.*

The yearly issue consists of 1,000 pages, super-royal 8vo, and the Subscription is Two Guineas, payable in advance. Vols. I. to X. may now be had. Price 10l. 10s. cloth.

---

## Manual of the Mercantile Law

Of Great Britain and Ireland.

*By Dr. Leone Levi.*

8vo. Price 12s. cloth.

---

## Commercial Law of the World.

*By Dr. Leone Levi.*

Two vols. royal 4to. Price 6l. cloth.

---

## A Handbook of Average.

With a Chapter on Arbitration.

*By Manley Hopkins.*

Second Edition, Revised and brought down to the present time.

8vo. Price 15s. cloth; 17s. 6d. half-bound law calf.

---

## Sea Officer's Manual.

Being a Compendium of the Duties of Commander and Officers in the Mercantile Navy.

*By Captain Alfred Parish.*

Second Edition. Small post 8vo. Price 5s. cloth.

---

## Victoria,

Or the Australian Gold Mines in 1857.

*By William Westgarth.*

Post 8vo, with Maps.    10s. 6d. cloth.

---

## New Zealand and its Colonization.

*By William Swainson, Esq.*

Demy 8vo. Price 14s. cloth.

---

## The Education of the Human Race.

*Now first Translated from the German of Lessing.*

Fcap. 8vo, antique cloth.    Price 4s.

---

## Life in Spain.

*By Walter Thornbury.*

Two Vols. post 8vo, with Eight Tinted Illustrations, price 21s.

---

## Captivity of Russian Princesses in the Caucasus.

*Translated from the Russian by H. S. Edwards.*

With an authentic Portrait of Shamil, a Plan of his House, and a Map. Post 8vo, price 10s. 6d. cloth.

---

A Treatise on Rifles, Cannon, and Sporting Arms.

## Gunnery:

*By William Greener,*

Author of "The Gun."

Demy 8vo, with Illustrations. Price 14s. cloth.

---

## On the Strength of Nations.

*By Andrew Bisset, M.A.*

Post 8vo.   Price 9s. cloth.

## Results of Astronomical Observations

Made at the Cape of Good Hope.
*By Sir John Herschel.*
4to, with Plates. Price 4*l.* 4*s.* cloth.

---

## Astronomical Observations.

Made at the Sydney Observatory in the year 1859.

*By W. Scott, M.A.*
8vo. 6*s.*

---

## On the Treatment of the Insane,

Without Mechanical Restraints,
*By John Conolly, M.D.*
Demy 8vo. Price 14*s.* cloth.

---

## Visit to Salt Lake.

Being a Journey across the Plains to the Mormon Settlements at Utah.
*By William Chandless.*
Post 8vo, with a Map. 2*s.* 6*d.* cloth.

---

## The Red River Settlement.

*By Alexander Ross.*
One vol. post 8vo. Price 5*s.* cloth.

---

## Fur Hunters of the West.

*By Alexander Ross.*
Two vols. post 8vo, with Map and Plate. Price 10*s.* 6*d.* cloth.

---

## The Columbia River.

*By Alexander Ross.*
Post 8vo. Price 2*s.* 6*d.* cloth.

---

## England and her Soldiers.

*By Harriet Martineau.*
With Three Plates of Illustrative Diagrams. 1 vol. crown 8vo, price 9*s.* cloth.

---

## Grammar and Dictionary of the Malay Language.

*By John Crawfurd, Esq.*
Two vols. 8vo. Price 36*s.* cloth.

---

## Traits and Stories of Anglo-Indian Life.

*By Captain Addison.*
With Eight Illustrations. 2*s.* 6*d.* cloth.

---

## Tea Planting in the Himalaya.

*By A. T. McGowan.*
8vo, with Frontispiece, price 5*s.* cloth.

---

## Signs of the Times;

Or, The Dangers to Religious Liberty in the Present Day.
*By Chevalier Bunsen.*
Translated by Miss S. WINKWORTH.
One vol. 8vo. Price 5*s.* cloth.

---

## Wit and Humour.

*By Leigh Hunt.*
Price 5*s.* cloth.

---

## Jar of Honey from Hybla.

*By Leigh Hunt.*
Price 5*s.* cloth.

Men, Women, and Books.
*By Leigh Hunt.*
Two vols.   Price 10s. cloth.

Zoology of South Africa.
*By Dr. Andrew Smith.*
Royal 4to, cloth, with Coloured Plates.

    MAMMALIA.............................£3
    AVES ....................................7
    REPTILIA ...............................5
    PISCES ..................................2
    INVERTEBRATA ....................1

Religion in Common Life.
*By William Ellis.*
Post 8vo.   Price 7s. 6d. cloth.

Life of Sir Robert Peel.
*By Thomas Doubleday.*
Two vols. 8vo.   Price 18s. cloth.

Principles of Agriculture;
Especially Tropical.
*By B. Lovell Phillips, M.D.*
Demy 8vo.   Price 7s. 6d. cloth.

Books for the Blind.
Printed in raised Roman letters, at
the Glasgow Asylum.

# SMITH, ELDER AND CO.'S SHILLING SERIES

OF

# STANDARD WORKS OF FICTION.

**Well printed, on good paper, and tastefully bound.**
**Price ONE SHILLING each Volume,**

*SECOND ISSUE.*

LOST AND WON.  By GEORGIANA M. CRAIK.
HAWKSVIEW.  By HOLME LEE.
FLORENCE TEMPLAR.  By Mrs. F. VIDAL.

COUSIN STELLA; OR, CONFLICT. By the Author of "Who Breaks—Pays."
HIGHLAND LASSIES; OR, THE ROUA PASS.

*FIRST ISSUE.*

CONFIDENCES.  By the author of "Rita."
ERLESMERE; OR, CONTRASTS OF CHARACTER.  By L. S. LAVENU.
NANETTE AND HER LOVERS.  By TALBOT GWYNNE.
THE LIFE AND DEATH OF SILAS BARNSTARKE.  By TALBOT GWYNNE.
TENDER AND TRUE.  By the Author of "Claran."

ROSE DOUGLAS; THE AUTOBIOGRAPHY OF A SCOTCH MINISTER'S DAUGHTER.
GILBERT MASSENGER.  By HOLME LEE.
MY LADY: A TALE OF MODERN LIFE.
THORNEY HALL: A STORY OF AN OLD FAMILY.  By HOLME LEE.
THE CRUELEST WRONG OF ALL.

# WORKS ON INDIA AND THE EAST.

Cotton; an Account of its Culture in the Bombay Presidency.
*By Walter Cassels.*
8vo, price 16s. cloth.

Narrative of the North China Campaign of 1860.
*By Robert Swinhoe.*
Staff Interpreter to Sir Hope Grant.
8vo, with Illustrations. 12s. cloth.

PRIZE ESSAY.

Caste:
Considered under its Moral, Social, and Religious Aspects.
*By Arthur J. Patterson, B.A., of Trinity College.*
Post 8vo. Price 4s. 6d. cloth.

The Sanitary Condition of Indian Jails.
*By Joseph Ewart, M.D.,*
Bengal Medical Service.
With Plans, 8vo. Price 16s. cloth.

District Duties during the Revolt
In the North-West Provinces of India.
*By H. Dundas Robertson,*
Bengal Civil Service.
Post 8vo, with a Map. Price 9s. cloth.

Campaigning Experiences
In Rajpootana and Central India during the Mutiny in 1857-8.
*By Mrs. Henry Duberly.*
Post 8vo, with Map. Price 10s. 6d. cloth.

Narrative of the Mutinies in Oude.
*By Captain G. Hutchinson,*
Military Secretary, Oude.
Post 8vo. Price 10s. cloth.

A Lady's Escape from Gwalior
During the Mutinies of 1857.
*By Mrs. Coopland.*
Post 8vo. Price 10s. 6d.

The Crisis in the Punjab.
*By Frederick H. Cooper, Esq., C.S., Umritsir.*
Post 8vo, with Map. Price 7s. 6d. cloth.

Views and Opinions of Gen. Jacob, C.B.
*Edited by Captain Lewis Pelly.*
Demy 8vo. Price 12s. cloth.

Papers of the late Lord Metcalfe.
*By John William Kaye.*
Demy 8vo. Price 16s. cloth.

The English in India.
*By Philip Anderson, A.M.*
Second Edition, 8vo. Price 14s. cloth.

Life in Ancient India.
*By Mrs. Spier.*
With Sixty Illustrations by G. Scharf.
8vo. Price 15s., elegantly bound in cloth, gilt edges.

---



## Indian Exchange Tables.
*By J. H. Roberts.*
8vo. Second Edition, enlarged. Price 10s. 6d. cloth.

## Christianity in India.
A Historical Narrative.
*By John William Kaye.*
8vo. Price 16s. cloth.

## The Parsees:
Their History, Religion, Manners, and Customs.
*By Dosabhoy Framjee.*
Post 8vo. Price 10s. cloth.

## The Vital Statistics
Of the European and Native Armies in India.
*By Joseph Ewart, M.D.*
Demy 8vo. Price 9s. cloth.

## The Bhilsa Topes;
Or, Buddhist Monuments of Central India.
*By Major Cunningham.*
One vol. 8vo, with Thirty-three Plates. Price 30s. cloth.

## The Chinese and their Rebellions.
*By Thomas Taylor Meadows.*
One thick volume, 8vo, with Maps. Price 18s. cloth.

## Hong Kong to Manilla.
*By Henry T. Ellis, R.N.*
Post 8vo, with Fourteen Illustrations. Price 12s. cloth.

## The Botany of the Himalaya.
*By Dr. Forbes Royle.*
Two vols. roy. 4to, cloth, with Coloured Plates. Reduced to 5l. 5s.

## The Defence of Lucknow.
*By Captain Thomas F. Wilson.*
Sixth Thousand. With Plan. Small post 8vo. Price 2s. 6d.

## Eight Months' Campaign
Against the Bengal Sepoys during the Mutiny, 1857.
*By Colonel George Bourchier, C.B.*
With Plans. Post 8vo. 7s. 6d. cloth.

### PRIZE ESSAYS.
*By B. A. Irving.*

## The Theory of Caste,
8vo. 5s. cloth.

## The Commerce of India with Europe.
Post 8vo. Price 7s. 6d. cloth.

## Moohummudan Law of Sale.
*By N. B. E. Baillie, Esq.*
8vo. Price 14s. cloth.

## Moohummudan Law of Inheritance.
*By N. B. E. Baillie, Esq.*
8vo. Price 8s. cloth.

## The Cauvery, Kistnah, and Godavery:
Being a Report on the Works constructed on those Rivers, for the Irrigation of Provinces in the Presidency of Madras.
*By Col. R. Baird Smith, F.G.S.*
Demy 8vo, with 19 Plans. 28s. cloth.

## Land Tax of India.
According to the Moohummudan Law.
*By N. B. E. Baillie, Esq.*
8vo. Price 6s. cloth.

# FICTION.

## Carr of Carrlyon.
*By Hamilton Aidé.*
Author of "Rita," &c.  3 vols.

## The Cotton Lord.
*By Herbert Glyn.*
Two Vols.

## Warp and Woof.
*By Holme Lee.*
Three Vols.

## Said and Done.
In One Vol.

## Who Breaks—Pays.
In Two Vols.
*By the Author of " Cousin Stella."*

## The Wortlebank Diary:
With Stories from Kathie Brande's
Portfolio.
*By Holme Lee.*   Three Vols.

## Over the Cliffs.
*By Mrs. Chanter,*
Author of " Ferny Combes."  2 vols.

## Scarsdale;
Or, Life on the Lancashire and York-
shire Border Thirty Years ago. 3 vols.

## Lovel the Widower.
*By W. M. Thackeray.*
With six Illustrations.   Post 8vo.
Price 6s. cloth.

## Esmond.
*By W. M. Thackeray.*
Third Edition, crown 8vo.  Price 6s.
cloth.

## Herbert Chauncey:
A Man more Sinned against than
Sinning.
*By Sir Arthur Hallam Elton, Bart.*
In 3 vols.

## Hills and Plains.
Two Vols.

## The Firstborn.
*By the Author of " My Lady."*
Three volumes.

## The Tragedy of Life.
*By John H. Brenten.*   Two Vols.

## Framley Parsonage.
*By Anthony Trollope,*
Illustrated by J. E. Millais, R.A.
Three Vols.  Post 8vo, 21s. cloth.
Also a cheap Edition. 1 vol., post 8vo .
Price 5s. cloth.

## Netley Hall;
or, the Wife's Sister.
Foolscap 8vo.   6s. cloth.

## Phantastes:
A Faerie Romance for Men and
Women.
*By George Macdonald.*
Post 8vo.  Price 10s. 6d. cloth.

## The Fool of Quality.
*By Henry Brooke.*
New and Revised Edition, with Biogra-
phical Preface by the Rev. Chas.
Kingsley, Rector of Eversley.
Two vols., post 8vo, with Portrait of
the Author, price 21s.

# CHEAP EDITIONS OF POPULAR WORKS.

### Lavinia.
Price 2s. 6d. cloth.

### Sylvan Holt's Daughter.
*By Holme Lee.*
Price 2s. 6d. cloth.

### The Autobiography of Leigh Hunt.
Price 2s. 6d. cloth.

**WORKS OF THE BRONTE SISTERS.**
Price 2s. 6d. each vol.
*By Currer Bell.*

### The Professor.
To which are added the POEMS of Currer, Ellis, and Acton Bell. Now first collected.

### Jane Eyre.
### Shirley.
### Villette.

### Wuthering Heights and Agnes Grey.
*By Ellis and Acton Bell.*
With Memoir by CURRER BELL.

### The Tenant of Wildfell Hall.
*By Acton Bell.*

### Life of Charlotte Brontë
(Currer Bell).
*By Mrs. Gaskell.*
Cheap edition. 2s. 6d. cloth.

### Lectures on the English Humourists
Of the Eighteenth Century.
*By W. M. Thackeray.*
Price 2s. 6d. cloth.

### The Town.
*By Leigh Hunt.*
With Forty-five Engravings.
Price 2s. 6d. cloth.

### Transformation.
*By Nathaniel Hawthorne.*
Price 2s. 6d. cloth.

### Kathie Brande:
The Fireside History of a Quiet Life.
*By Holme Lee.* Price 2s. 6d. cloth.

### Below the Surface.
*By Sir A. H. Elton, Bart., M.P.*
Price 2s. 6d. cloth.

### British India.
*By Harriet Martineau.* 2s. 6d. cloth.

### Italian Campaigns of General Bonaparte.
*By George Hooper.*
With a Map. Price 2s. 6d. cloth.

### Deerbrook.
*By Harriet Martineau.* 2s. 6d. cloth.

### Tales of the Colonies.
*By Charles Rowcroft.* 2s. 6d. cloth.

### A Lost Love.
*By Ashford Owen.* 2s. cloth.

### Romantic Tales
(Including "Avillion").
*By the Author of "John Halifax, Gentleman."* 2s. 6d. cloth.

### Domestic Stories.
*By the same Author.* 2s. 6d. cloth.

### After Dark.
*By Wilkie Collins.* 2s. 6d. cloth.

### School for Fathers.
*By Talbot Gwynne.* 2s. cloth.

### Paul Ferroll.
Price 2s. cloth.

## JUVENILE AND EDUCATIONAL.

### The Parents' Cabinet

Of Amusement and Instruction for Young Persons.

New Edition, revised, in Twelve Shilling Volumes, with numerous Illustrations.

\*\*\* The work is now complete in 4 vols. extra cloth, gilt edges, at 3s. 6d. each; or in 6 vols. extra cloth, gilt edges, at 2s. 6d. each.

Every volume is complete in itself, and sold separately.

By the Author of "Round the Fire," &c.

### Round the Fire:

Six Stories for Young Readers.

Square 16mo, with Four Illustrations. Price 2s. 6d. cloth.

### Unica:

A Story for a Sunday Afternoon.

With Four Illustrations. 2s. 6d. cloth.

### Old Gingerbread and the Schoolboys.

With Four Coloured Plates. 2s. 6d. cl.

### Willie's Birthday:

Showing how a Little Boy did what he Liked, and how he Enjoyed it.

With Four Illustrations. 2s. cloth.

### Willie's Rest:

A Sunday Story.

With Four Illustrations. 2s. cloth.

### Uncle Jack, the Fault Killer.

With Four Illustrations. 2s. 6d. cloth.

### Philo-Socrates.

Parts I. & II. "Among the Boys."
Part III., IV.—"Among the Teachers."
*By William Ellis.*
Post 8vo. Price 1s. each.

### Legends from Fairy Land.

*By Holme Lee,*

Author of "Kathie Brande," "Sylvan Holt's Daughter," &c.

With Eight Illustrations. 3s. 6d. cloth.

### The Wonderful Adventures of Tuflongbo and his Elfin Company in their Journey with Little Content, through the Enchanted Forest.

*By Holme Lee,*

Author of "Legends from Fairy Land," &c.

With Eight Illustrations. Fcap 8vo. Price 3s. 6d. cloth.

### The King of the Golden River;

Or, the Black Brothers.

*By John Ruskin, M.A.*

Third Edition, with 22 Illustrations by Richard Doyle. Price 2s. 6d.

### Elementary Works on Social Economy.

*By William Ellis.*

Uniform in foolscap 8vo, half-bound.

I.—OUTLINES OF SOCIAL ECONOMY. 1s. 6d.
II.—PROGRESSIVE LESSONS IN SOCIAL SCIENCE.
III.—INTRODUCTION TO THE SOCIAL SCIENCES. 2s.
IV.—OUTLINES OF THE UNDERSTANDING. 2s.
V.—WHAT AM I? WHERE AM I? WHAT OUGHT I TO DO? &c. 1s. sewed.

### Rhymes for Little Ones.

16 Illustrations. 1s. 6d. cl., gilt edges.

### Stories from the Parlour Printing Press.

*By the Authors of the "Parent's Cabinet."*

Fcap 8vo. Price 2s. cloth.

### Juvenile Miscellany.

Six Engravings. Price 2s. 6d. cloth.

## RECENT POETRY.

### Poems.
By the Rev. George E. Maunsell.
Fcap 8vo. Price 5s. cloth.

### Prometheus' Daughter:
A Poem.
Crown 8vo. Price 7s. 6d. cloth.

### Christ's Company, and other Poems.
By Richard Watson Dixon, M.A.
Fcap 8vo, price 5s. cloth.

### Sybil, and other Poems.
By John Lyttelton.
Fcap 8vo, price 4s. cloth.

### Stories in Verse for the Street and Lane:
By Mrs. Sewell.
3rd Thousand. Post 8vo. Cloth, 1s.

### Hannibal; a Drama.
Fcap 8vo. Price 5s. cloth.

### A Man's Heart: a Poem.
By Dr. Charles Mackay.
Post 8vo. Price 5s. cloth.

### Edwin and Ethelburga:
A Drama.
By Frederick W. Wyon.
Fcap 8vo. Price 4s. cloth.

### Shelley; and other Poems.
By John Alfred Langford.
Fcap 8vo. Price 5s. cloth.

### Isabel Gray; or, The Mistress Didn't Know.
By Mrs. Sewell,
Post 8vo. Cloth. Gilt edges. 1s.

### Homely Ballads
For the Working Man's Fireside.
By Mary Sewell.
13th Thousand. Post 8vo. Cloth, 1s.

### Memories of Merton.
By John Bruce Norton.
Fcap 8vo. Price 5s. cloth.

---

## THE CORNHILL MAGAZINE:
### Edited by W. M. Thackeray.

Price One Shilling Monthly, with Illustrations.

VOLUMES I., II., III., and IV., each containing 768 pages of Letterpress, with 12 Illustrations, and numerous Vignettes and Diagrams, are published, handsomely bound in Embossed Cloth. Price 7s. 6d. each.

For the convenience of Subscribers, the Embossed CLOTH COVERS for each Volume are sold separately, price One Shilling.

READING COVERS for separate Numbers have also been prepared, price Sixpence in plain Cloth, or One Shilling and Sixpence in French Morocco.

London : Printed by SMITH, ELDER and Co., Little Green Arbour Court, Old Bailey, E.C.

CPSIA information can be obtained
at www.ICGtesting.com
Printed in the USA
BVHW040236261120
594260BV00003BA/11